A CORNISH
DICTIONARY
FOR CONVERSATION

# GERLYVER KESCOWS

Ian Jackson

Agan Tavas • Redruth
2017

© 2017 Ian Jackson
1st impression / 1sa pryntyans, Nov / Du 2017
2nd impression (corrected) / pryntyans (amendys), Mar / Mer 2018
3rd impression (corrected) / pryntyans (amendys), Nov / Du 2018

The opinions expressed by the author of this dictionary are not necessarily those of the publishers.
*Ny dal kemeres pùb tybyans rës gans auctour an gerlyver-ma avell prederow an dhylloryon.*

ISBN-10: 1-901409-20-1
ISBN-13: 978-1-901409-20-8

All rights reserved. No part of this publication may be reproduced, stored in a retrieval system or transmitted, in any form or by any means, electronic, mechanical, photocopying, recording or otherwise whatsoever, without prior permission of the publishers.
*Pùb gwir gwethys. Ny yll radn vëth a'n pùblycacyon-ma naneyl bos copies, sensys aberth in system dascafos na treuscorrys in form vëth oll na dre vain vëth oll, poken electronek, jynweythek, dre fotocopians, dre recordyth bò fordh vëth aral, heb recêva cubmyas dhyrag dorn dhyworth an dhylloryon.*

Typeset by the author in Arial.
*Olsettyans gans an auctour in Arial.*

| | |
|---|---|
| Published by | Agan Tavas |
| *Dyllys gans* | Chy Gordon / Gordon Villa |
| | Fordh Nans Howlek / Sunnyvale Road |
| | Por'treth / Portreath |
| | Ewny Redrudh / Redruth |
| | Kernow TR16 4NE |
| Cover / *Cudhlen* | Bethany Hall |

Printed and bound by Lulu.
*Pryntys ha kelmys gans Lulu.*

# CONTENTS

| | |
|---|---|
| Preface | 5 |
| Introduction | 7 |
| Cornish-English Section | 15 |
| Grammar Words | 160 |
| English-Cornish Section | 179 |
| Key Verb Tables for Reference | 275 |
| Numerals for Reference | 281 |
| Contact Mutations for Reference | 284 |
| 'Outbursts' | 286 |
| Appendix of Place Names | 294 |

# PREFACE

*'Cows Kernowek yw moy y vern agès cows adro dhe'n Kernowek.'*
(A.S.D. Smith *'Caradar'*, respelled)

This *Gerlyver Kescows* is designed specifically for those who speak, or are learning to speak, 'Unified Cornish' or 'Unified Cornish Revised' or 'Standard Cornish', all of which are based on the Cornish texts that have survived from the 14th to the 18th centuries.

The Cornish in this dictionary takes William Jordan's *Gwrians an Bÿs* as its 'foundation text', while looking forward to John Keigwin, William Rowe and Nicholas Boson, and back to John Tregear, *Sacrament an Alter*, *Bêwnans Ke*, and *Bêwnans Meriasek*. Spellings are those of 'Standard Cornish'. This particular orthography has been developed under the leadership of Michael Everson in close cooperation with Professor Nicholas Williams 'Golvan'. It aims for spellings that are as unambiguous as possible in their representation of the sounds of Cornish, and which at the same time remain faithful to the forms we encounter in the traditional Cornish texts – since these are our chief source for the language. The whole corpus of traditional Cornish has been used to enlarge the vocabulary. This has been a necessary principle of the revival from the outset.

Standard Cornish is the language of the complete Cornish Bible (*An Beybel Sans*, Evertype 2011) and many other published works, including recent translations by Nicholas Williams of 'The Wind in the Willows' (*An Gwyns i'n Helyk* 2013), 'The Hobbit' (*An Hobys* 2014), 'Pride and Prejudice' (*Gooth ha Gowvreus* 2015), 'She' and 'Dracula' (*Honna* and *Dracùla*, both 2016), all published by Evertype.

The dictionary contains:
- 5000 Cornish entries in the main Cornish-English section
- a separate list of 'grammar words'
- an English-Cornish index of these words and phrases
- reference charts of essential verbs, numerals, and contact mutations
- a collection of 200 'outbursts' (a portmanteau term for greetings and exclamations)
- an appendix of 250 place names

Everything has been selected as a practical aid to **conversation**. The main source has been Nicholas Williams's *Gerlyver Sawsnek-Kernowek* (Agan Tavas & Evertype, 2nd edition 2006); this takes full account of the earlier work of R. Morton Nance 'Mordon'. Much has been adopted from Prof. Williams's *Geryow Gwir* (Evertype, 2nd edition 2014); but vigorous coinages by Nance have been retained. And there are some new expressions. It is hoped the chosen vocabulary will prove useful wherever folk are eager to speak Cornish in a vibrant manner, balancing the needs of modern communication with cherished tradition.

I am grateful to Ray Chubb 'Map Essa' for all the work he has put into the publication of this dictionary; to the Committee of Agan Tavas for its enthusiastic support; and to Nicholas Williams for his advice on several matters of inflection, pronunciation and spelling.

Ian Jackson, An Dhyw Rës, Hâv 2017

iacobianus@googlemail.com

# INTRODUCTION

## The alphabet

Here are Cornish names for the letters of the alphabet in case you need to spell out a word: **a**, **be**, **ce**, **de**, **e**, **ef**, **ge**, **ha**, **i**, **je**, **ke**, **èl**, **èm**, **èn**, **o**, **pe**, **qwo**, **èr**, **ès**, **te**, **û** (pronounced oo or yoo as you like), **ve**, **we**, **ex**, **ye**, **zèd**. These expressions will also be useful: aken dhieskydnus (`` ` ``), aken grobm (^), aken dhewboynt (¨), collverk ('), nos jùnya (-), lytheren vrâs (capital letter), lytheren vian (small letter).

## Reading each entry

### Cornish-English

In the Cornish-English section the following abbreviations apply to Cornish words and phrases:

*adj* adjective, *adv* adverb, *du* dual, *col* collective, *conj* conjunction, *f* feminine, *interj* interjection, *intr* used intransitively, *m* masculine, *phr* phrase, *pl* plural, *pp* past participle, *pref* prefix, *prep* preposition, *v* verb-noun.

A verb-noun is not used with the definite article; it is qualified by an adverb rather than an adjective; and possessive pronouns are used with it in the rôle of object. The designation *m/v* means that the relevant word may be used as an ordinary masculine noun as well; in which capacity it may have a plural, according to sense.

In entries for Cornish nouns, the plural form is also given (just the portion that changes in the case of an expression comprising more than one word); except that for collective nouns it is the singulative that is often added. All singulative nouns in -en are feminine with a plural in -ednow.

It is worth noting that plural nouns employed in an abstract sense are much less common in good Cornish than in English.

A reference to the 'infinitive construction' is to the pattern *noun or pronoun* + dhe² + *verb-noun*.

Anything between square brackets is optional.

### *English-Cornish*

In the English-Cornish section the following abbreviations apply to English words and entries:

*adj* adjective, *adv* adverb, *conj* conjunction, *interj* interjection, *n* noun (singular or plural), *phr* phrase, *pref* prefix, *prep* preposition, *pron* pronoun, *v* verb.

### *Throughout the dictionary*

Commas separate close synonyms. Semi-colons separate definitions that are not synonyms.

An asterisk indicates that the Cornish word functions in a verbal phrase. If the word is an adjective, the phrase structure will be *adjective* + yw ganso. If the word is a noun, the phrase will be yma + *noun* dhodho a², or y'n jeves + *noun* a²; the a² is often omitted before a verb-noun, and is always dropped before the infinitive construction or a na²-clause. Nouns of emotion may alternatively use the same structure as adjectives when put with a verb-noun: thus, bern, cas, edrek, màl, marth, meth; but not nouns of deliberation or fact: dowt, govenek, othem, own, sehes, trèst, whans.

Many phrases containing a personal pronoun or inflected preposition appear in the dictionary in the masculine third person singular (ev / va / y² / 'he' / 'him' / 'his'); you will need to adjust them for the appropriate person. Clipped 'incl' means 'including', 'sb' means 'somebody', 'sth' means 'something'.

Superscript numbers indicate a contact mutation, or its absence, by state: first (no mutation – only marked for prefixes), second (lenition), third (spirantization), fourth (provection), fifth (mixed).

## Pronunciation

The pronunciation of Revived Cornish is a matter of *reconstruction* and there is room for a range of opinion. Among textbooks, *Desky Kernowek* (Nicholas Williams, Evertype 2012) is a good starting-point. Listen to the spoken Cornish of as many people as you can. Try to follow the example of those whose pronunciation consistently reflects the spellings of traditional Cornish. You will find there is quite a lot of scope to personalize your own speech patterns within the wider framework.

Here are a few important things to remember when pronouncing according to the spellings given in this dictionary. The description avoids very technical language, so it is only approximate. Note that ch dh gh sh th count as single consonants.

An unmarked vowel in a word of one syllable is usually pronounced short; but it is *long* if followed by a single voiced consonant or gh sk st th. An unmarked vowel in a word of several syllables is always pronounced short.

A circumflex accent (^) on a e i o in any word means it is pronounced *long*. But in the case of yê at the beginning of a word, the accent merely indicates that the y may be elided if you prefer. A grave accent (`) on a e i o in any word means it is pronounced *short*.

Many speakers of traditional Cornish give unmarked u the same pronunciation as unmarked i. But note that unmarked u before another vowel is pronounced as ù: *e.g.* cruel.

Unmarked y as a vowel is always short except when stressed at the end of a word.

Both ë and ÿ are long, and they are interchangeable according to preference. But it is usual to reserve ë for bës 'finger' and ÿ for bÿs 'world'.

û is always long like the vowel in 'cool', except that in loan-words from English both û and ew sound like the whole of the word 'you' if that is also the English sound. ù is always short like the vowel in 'cook'. Note that -ury occurs alongside -ùry.

Stressed ai has the same sound as ê, stressed au is very like ô.

HOWEVER, as in English, unstressed short vowels in normal speech (that is, with no special emphasis) tend to be 'reduced' to the sound known as *schwa*. This is what you hear in the word 'the', except when it is occasionally pronounced like 'thee'. Though when the schwa replaces a short i or u sound, again as in English, it may still retain a 'colouring' of i / u.

Double consonants are generally pronounced the same as single consonants, though reconstructed mediaeval pronunciation may distinguish them. If you do not apply 'pre-occlusion' in your speech, you may change every Cornish bm and dn in this dictionary to mm and nn. Incorporation of pre-occlusion into spellings is particularly associated with more westerly parts of the Cornish mainland.

Here is a further point, relevant only to those applying pre-occlusion. If a word ending in bm / dn becomes the first part of a compound word, it is simplified to m / n, but it can still optionally be pronounced 'bm' / 'dn' where it follows a vowel carrying primary (main) stress, or occasionally even secondary stress. Thus some will pronounce penscol as 'pednscol'; a few might pronounce peneglos as 'pedneglos'.

You may assume that a Cornish word has primary stress on its penultimate syllable (the last but one) unless a dot placed after the vowel of another syllable indicates that primary stress falls on that syllable. When two elements are linked by a hyphen, primary stress is located in the second element. Occasionally equal stress is an option: *e.g.* pùptra, solabrës. For words of one syllable, the stress is reduced or disappears completely if the word is a *possessive* pronoun, or a preposition or conjunction (unemphasized); or if it is an unemphasized *personal* pronoun. A particle is always unstressed.

## Extending the vocabulary in this dictionary

Generally a word for the action of a verb or for its result can be formed regularly with the suffix -ans (plural -answow). The suffix is added to the verb-noun. If the verb-noun ends in a suffix (the most common are -as, -el, -es, -os), this is first removed; in the case of -el, it is also necessary to reverse the 'affection' (e.g. gelwel > galwans 'calling'). When the verb-noun ends in the suffix -ya (or -yas), the a(s) is removed but the y is retained. Elsewhere the suffix -ans occasionally grows a y of its own to become -yans.

A word for the doer of the action of a verb can usually be formed regularly with the suffix -or (plural -oryon). This suffix works in the same way as -ans; except that it never grows a y of its own. Another suffix for the doer of an action is -yth (plural -ydhyon), which has a flavour of 'dedication'; it is often used where English has -ist. A third suffix is -yas (plural -ysy), which has a flavour of 'professionalism'; it causes affection (preceding a changes to e).

Any word in -or / -yth referring to a person can be given specific female reference by adding -es (first changing th to dh). A word in -yas changes to -yades. The noun is then feminine, with plural -ow. The suffix -es can also be added to nouns in -ak, -ek, -yk (first changing k to g). Words in suffix -ak and many in -ek also change the a or e to o when making both plurals and feminine forms; so check the plural in the Cornish-English section. Thus for tevysak there is a plural tevysogyon and a feminine form tevysoges. You are not obliged to use -es; without it the word, though masculine, refers not to a male specifically, but to any person.

An adjective meaning -able / -ible can be formed by adding the suffix -adow to the stem of the verb (dropping any final y). But these words have a weighty feel, and should be used sparingly. Heavier still are the related masculine abstracts in -adêwder. For instance, cafadow 'available', cafadêwder 'availability'.

There are a number of suffixes forming abstract nouns: -der, -ter, -ys, -eth, -neth. A few generalizations may assist; the detail belongs to a book on grammar. Choosing between -der and -ter depends on sound; the system is very regular, including the effect of these suffixes on the consonant that precedes them. Nouns in suffix -der / -ter are always masculine; the plural forms are -derow / -terow. The plural of suffix -sys is -sesow. Be particularly careful with -eth. Revived Cornish recognizes *two* suffixes: -eth (plural -edhow) and -eth (plural -ethow). The first forms masculine nouns. The second mostly makes feminines, and has an extended version -ieth which is also feminine but usually singular only. In most cases both of the syllables in -ieth are unstressed. The suffix -neth is apparently a combination of English -ness and -eth; in traditional Cornish it is usually masculine, occasionally feminine. If you need a plural, it would be best to to follow the gender of the singular: so -nedhow (perhaps -nethow) for masculines, and -nethow for feminines.

## A note on Common Cornish

Common Cornish is a form of Revived Cornish that has become increasingly distinct. Its own reconstructed phonology gives less weight to the evidence of the surviving texts. But its vocabulary too has moved in a different direction, so that it remains apart even when spelled in the Standard Written Form. Genders, plurals, verb-noun endings sometimes differ; there are fewer loan-words from English, and international technical terms are more radically adapted; suffixes are employed differently when coining new terms; and a different semantic approach is taken with many words. The promoters of Common Cornish are Kesva an Taves Kernewek and Kowethas an Yeth Kernewek. If you wish to make comparisons with the Cornish in this book, here are two comprehensive volumes to consult: *An Gerlyver Meur* (2009), edited by Dr Ken George in the Common Cornish spelling system; and *A Learners' Cornish Dictionary* (2016), edited by

Steve Harris in the 2014 version of the SWF (see below). Both publications are available from the Kowethas.

## A note on the Standard Written Form

The Standard Written Form is a spelling system designed to be applicable to every kind of Revived Cornish. In theory each Cornish word has a single spelling in the SWF, with only a small number of permitted variants. This however assumes unanimity about the etymology of old words, and the way in which new words are coined or borrowed.

There is no general obligation to employ the Standard Written Form, and heavy limitations make it unsuitable for widespread application to traditional Cornish. Spellings with c q wh x, and most with final y, are not permitted in 'elementary language textbooks or official documents produced by public bodies'. A few spellings with final y are prohibited absolutely. Diacritical marks may only appear in 'dictionaries and teaching materials'.

The original version of the SWF and a few minor emendations were published in 2008. Recommendations for a number of significant changes were made in March 2014. Unfortunately the review board was not representative of all forms of Revived Cornish, and these recommendations would upset the delicate balance achieved by the original project. The changes have not been universally accepted.

## Improvements

All varieties of Revived Cornish are work-in-progress to some extent, and living languages are never entirely uniform.

Suggestions for improving the Standard Cornish in this dictionary may be sent to the author or the publishers. Any errors are the sole responsibility of the author.

# CORNISH-ENGLISH SECTION

Alternative forms of some Cornish words, sometimes even alternative words, are supplied between round brackets; they can be used with confidence, but such alternatives will occasionally involve different grammar. Definitions are confined to those most relevant for everyday conversation. Refer to the Introduction for entries containing an asterisk.

Bear in mind that Cornish words often span several grammatical categories. Adjectives in Cornish can be used as adverbs or nouns, adverbs may also function as adjectives, prepositions may serve as conjunctions; and many nouns can be employed with adjectival force. The categories marked in this dictionary are only a starting-point.

You will find a separate list of 'grammar words' (particles, pronouns, inflecting prepositions, conjunctions, question words) at the end of this section.

# A

**a boos brâs** *phr* important
**a bris** *phr* significant
**a brow** *phr* useful
**a les** *phr* interesting
**a'n barth / tu-ma dhe**[2] *phr* on this side of
**a'n par-ma** *phr* of this kind
**a'n par-na** *phr* such, of that kind
**a'n sêson** *phr* seasonal
**a res** *phr* necessary
**a varhas dhâ** *phr* a bargain (good value)
**a vresel** *phr* military
**a vry** *phr* notable
**a'y anvoth** *see* [oll] a'y anvoth
**a'y vodh** *see* [oll] a'y vodh
**aba·rth** *prep + noun*
**aba·rth dhe**[2] *prep + pronoun* on behalf of; in favour of (arguing etc)
**abatty** *m abattiow* abbey

**abecedary** *m abecedarys* alphabet
**abe·rth in** *phr* inside, within; into
**aberveth** *adv* in[side]
**aberveth in** *phr* inside, within; into
**abhorrya** *v* loathe
**abm** *m abmow* kiss
**abma** *v* (dhe²) kiss *Note pp* ibmys
**aborpos** *adv* intentionally, on purpose
**abo·ynt** *adv* punctually
**abrans** *m abransow* eyebrow
**absù·rd** *adj* absurd
**abyl** *adj* capable, competent
**aca·demy** *m aca·demys* academy
**aco·rd** *m acordys* accord, agreement
**acordya** *v* (gans, orth) agree (with)
**acordyon** *m acordyons* accordion
**aco·wnt** *m acowntys* account (financial)
**aco·wnt arhow** *m acowntys* deposit account
**aco·wnt erbysyon** *m acowntys* savings account
**aco·wnt kesres** *m acowntys* current account
**acowntya** *v* account; have a high regard for
**acowntyas** *m acowntysy* accountant
**act** *m actys* act (incl of Parliament)
**adâ·l** *prep + noun* **adâ·l dhe²** *prep + pronoun* opposite; compared with
**a·damant** *m adamantys* diamond
**addys** *adj* extra
**aden gales** *f adenyow cales* hardback
**aden vedhel** *f adenyow medhel* paperback
**aderdro** (ade·r dro) *adv* around; approximately
**adermyn** *adv* on time
**adhevî·s** *adv* exactly; first class; ideal
**adhewedhes** *adv* late (in time)
**adhewys** *adv* optionally
**adhvejy** *v* ripen, mature
**adhves** *adj* ripe, mature

**adhvetter** *m* ripeness, maturity
**adhyhow** *adv* on the right
**adhyhow dhe**[2] *prep* on / to the right of
**adhyscans** *m* education
**adhyscansek** *adj* educational
**adneth** *f anedhow* abode
**adrë·v** *prep + noun*
**adrë·v dhe**[2] *prep + pronoun* behind *position*
**adro·** *adv* around
**adro· dhe**[2] *prep* around; relating to, concerning, about
**adverb** *m adverbys* adverb
**afîna** *v* decorate
**afinuster** *m afinusterow* decoration; cosmetic
**afydhya** *v* (dhe[2]) assure (sb); confirm
**afydhyans** *m afydhyansow* assurance; confirmation
**agensow** *adv* recently
**agle·dh** *adv* on the left
**agle·dh dhe**[2] *prep* on / to the left of

**agria** *v* (gans) agree (with)
**agrians** *m agriansow* agreement
**ahë·s** *adv* along
**air** *m airys* air
**airborth** *m airborthow* airport
**aireth** *m airedhow* climate
**airgelgh** *m airgelhow* atmosphere
**ajwy** *f ajwiow* gap; loophole (figuratively)
**ajy·** *adv* in[side]
**ajy· dhe**[2] *prep* in[side], within; into
**a·lamand** *m alamandys* almond
**ala·rm** *m ala·rms* alarm (for security)
**albùm** *m albùms* album (music)
**a·lcohol** *m* alcohol
**alebma** *adv* from here; ago (viewed from present)
**alena** *adv* from there
**alge** *m* algae
**Allâ·h** *m* Allah

**allergek** *adj* (orth) allergic (to)
**alowa** *v* allow; admit, acknowledge
**alowadow** *adj* legitimate
**âls** *f âlsyow* cliff
**alsen** *f alsednow* razor
**alû·mynùm** *m* aluminium
**alusen** *f alusednow* charitable gift
**alwhedha** *v* lock
**alwhedhel** *f alwhedhellow* keyboard
**alwhedhen** *f alwhedhednow* key (keyboard)
**alwhedhor** *m alwhedhoryon* treasurer
**alwheth** *m alwhedhow* key (for lock)
**alwheth corkyn** *m alwhedhow* corkscrew
**amal** *m emlow* edge
**amanyn** *m* butter
**a·mary** *m a·marys* cupboard
**amatorek** *adj* amateur
**amatorus** *adj* amateurish
**amatou·r** *m amatou·rs* amateur

**ambos** *m ambosow* (orth) undertaking (to); condition
**ambosek** *adj* conditional
**ambosow aco·rd** *pl* terms and conditions
**amendya** (mendya) *v* put right, mend; revise
**amethy** *v* farm
**amethyans** *m* farming, agriculture
**amowntyor** (kevrivyador) *m amowntyoryon* computer
**amowntyor dewlin** *m amowntyoryon* laptop
**amseryow** *pl* period (of woman)
**amuvyansek** *adj* sentimental
**amyttya** *v* admit (all senses)
**an** + *noun* **a dheu** *phr* next (in time)
**an** + *noun* **lacka oll** *phr* the worst
**An Avar** *f* Capricorn
**An Benscol Egor** *f* The Open University
**an bobel** *f* the public

**an bobel vian** *f* the fairies
**An Bobm Brâs** *m* The Big Bang
**An Canker** *m* Cancer
**an cans** *phr* per cent
**An Colmeth Adhevî·s** *m* The Premier League
**an dâ** *m* right (as opposed to wrong)
**An Democratyon Lybral** *pl* The Liberal Democrats
**An Dowror** *m* Aquarius
**an drog** *m* wrong (as opposed to right)
**An Enebyans** *m* The Opposition (in Parliament)
**An Evellas** *pl* Gemini
**An 'Furv Scrifys Savonek' (FSS)** *f* The Standard Written Form (SWF)
**An Fydhyans Kenedhlek** *m* The National Trust
**An Gov** *m* The Smith (Michael Joseph)
**an gowethas** *f* society
**An Gwariow Olympek** *pl* The Olympics

**an gwedhyl** *m* ($a^2$) the rest (of)
**an gwelha** (an gwella) *adj* the best
**an gwelha oll ganso** *phr* his favourite
**An Hordh** *m* Aries
**an jowl** *phr after question word* the hell
**An Kenedhlow Unyes** *pl* The United Nations
**An Kesrosweyth** *m* The Internet
**An Lew** *m* Leo
**An Lo·ttery [Kenedhlek]** *m* The National Lottery
**an mainys [kemenessa]** *pl* the media
**An 'Pewas Perghyryn'** *m* The Palmer Award
**An Pùscas** *pl* Pisces
**an remnant** *m* ($a^2$) the remainder (of)
**An Scorpyon** *m* Scorpio
**An Servys [Kenedhlek] Yêhes** *m* The National Health Service (NHS)
**An Sethor** *m* Sagittarius
**An Spyrys Sans** *m* The Holy Spirit

**an stairys wàr nans** *phr* downstairs *motion*
**An Tarow** *m* Taurus
**an termyn a dheu** *m* the future
**an termyn eus passys** *m* the past
**An Unyans Ewropek** *m* The European Union
**An Vantol** *f* Libra
**An Werhes** *f* Virgo
**anabyl** *adj* incapable
**anal** *f* breath
**ana·lojy** *m ana·lojys* analogy
**ancertan** *adj* uncertain
**ancombra** *v* confuse (sb); inconvenience
**ancombrus** *adj* confusing; inconvenient
**ancombrynjy** *m* confusion; inconvenience
**andenythek** *m andenythegow* contraceptive
**andesedhus** *adj* inappropriate
**andyblans** *adj* imprecise
**anella** *v* breathe
**anê·s** *adj* uncomfortable (sb)

**ane·wn** *adj* unfair
**anfel** *adj* naive
**anfelder** *m* naivety
**anfurvus** *adj* informal
**anfusyk** *adj* unlucky, unfortunate
**A·nglycan** *adj/m A·nglycans* Anglican
**ania** *v* annoy, irritate
**anians** *m aniansow* annoyance
**anjù·st** *adj* unjust
**ankevy** *v* forget
**anowy** *v* kindle
**anserhak** *adj* independent (conduct, country)
**ansur** *adj* unsure
**a·nterlyk Nadelyk** *m anterlygow* pantomime
**anteythy** *adj* incompetent; hopeless (sb)
**antybiotek** *m antybiotygyon* antibiotic
**anvodhek** *adj* unwilling
**anwhek** *adj* unpleasant
**anwos** *m* cold, chill (illness)
**anwosva** *f* flu
**anwyw** *adj* unsuitable

**anyagh** *adj* unhealthy (sb and figuratively)
**anyahus** *adj* unhealthy (sth)
**anyen** *f* instinct(s)
**ape·rt** *adj* obvious
**apo·tecary** *m apo·tecarys* pharmacist
**appa** *m appys* ape
**apposyans** *m apposyansow* examination (academic)
**apron** (apern) *m aprodnyow* apron
**aqwîrya** *v* acquire
**aqwîtyans** *m aqwityansow* receipt (document)
**a·radar** (ardar) *m e·reder (erder)* plough
**arâ·g** *adv* in front
**aral** *adj* (*pl* **erel**) other See also 'Grammar Words'
**aras** *v* plough
**ara·y** *m arayes* arrangement; layout
**araya** *v* arrange
**arbenegor** *m arbenegoryon* specialist, expert

**arbenegy** *v* specialize
**arbrevy** *v* experiment
**arbrof** *m arbrovow* experiment
**arbrôjy** *m arbrojiow* laboratory
**ardak** *m ardagow* delay; reservation (about sth); check (in chess)
**arenep** *m arenebow* surface
**areth** *f arethyow* lecture, talk, speech
**arethek** *adj* rhetorical
**arethva** *f arethvaow* podium
**arethya** *v* lecture, talk
**argebmyn** *m argemydnow* advert[isement]
**argemydna** *v* advertise
**argen** *f argenow* veneer
**argerdh** *m argerdhow* process
**argh** *f arhow* bin, tank (for storage / disposal of bulk: litter, rubbish, water etc)
**argh-**[1] *pref* arch-
**argh atal** *f arhow* wheelie bin

**arghpedrevan** *f arghpedrevanas* dinosaur
**argibya** *v* kidnap; hijack
**argip** *m argibyow* kidnap[ping]; hijack[ing]
**argraf** *m argrafyow* impression
**a·rgùment** *m argùmentys* argument (specific)
**argya** *v* argue (develop an argument)
**arhadow** *m* order
**arhans** *m* silver
**arhansek** *adj* financial
**arhanso·rieth** *f* finance
**arhanty** *m arhantiow* bank
**arhas** *m arhasow* fund
**arhasa** *v* fund
**arlodhes** *f arlodhesow* lady (peer)
**arlùth** *m arlydhy* lord
**arlyw** *m arlywyow* tint, shade; nuance
**arlywa** *v* tint; nuance
**arnowedhy** *v* modernize
**arnowyth** *adj* modern
**arolegyth** *m arolegydhyon* inspector
**arsmetryk** *m* arithmetic

**art** *m artys* art
**arta** *adv* again; back again
**artykyl** *m artyclys* article (written)
**arv** *f arvow* weapon
**arva** *v* arm
**arvedhesyk** *m arvedhesygyon* employee
**arvedhor** *m arvedhoryon* employer
**arvedhyth** *m arvedhydhyon* attacker
**arveth** *m/v* employ(ment)
**arveth** *v* harass, attack (physically or by actions / words)
**arvrusy** (arvrujy) *v* assess
**arvrusyans** *m arvrusyansow* assessment
**arwedha** *v* signal
**arwedhek** *adj* symbolic
**arwedhyk** *f arwedhygow* badge
**arweth** *f arwedhyow* sign, signal (incl radio etc); symbol; character (keyboard)

**arwhythrans** *m arwhythransow* survey
**ascendya** *v* ascend
**asclas** *col asclejen* chips (potato)
**ascor** *v* produce
**ascoras** *m ascorasow* product
**ascorn** *m eskern* bone
**ascû·s** *m ascûsys* excuse
**asen** *m & f asenas* donkey
**asfalt** *m* asphalt
**askel** *f eskelly* wing; fin
**asnodhow** *pl* resources
**asow** *col asowen* ribs
**asper** *adj* grim
**aspe·ryta** *m aspe·rytys* grimness; austerity
**aspia** *v* catch sight of
**aspia orth** *v* look out for; observe
**aspians** *m aspiansow* reconnaissance; surveillance
**aspias** *m/v no inflection aspiesy* (orth) spy (on)
**asran** *f asradnow* department

**[Asran] Droglabmow ha Gorothobmow** *f* Accidents and Emergencies Department (A&E)
**âss** *m âcys* ace
**assaultya** *v* assault, attack
**assaultyans** *m assaultyansow* assault, attack
**assa·y** *m assa·ys* attempt; rehearsal
**assaya** *v* attempt (sth); rehearse
**assentya** *v* (dhe$^2$, orth) consent (to), agree (with)
**assentyans** *m assentyansow* (dhe$^2$, orth) consent (to), agreement (with)
**assoylya** *v* solve
**assoylyans** *m assoylyansow* solution
**astel** *v* discontinue; suspend
**astel ober** *m/phr astellow* (go on) strike
**astell** *f estyll* board
**astell dartys** *f estyll* dartboard

**astell dîvya** *f estyll* diving board
**astell gool** *f estyll* sailboard, windsurfer
**astell mordardha** *f estyll* surfboard
**astell omborth** *f estyll* see-saw
**astell-wolya** *v* go sailboarding / windsurfing
**astelor** *m asteloryon* striker
**astevery** *v* (nampy·th dhe[2] nebonen) compensate (sb for sth)
**asvaba** *v* adopt (child)
**aswon** (ajon) *v* know (be acquainted with); recognize, identify; acknowledge
**aswon grâss dhe**[2] *phr* (a[2]) thank (for)
**aswywa** *v* adapt
**aswywor** *m aswyworyon* adapter
**atal** *col* rubbish
**athlet** *m athletys* athlete
**atom** *m atomow* atom
**atorny** *m atornys* solicitor (loosely)

**atta·l** *m attallow* repayment; retaliation
**attendya** *v* pay attention (to)
**atte·nt** *m attentys* attempt
**attê·s** *adj/m* comfort(able) (sb)
**attylly** *v* repay; retaliate
**aucto·ryta** *m aucto·rytys* authority
**auctour** *m auctours* author
**aval** *m avallow* apple
**aval gwlanek** *m avallow* peach
**aval kerensa** *m avallow* tomato
**aval pa·radhys** *m avallow* grapefruit
**avan** *col avanen* raspberries
**ava·rr** *adv* early (incl before due time)
**avauncya** *v* advance; progress; promote
**avauncyans** *m avauncyansow* advance; progress
**aventu·r** *m aventu·rs* adventure

**aventurya** *v* venture
**aventuryans** *m aventuryansow* venture, enterprise
**avê·s** *adv* out[side] *position*
**avê·s dhe**² *prep* outside *position*
**avî·s** *m avîsyow* notice (formal); motion (for debate)
**avlavar** (aflavar) *adj* mute
**avles** (afles) *m* disadvantage
**avorow** *adv* tomorrow
**avortans** *m avortansow* abortion
**avowa** *v* admit, acknowledge
**avoydya** (voydya) *v* depart
**avresonus** *adj* unreasonable
**avy** *m* **aviow** liver
**awartha** *adv* at the top
**awayl** *f awaylow* gospel
**awaylek** *adj* evangelical
**awedhus** *adj* influential

**awedhya** *v* influence
**awedhyans** *m awedhyansow* influence
**awednow** *pl* jaws
**awel** *f awellow* gale; weather (windy or in general)
**awen** *f* inspiration, muse; creativity
**awenek** *adj* creative
**aweny** *v* inspire
**awenyth** *m awenydhyon* genius (sb)
**awgrym** *m awgrymow* algorithm
**awhesyth** *m awhesydhas* [sky]lark
**awoles** *adv* at the bottom; downstairs *position*
**awo·s** *prep + noun, indefinite pronoun, verb-noun, infinitive construction, relative clause* because (of) (affirmative only); in spite of, despite
**awosa** (a'y wosa) *adv* afterwards
**aysel** *m* vinegar

# B

**baby** *m & f babiow* baby
**backa** *m* tobacco
**backen** *m* bacon
**bacterya** *pl* bacteria
**badhya** *v* bathe
**badna** *m literally* 'drop': *with express negative* any, *with implied negative* no (of sth liquid or abstract)
**bagas** *m bagasow* group; troop (actors)
**bagas dyba·rth** *m bagasow* splinter group
**bagas kevos** *m bagasow* year group
**bagas lavur** *m bagasow* working party
**bagas tyckly** *m bagasow* awkward squad
**bagh** *m bahow* hook; hinge
**bagh** *f bahow* cage; prison (slang)
**baha** *v* hook
**bal** *m balow* mining complex
**balcon** *m balconow* balcony; circle (in theatre)
**balegy** *v* jut out; stand out
**balou·n** *m balou·ns* balloon
**balyer** *m balyers* barrel
**balyer fortydnys** *m balyers* lucky dip
**bàn** *m badnow* height (high place)
**banâna** *m banânas* banana
**baner** *m banerow* flag, banner
**bank botel** *m bancow* bottle bank
**banket** *m bankettys* banquet
**banknôta** *m banknôtys* banknote
**Baptyst** *m Baptystyon* Baptist
**bara** *m* bread
**bara cras** *m* toast (food)
**ba·rbecû** *m barbecûys* barbecue
**barbour** *m barbours* barber
**bardh** *m berdh* bard

**Bardh Meur** *m Berdh Veur* Grand Bard
**bardhonek** *m bardhonegow* poem
**bargednya** *v* bargain, haggle
**bargen** *m bargenys* bargain (deal)
**bargen tir** *m bargenys* farm
**barlen** *f barlednow* lap
**barlys** *col* barley
**barr** *m barrow* summit
**barr** *m barrys* bar (incl for drinks)
**barryth** *m barydhyon* barman, barista
**barthusek** *adj* marvellous, phenomenal
**barv** *f barvow* beard
**barvus** *m barvusy* cod
**barya** *v* bar
**baryas** *m barysy* barrier
**bas** *adj* shallow
**basa·r trog** *m basa·rs* car boot sale
**basnet** *m basnettys* helmet
**bason** *m basonys* basin
**baster** *m* shallowness
**batalyas** *v* battle, fight

**batel** *f batellyow* battle
**bath** *m bathow* coin
**bathador** *m bathadoryon* slot machine
**batry** *m batrys* battery
**bay** *m bays* bay
**bedh** *m bedhow* tomb, grave
**bednath** *f benothow* blessing
**begel** *m begelyow* navel
**behek** *adj* pregnant
**benega** *v* bless
**Benenes** (Myrhas) *pl* Ladies (toilet)
**benow** *adj* female; feminine (grammar)
**benthygya** *v* borrow (sth specific)
**benyn** *f benenes* woman
**benyn ambosys** *f benenes* fiancée
**bern** *m* concern; *care about
**berry** *m* fat
**berus** *adj* fluid
**berusen** *f berusednow* fluid
**bës** *m besias* finger; hand (clock)
**bës troos** *m besias* toe

**besow** *m besewow* ring
**best** *m bestas* animal
**besydhya** *v* baptize, christen
**besyth** (bejyth) *m besydhow* baptism, christening
**betys rudh** *col betysen* beetroot
**bew** *adj* alive; live (TV etc); lively
**bewa** *v* (orth) live (on – food etc)
**bewder** *m* liveliness
**bewek** *adj* lively
**bewekhe·** *v* liven up
**bewhe·** (bew'he·) *v* animate; activate
**bêwnans** *m bewnansow* life
**beyt** *m beytys* byte
**bian** *adj* small, little
**bîbyn-bûbyn** *m bîbyn-bûbynas* shrimp
**biologyl** *adj* biological
**blam** *m* blame
**blâmya** *v* blame
**bla·sfemy** *m bla·sfemys* blasphemy
**bledhednek** *adj* annual

**bledhen** *f bledhydnyow* year
**blejen an gùcû** *f* bluebell
**blejen tù·lyfant** *f blejednow* tulip
**blesys dâ** *phr* tasty
**bleus** *m* flour
**blew** *col blewen* hair
**blew an lagas** *col blew an lagasow* eyelash
**bleydh** *m bleydhas* wolf
**bleyn** *m bleynow* tip; peak (incl of cap)
**blòg** *m bloggys* blog
**bloggyor** *m blogyoryon* blogger
**blogh** *adj* hairless
**blonegek** *adj* greasy
**blonek** *m* fat, grease
**bloodh** *m* year (of age)
**blou** *adj* blue (contrasted with green)
**blùbber** *m blùbbers* jellyfish
**bludh** *adj* delicate
**bludhecter** *m bludhecterow* delicacy
**bludhyans menowghter** *m* frequency modulation (FM)

**bobansus** *adj* pompous
**bobba** *m bobbys* idiot
**bobm** *m bobmyn* bang
**bobmen** *f bomednow* blow
**bobmen scav** *f bomednow* flick
**bockyl** *m boclys* buckle
**bodh dâ** *m* goodwill
**bodhar** *adj* deaf
**bodharus** *adj* deafening
**bodhek** *adj* voluntary
**bodhogyon** *pl* volunteers
**bogh** *f bohow* cheek
**bohes** (**bohes**[2] before b, g, gw, m) *adj + singular or collective noun* little; few
**bohes venowgh** *phr* rarely, seldom
**bohes y vern** *phr* indifferent; unimportant
**bohosek** *adj* poor
**bohosogneth** *m* poverty
**bojet** *m bojettys* budget
**bolder** *m* boldness
**bolhen** *f bolhednow* capsule (for medication)
**boll** *adj* see-through
**bolla** *m bollys* bowl (deep)

**bollen** *f bollednow* bulb (electric)
**bolùnje'ek** *adj* willing
**bond codna** *m bondys* collar
**bonden** *f bondednow* tyre
**bonk** *m bonkys* bump
**bool** *f bolow* axe
**boos** *m bosow* food
**boos soper** *m* supper
**bord** *m bordys* board; table (especially for eating)
**borger** *m borgers* burger
**bos** (bones) *v* be
**bos a'y eseth** *phr* be sitting / sat
**bos a'y sav** *phr* be standing / stood
**bos a'y wroweth** *phr* be lying (position)
**bos balgh a**[2] *phr* take pride in
**bos desedhys** *phr* be situated
**bos determys dhe** *phr + verb-noun* be determined to
**bos genys** *phr* be born
**bos heb** *v* lack

**bos in** *v* attend
**bos in kendon rag** *phr* owe
**bos kemerys yn frâs gans** *phr* be impressed by
**bos porposys dhe**[2] *phr* + *verb-noun* intend to
**bos res porre·s** *phr* be urgent
**bos rêson** *phr* make sense (idea, proposal)
**bos sensys dhe**[2] *phr* be grateful to
**bos tregys in** *phr* live in
**bos unverhë·s** *phr* (gans) be in agreement (with)
**bos whensys dhe**[2] *phr* + *verb-noun* want to, wish to, be inclined to
**bosa** *v* feed (animal, machine, media)
**bost** *m bôstow* boast
**bosty** *m bostiow* restaurant
**bôstya** *v* boast
**botas** *col botasen* boots
**botas palvek** *col botasen* flippers (for wearing)
**botel** *f botellow* bottle
**bothan** *m bothadnow* hump; bulge
**bothel** *f bothlow* bubble
**boton** *m botodnow* button
**bownder** *f bownderyow* lane
**bowyn** *see* [kig] bowyn
**box** *m boxys* box
**boxesy** *v* box
**brabm** *m brebmyn* fart
**brabma** *v* fart
**bran** *f breyny* crow
**brâs** *adj* big, large; greatly
**bras** *m brasow* plot, conspiracy
**brâster** *m brasterow* size
**brastir** *m brastiryow* continent
**brathy** *v* bite (to hurt)
**brav** *adj* fine, grand
**brawehy** *v* terrify
**bre** *f breow* hill
**brednya** *v* give directions; run (event, organization)
**brednyk** *col brenygen* limpets
**bregh** *f brehow* arm

**breghtan** *m breghtanow* sandwich
**breha** *v* inoculate
**brehal** *m brehellow* sleeve
**brentyn** (bryntyn) *adj* noble; excellent
**brës** *m bresyow* mind
**bresel** *f breselyow* war
**brest** *m* brass
**brèst** *m brestys* chest (anatomy)
**Bretonek** *m* Breton (language)
**breus** *f breusow* judgement, opinion
**breusor** *m breusoryon* referee
**brew** *adj/m brewyon* injured; bruise, sore, wound (minor)
**brewy** *v* bruise; crush; smash, shatter; mash
**Brexyt** *m* Brexit
**briansen** *f briansednow* throat
**briel** *m brilly* mackerel
**bris** *m brisyow* womb
**brith** *adj/col brithen* spotted, speckled, freckled; spots, speckles, freckles
**brîvya** *v* bleat
**bro** *f broyow* land, country (often with sense of intimacy)
**brôcha** *m brôchys* brooch
**broder** *m breder* brother
**brodn** *f brodnow* breast (particularly female)
**brodn-noth** *adj* topless
**brogh** *m brohas* badger
**brongolm** *m brongolmow* bra
**bronlen** *f bronlednow* bib
**brons** *m* bronze
**bronvil** *m bronvilas* mammal
**bros** *adj/m brosow* very hot; great heat; stew
**bros** *m brojow* sting
**brosa** *v* sting
**brosweyth** *m* embroidery
**brosya** *v* embroider
**browsyon** *pl* crumbs
**bry** *m* regard, respect
**bryck** *m bryckys* brick
**bryjyon** *v* boil *intr*
**bryketh** *col brykethen* apricots

**bùcka** *m bùckyas* gremlin; ghost; scarecrow
**Bùdda** *m* Buddha
**Bù·ddieth** *f* Buddhism
**Bùddyst** *m Bùddystyon* Buddhist
**budhy** *v* drown; sink
**budhyans** *m* flooding
**bùffê·** *m bùffê·s* buffet
**bùhyk Duw** *f bùhygow* ladybird
**bùlet** *m bùlettys* bullet
**bùlgh** *m bùlhow* slot
**bùlly** *m bùllys* bully
**bùllya** *v* bully
**bùltyn** *m bùltyns* bulletin
**bùluk** *col bùlugen* earthworms
**bùly bian** *col bùlien vian* pebbles
**bùsh** *m bùshys* bush
**bùsh brâs a**[2] *phr* a whole lot of
**buwgh** *f buhas* cow
**byckenus** *adj* eternal
**byckenuster** *m* eternity
**bykîny** *m bykînys* bikini
**bylder** *m bylders* builder
**byldya** *v* build
**bylyard tavern** *m* pool (game)

**bylyonê·r** *m bylyonê·rs* billionaire
**byrla** *v* hug, embrace
**byrlans** *m byrlansow* hug, embrace
**bÿs** *m bysow* world
**bys** *prep + adverb* until
**bys dhe**[2] *prep + pronoun*
**bys in** *prep + noun* [up] to; until
**bys i'n eur-ma** *phr* up to now
**bys vycken [ha bys venary]** *phr* for ever [and ever]
**bÿs-estren** *m bÿs-estrenyon* alien, extraterrestrial
**byskyt** *m byskyttys* biscuit (sweet or savoury)
**bysmê·r** *m bysmêrys* smear (defamatory); scandal (specific)
**bysy** *adj* busy; engaged (telephone, toilet)
**bysy yw** *phr + verb-noun, infinitive construction, na*[2]*-clause* it is important
**bytegy·ns** *adv* however

**bÿth na lavar a'n dra** *phr* don't mention it (in response to thanks)
**bythqweth** *adv with express negative* ever, *with implied negative* never (past reference)
**bythwer** *adj* evergreen
**byttele·** *adv* nonetheless, nevertheless

# C

**cabel** *m* criticism (adverse)
**cabel sclandrus** *m* libel, slander
**cabester** *m cabestrow* loop; noose; strap (shoulder)
**cablek** *adj* critical (adverse), derogatory
**cablus** *adj* guilty
**cably** *v* criticize (adversely)
**cabm** *adj* crooked; wrong
**cabma** *v* distort
**cabmas** *m camasow* bay (wide – e.g. Mount's Bay)
**cabmen** *f literally* 'single step': *with express negative* at all, *with implied negative* not at all
**cabùlva** *f cabùlvaow* muddle
**cabùly** *v* stir (liquid)

**cabyn** *m cabyns* cabin; deck (aircraft)
**cabyn lewyador** *m cabyns* cockpit
**ca·bynet** *m cabynettys* cabinet (incl government)
**cachya** *v* catch; catch up with *Note pp* kychys
**cactùs** *m ca·ctùsow* cactus
**cadar herdhya** *f caderyow* pushchair
**cadar rosow** *f caderyow* wheelchair
**caderya** *v* chair, preside (over)
**caderyor** *m caderyoryon* chairman
**cadna** *m cadnys* tin, can (*e.g.* for baking / roasting, for petrol)
**cadnas** *f canajow* delegate, representative; messenger; message

**cadnas vôtya** *f canajow* proxy
**cafas** *m cafasow* container; tin, can (incl of / for food / drink)
**cafas dowrhe·** *m cafasow* watering can
**cafos** (cavos, cawas, gawas *fixed 2nd state*) *v* have, get; find (incl by experience)
**cafos cowas** *phr* take a shower
**cafosyans** *m cafosyansow* acquisition
**caja** *f* daisy
**càl** *m calyow* penis, cock
**cala** *col* straw
**calco·rieth** *f* mathematics
**cales** *adj* hard; difficult
**calesen** *f calesednow* corn, callus
**caletter** *m caletterow* difficulty; problem
**calhen** *f calhednow* chalk (piece for drawing)
**cals a**[2] *phr + uncountable noun* plenty of
**caltor** *f caltoryow* kettle

**camdremenyas** *m camdremenysy* trespasser (incl on land)
**ca·mera** *m ca·meras* camera
**ca·mera gwias** *m ca·meras* webcam
**ca·mera kelgh clos** *m ca·meras* CCTV camera
**ca·mera toth** *m ca·meras* speed camera
**camhensek** *adj* wrong, immoral, unethical, wicked
**camhùmbronk** *v* mislead
**camnedhys** *adj* tangled
**camp** *m campys* camp
**campoll** *m campollow* reference (to sth); comment
**campolla** *v* refer to; comment on
**campolla andydro** *phr* allude to
**campùs** *m ca·mpùsow* campus
**campva** *f campvaow* campsite
**campya** *v* camp
**campyor** *m campyoryon* champion

**campyorsys** *m campyorsesow* championship
**camùnderstondyng** *m* misunderstanding
**camva** *f camvaow* stile
**camwonys** *v* bungle
**càn** *m* shine
**cân** *f cânow* song
**cana** *v* sing
**canasa** *v* (nebonen a nampy·th) delegate (sth to sb)
**canaseth** *m canasedhow* delegation; embassy
**canasor** *m canasoryon* ambassador
**canel** *f canellow* channel (incl TV)
**canker** *m kencras* crab; cancer
**canor** *m canoryon* singer
**cansran** *f cansradnow* percentage
**canstel** *f canstellow* basket
**cansvledhen** *f cansvledhydnyow* century (100 years)
**cantol** *f cantolyow* candle
**capel** *m caplys* cable
**cappa** *m cappys* cap; topping (cookery)
**capten** *m captens* captain
**cara** *v* love See also ev a garsa
**cara warba·rth** *phr* (gans) make love (to)
**caradow** *adj* kind; likeable
**ca·ramel** *m* caramel
**ca·ravan** *m caravanow* caravan
**ca·rdygon** *m ca·rdygons* cardigan
**caregek** *adj* rocky
**cares** *f caresow* girlfriend
**caretys** *col caretysen* carrots
**carg** *m cargow* load; charge (electricity)
**carga** *v* load; charge (electricity)
**cargor** *m cargoryon* charger
**carjy** *m carjiow* garage
**carn** *m carnow* hoof
**carn** *m carnow* tor; cairn
**carnak** *adj* rocky (exposed bedrock)

**carnal joy** *m* sex (sexual activity)
**ca·rnyval** *m carnyvalow* carnival
**caror** *m caroryon* lover, boyfriend
**caro·rieth** *f caroriethow* relationship (sexual)
**carow** *m kyrwas* deer
**carow Loghlyn** *m kyrwas* reindeer
**carr clôjy** *m kerry* ambulance
**carr slynkya** *m kerry* sleigh, sledge
**carr [tan]** *m kerry* car
**carrek** *f ca·rrygy* rock
**carten** *f cartednow* card (individual)
**carten cravas** *f cartednow* scratch card
**carten crejys** *f cartednow* credit card
**carten debys** *f cartednow* debit card
**carthpîp** *m carthpibow* drain[pipe]
**carven** *f carvenow* van
**carven campya** *f carvenow* camper van
**carya** *v* transport

**caryach** *m caryajys* carriage; coach (train)
**caryach baby** *m caryajys* pram
**caryans** *m* transport[ation]
**cas** *m* hatred; *dislike, disapprove of
**casadow** *adj* horrible, repulsive
**casek** *f ca·sygy* mare
**casek coos** *f ca·sygy* woodpecker
**caskergh** *m caskerhow* campaign
**caslewyth** *m caslewydhyon* general
**câss** *m câssys* case (all senses)
**cast** *m castys* trick, hoax
**castel** *m castylly* castle
**castya** *v* trick, hoax
**ca·talog** *m catalogow* catalogue
**cath** *f cathas* cat
**Catholyk** *adj/m Catholygyon* Catholic
**cathyk** *f cathygas* kitten
**caudarn** *m caudarns* boiler
**caugh** *m* shit

**cauha** *v* shit
**caulvlejen** *f caulvlejednow* cauliflower
**caulvlejen gales** *f caulvlejednow cales* broccoli
**caulygen** *f caulygednow* Brussels sprout
**cauns** *m cauncys* pavement; courtyard (open)
**causya** *v* cause
**cav** *m câvyow* cave
**cavach** *m* cabbage
**cavylek** *adj* contentious
**cay** *m cays* quay; pier; platform (for train)
**centy-**[1] *pref* centi-
**certan** *adj* certain
**cessya** *v* cease
**cessyans tedna** *m cessyansow* ceasefire
**chacya** *v* chase
**chain** *m chainys* chain
**chair** *m chairys* chair
**chair brehek** *m chairys* armchair
**chair howl** *m chairys* deck chair
**chalynjya** *v* challenge (sth)
**chambour** *m chambours* chamber; bedroom
**chapel** *m chapelyow* chapel
**chaptra** *m chaptrys* chapter
**charj** *m charjys* responsibility (to perform specific task/s)
**chauncya** *v* risk
**chaunj** *m chaunjys* change, modification
**chaunjus** *adj* variable
**chaunjya** *v* change, modify
**chauns** *m chauncys* chance; opportunity
**checken** *f checkednow* cheque
**checker** *m checkeryow* chessboard; check (pattern)
**checkva** *f checkvaow* security [check] (at airport etc)
**checkya** *v* check
**chemyk** *m chemygow* chemical
**chêny** *m* china (material)
**cher** *m cheryow* mood
**chersya** *v* caress, pet

**chersya re** *phr* spoil
**cherya** *v* care for (sb)
**che·ryta** *m che·rytys* charity (organization)
**chêson** *m chêsonys* (a) reason, motive
**chif-**[1] *pref* chief, main, principal
**choclat** *m choclats* chocolate
**chôk** *m chôkys* jackdaw
**chy** *m treven* house, building *See also* [in] chy
**Chy an Arlydhy** *m* The House of Lords
**Chy an Gemyn** *m* The House of Commons
**chylly** *m* chilli
**chymbla** *m chymblys* chimney; funnel
**chyrù·rjery** *m* surgery (operation)
**chyrùrjyen** *m chyrùrjyens* surgeon
**cîder** *m* cider
**clamder** *m* faint, blackout; anaesthesia
**clamdera** *v* faint, black out
**clamderyas** *m clamderysy* anaesthetic

**clapes** *m clapesow* valve
**clappya** *v* chat
**class** *m classys* class; category
**classya** *v* classify
**classyk** *adj/m classygyon* classic
**clattra** *v* clatter; chatter, babble
**clâv** *adj/m clevyon* ill, sick; patient
**clavhun** *m clavhunow* coma
**cledh** *adj/m* left (as opposed to right)
**cledh** *m cledhyow* ditch, trench
**cledha** *m cledhydhyow* sword
**cledhek** *adj* clumsy
**cledhyas** *m cledhysy* left-handed person
**clegar** *m clegrow* precipice
**cler** *adj* clear
**clerhe·** *v* clarify, explain
**cles** *adj* cosy, snug
**clether** *col clethren* rails; railings
**clevejus** *adj* infectious
**clevejy** *v* infect

**clevejyans** *m clevejyansow* infection
**cleves** *m clevejow* illness, disease
**cleves dyglon** *m* depression
**cleves epydemek** *m clevejow* epidemic
**cleves esyly** *m* rheumatism
**cleves melys** *m* diabetes
**cleves strewy** *m* hayfever
**client** *m cliens* client
**clock** *m clockys* clock
**cloffy** *v* limp
**clogh** *m clegh* bell
**clojior** *m clojioryon* nurse
**clôjy** *m clojiow* hospital
**clôk** *m clôkys* cloak
**clôkva** *f clokvaow* cloakroom
**cloos** *f clojow* lattice, framework; rack, crate; hurdle
**cloppek** *adj* lame
**clor** *adj* gentle, mild
**clorder** *m* gentleness, mildness
**clos** *adj/m closys* enclosed; stuffy; enclosure (place)
**cloud** *m cloudys* cloud
**cloweles** *adj* audio-visual
**clôwes** *v* hear; smell (sth); feel (sensation)
**clowt** *m clowtys* cloth (small piece); patch
**clowtya** *v* patch
**clùb** *m clùbbys* club
**clùbba** *v no inflection* go out clubbing
**clun** *f clunyow* hip
**clyckya** *v* click (incl on device)
**clyjjy** *m* toffee
**clynyk** *m clynygow* clinic
**clyp** *m clyppys* clip
**cober** *m* copper
**côcha** *m côchys* coach (road vehicle)
**cocktail** *m cocktails* cocktail
**côco** *m* cocoa
**cod** *m côdyow* code
**cod marhasa** *m côdyow* promotional code
**codha** *v* fall; befall
**codha in dyfyk** *phr* crash (device)
**codna** *m conaow* neck

**codna bregh** *m conaow* wrist
**codnek** *adj* clever
**coffy** *m* coffee
**co·ffyva** *f coffyvaow* café
**cofyr** *m cofrow* chest, trunk (box)
**cog** *adj* silly, pointless
**côk** *m cûcow* fishing boat
**côla** *m* cola
**cola orth** *v* listen to (heed)
**colhes** *f colhesow* mattress
**coljy** *m coljiow* college
**coll** *m collow* loss
**collel** *f kellyl* knife
**collenwel** *v* complete; fulfil; accomplish; complement
**collor** *m colloryon* loser (as opposed to winner)
**colm** *m colmow* bond, tie; knot, bow
**colm codna** *m colmow* tie (for neck)
**colmen bleg** *f colmednow pleg* bow tie
**colmeth** *m colmedhow* league

**colodhyon** *pl* bowels, intestines
**colodnek** *adj* brave
**colom** *f colmas* dove, pigeon
**colon** *f colodnow* heart (incl in cards)
**colonecter** *m* bravery
**colonen** *f colonednow* core
**colour** *m colours* colour
**coloven** *f colovednow* column
**colpes** *m colpesow* lever
**colpon** *m colponys* coupon, voucher
**colyn** *m kelyn* puppy
**co·medy** *m co·medys* comedy
**comedyan** *m comedyans* comedian
**comek** *adj* comic
**comendya** *v* approve; recommend; introduce (sb to sb)
**comendyans** *m comendyansow* approval; recommendation
**comolek** *adj* cloudy
**comondya** *v* command

*Note constructions*
comondya dhe² nebonen gwil nampy·th *and* may whrella / na wrella nebonen nampy·th command sb to do / not to do sth
**compact** *adj* compact
**comparya** *v* compare
**comparyans** *m comparyansow* comparison; simile
**compas** *m compassys* extent; compass
**compassus** *adj* comprehensive
**compes** *adj* straight; even; right (morally)
**complek** *adj* complex
**completh** *adj* complicated
**completha** *v* complicate
**complethter** *m complethterow* complication
**composa** *v* straighten; verify
**composya** *v* compose (music, poetry etc)
**composyth** *m composydhyon* composer

**comprehendya** *v* include
**compressa** *v* oppress
**comptya** *v* count (how many)
**comùn** *m* communion (sacrament)
**comyk** *m comygow* comic (periodical)
**comyssyon** *m comyssyons* commission (body)
**conar** *f* fury; mania
**concêvya** *v* conceive (all senses)
**conce·yt** *m conceytys* concept
**concrît** *m* concrete
**condom** *m condoms* condom
**coneryak** *adj* furious; manic
**confessya** *v* confess
**confessyon** *m confessyons* confession
**confort** *m confortys* comfort; consolation
**confortya** *v* comfort, console
**cons** *f consyow* vagina, cunt
**consel** *m consels* council

**Consel Kernow** *m* Cornwall Council
**conse·nt** *m consentys* (dhe²) consent (to)
**conservegor** *m conservegoryon* conservative
**constrîna** *v* compel, oblige; enforce
**constrînus** *adj* compulsory, obligatory
**consûmyor** *m consûmyoryon* consumer
**consystya** a² *v* consist of
**contens** *m* contents
**contentya** *v* satisfy
**contentyans** *m* satisfaction
**conterfeytya** *v* fake, forge
**contrary** *adj/m contrarys* (dhe²) contrary (to), opposite; opponent, adversary
**contreweytya** *v* intercept; ambush
**controllya** *v* control
**convedhes** *see* godhvos convedhes
**conversacyon** *m* morals (of an individual); lifestyle

**convyctya** *v* convict
**conyn** *m conynas* rabbit
**coodh** *m codhow* fall
**coos** *m cosow* wood (place of trees)
**copel** *m coplow* couple, pair
**copia** *v* copy
**copy** *m copys* copy
**cor** *m* wax
**cor-²** *pref* dwarf, mini-
**cor lenter** *m* polish
**cora** *v* wax
**Corawys** *m* Lent
**corbref** *m corbrevas* microbe, bug
**cord** *m cordys* chord
**corden** *f kerdyn* string
**cordodnor** *m cordonoryon* microwave [oven]
**coref** *m* beer, ale
**coref gell** *m* pale ale
**coref gorm** *m* brown ale
**coref scav** *m* lager
**corf** *m corfow* body
**corf eskern** *m corfow* skeleton
**corfassa·y** *m* gymnastics
**corflaha** *m corflahys* constitution

**corflan** *f corfladnow* churchyard
**corfloskva** *f corfloskvaow* crematorium
**corflywans** *m corflywansow* tattoo
**corkyn** *m corkydnow* cork; stopper
**corn** *m kern* horn, antler
**corn denewy** *m kern* funnel
**cornel** *f cornellow* corner
**cors** *m corsow* course (study)
**corsyans** *m corsyansow* cruise
**cort** *f cortys* courtyard (closed); court (law)
**cortes** *adj* polite, courteous
**co·rtesy** *m co·rtesys* politeness, courtesy
**corvarvus** *m corvarvusy* haddock
**corynt du** *m coryns* blackcurrant
**cosa** *v* itch; tingle
**cosel** *adj* quiet, peaceful
**coselhe·** *v* calm

**cosmer** *m cosmers* customer
**cosmos** *m* cosmos
**cosolek** *adj* calm, tranquil
**cosoleth** *m* calm, tranquility, peace and quiet
**còst** *m costow* cost
**cost** *m côstys* coast
**còst spênys** *m costow* expense
**costen** *f costednow* basket (flat – *e.g.* for dog); target
**costrel** *m costrels* flask
**costya** *v* cost
**cosva** *f* tickle, itch; tingle
**cot** *adj* short, brief
**cot y berthyans** *phr* impatient
**cot y wolok** *phr* short-sighted
**côta** *m côtys* coat
**coth** *adj* old; stale
**cot'he·** *v* shorten
**cot'hens** *m cot'hensy* shortcut
**cothhe·** *v* grow old
**cothman** *m cothmans* friend

**coton** *m* cotton
**cov** *m covyon* memory
**covath** *m covathow* record
**covep** *f covebow* monument
**covlen** *f covlednow* dossier
**covnôtyans** *m covnotyansow* minute(s)
**covrol** *f covrolyow* register
**covscrefa** *v* register
**covscrevva** *f covscrevvaow* archive
**covva** *f covvaow* hideout
**cow** *adj/m cowyow* hollow; cavity
**cowal** *adj* whole, entire; gross (finance)
**coward** *adj/m cowardys* coward(ly)
**cowas** *f cowosow* shower (rain, washing)
**cowasva** *f cowasvaow* shower (cubicle)
**cowel** *m kewel* basket (deep – *e.g.* for laundry); cage (for bird)

**coweth** *m cowetha* companion; friend, comrade
**cowethas** *f cowethasow* association, society; firm, company
**cowethyans** *m cowethyansow* organization
**cowl** *m* soup
**cowl-**[2] *pref* complete(ly)
**cowlardak** *m* checkmate
**cowles** *col* jelly
**cowlsùm** *m cowlsùmys* total
**cowlwil** *v* complete; fulfil; achieve
**cowlwrians** *m cowlwriansow* achievement
**cowntnans** *m cowntnancys* attitude
**cowrek** *adj* gigantic, enormous
**cowrvargh** *m cowrvergh* camel
**cows** *m cowsow* speech, talk
**côwsel** *v* (orth) speak, talk (to)

**coynt** *adj* curious, odd
**co·yntùry** *m* oddness
**coyntys** *m coyntysow* peculiarity, quirk
**crambla** *v* climb, scramble
**cramblor** *m crambloryon* climber
**crampeth** *col crampethen* pancakes
**crampeth tellek** *col crampethen* crumpets
**cramvil** *m cramvilas* reptile
**cramyas** *v* crawl
**cravas** *v* scratch, scrape
**cravell** *f cravellow* scraper
**cravell defendya** *f cravellow* eraser
**cravyon mogh** *pl* pork scratchings
**crefhe·** *v* strengthen; reinforce; intensify
**crefny** *adj/m* greed(y)
**creft** *f creftow* craft, skill
**crefter** *m crefterow* strength; intensity; validity
**creftor** *m creftoryon* craftsman
**creftus** *adj* artificial

**cregy** *v* hang
**cregy wàr**[2] *v* depend on
**crejy** (cresy) *v* (nampy·th / dhe[2] nebonen) believe
**crejyans** *f crejyansow* belief; faith, religion
**crejys** *m crejysow* credit
**crena** (kerna) *v* tremble, shake *intr*
**crenwrë·dh** *col crenwredhen* bulbs (plant)
**cres** *adj/m cresyow* middle
**cres** *m* peace
**cresek** *adj/m cresegow* average
**cresen** *f cresednow* centre (for particular activity)
**creslu** *m cresluyow* police [force]
**crespoynt** *m crespoyntys* hub (figuratively)
**crespoyntya** *v* focus (sth)
**cresten** *f crestednow* crust
**cresyk** *m cresygow* crisp
**creunyon** *pl* reserves

**crev** *adj* strong; intense; valid
**cria** (*pronounced* 'creya') *v* shout, cry; summon
**cria in mes** *phr* exclaim
**crib** *f cribow* comb; ridge
**cribya** *v* comb
**crig** *m crigow* crack
**crigh** *adj/m crighyon* wrinkle; wrinkled, crinkled, rumpled
**cris** *m crisyow* shirt, blouse
**cris T** *m crisyow* T-shirt
**cris whës** *m crisyow* sweatshirt
**crispows** *f crispowsyow* waistcoat
**Cristyon** *adj/m Cristonyon* Christian
**Cristyoneth** *f* Christianity
**crithen** *f crithednow* scar
**criv** *adj* raw; unripe; crude
**crobm** *adj* bent; crumpled; numb with cold (fingers, toes)
**crobma** *v* bend; crumple; go numb with cold (fingers, toes)
**croch** *m crochys* crutch

**cro·codyl** *m cro·codyls* crocodile
**crôder** *m crôdrow* sieve (for kitchen)
**croffal** *m croffolow* grumble; complaint
**croffolas** *v* (wàr[2]) grumble (at); complain
**crogen** *f cregyn* shell (animal)
**crogen pedn** *f cregyn* skull
**croglen** *f croglednow* curtain
**crohen** *f crehyn* skin; leather
**crohen an lagas** *f crehyn an lagasow* eyelid
**cromgenter** *f cromgentrow* staple (fastening)
**cromgentra** *v* staple
**cron** *m cronow* strap, thong
**cronak** (cronek) *m cronogas* toad
**cronak ervys** *m cronogas* tortoise
**cronk** *m cronkys* bang
**cronkya** *v* bang; thrash

**croust** *m croustys* snack; picnic
**crow** *m crewow* socket
**crow** *m crowyow* hut
**crowd** *m crowdys* violin, fiddle
**crowjy** *m crowjiow* cottage
**crows** *f crowsow* cross
**crowsek** *adj* crossed; cross, irritable, grumpy
**crowseryow** *pl* crossword
**cruel** *adj* cruel
**crug** *m crugyow* mound
**crùllys** *adj* curly
**cruskyn** *m cruskydnow* mug
**cry** *m criow* shout, cry, call
**crycket** *m* cricket
**cryjyk** *adj* religious
**cûb** *m cûbys* cube
**cubmyas** *m cumyasow* permission, licence
**cubmyas lewyas** *m cumyasow* driving licence
**cùcû** *m cùcûs* cuckoo
**cû·cùmber** *m cû·cùmbers* cucumber (for salad)

**cudh** *adj* covert
**cudha** *v* cover, veil
**cudhlen** *f cudhlednow* cover (incl of book)
**cudyn** *m cudydnow* lock (hair); snag; problem
**cûgol** *m cûgollow* hood
**cùhudha** *v* accuse
**cùhudhans** *m cùhudhansow* accusation
**cùhudhor a'n tu aberveth** *m cùhudhoryon* whistle-blower
**cul** *adj* narrow
**culder** *m* narrowness
**culhe·** *v* narrow; restrict (sth)
**cùlt** *m cùltys* cult
**culyak** *m culyogas* cock[erel]
**culyak reden** *m culyogas* grasshopper; locust (incl figuratively)
**cunor** (keunor) *m cunoryon* lighter (for cigarettes, gas etc)
**cùntell** *v* gather, collect
**cùntellek** *adj* collective
**cùntelles** *f cùntellesow* congress

**cùntellva** *f cùntellvaow* congregation; assembly
**cùntellyans** *m cùntellyansow* collection; meeting (formal)
**cunys** *col* fuel
**cur** *m* care (community, day, social etc)
**cur** *m curyow* choir
**cûr** *m cûrow* boundary; limit
**cùriak** *m cùriogas* pimple
**cùrry** *m cùrrys* curry
**cùrun** *f cùrudnow* crown
**cùruna** *v* crown
**cùsca** *v* sleep
**cùsk** *m* sleep; dry rot
**cùssul** *f cùssulyow* advice; suggestion; plan
**cùssulya** *v* advise; suggest; plan *Note construction* cùssulya nebonen a wil / na wrella nampy·th = advise sb to do / not to do sth
**cùssulyor** *m cùssulyoryon* adviser
**cùssya** *v* swear (bad language)
**cùstard** *m* custard
**cuv** *adj* kind
**cyber-**[1] *pref* cyber-
**cygaryk** *m cygarygow* cigarette
**cy·lynder** *m cylyndrow* cylinder
**cyment** *m* cement
**cy·nema** *m cy·nemas* cinema
**cy·nycus** *adj* cynical
**cy·rcùmstans** *m cyrcùmstancys* circumstance
**cyrcùs** *m cy·rcùsow* circus
**cyta** *f cytys* city

# D

**dâ** *adj* good; *like
**dâ lowr** *phr* okay
**dâ y vlas** *phr* appetizing
**dadhel** *f dadhlow* debate
**dadhla** *v* debate
**dadhlak** *adj* controversial
**dadhlor** *m dadhloryon* barrister
**daffar** *m* instrument(s), equipment; material(s)

**daffar lybm** *m* cutlery
**dager** *m dagrow* tear
**dainty** *adj* nice, delicate
**dalathfos** *m* origin(s)
**dalathor** *m dalathoryon* beginner
**dalhedna** *v* grasp, grip; seize; arrest
**dalhen** *f dalhednow* grasp, grip; arrest
**dall** *adj* blind
**dallath** *m/v* begin(ning), start; take(-)off (aircraft)
**dallhe·** *v* blind (figuratively); dazzle
**dalva** *f dalvaow* quarrel; dispute
**dama dhâ** *f damyow dâ* mother-in-law
**dama wydn** *f damyow gwydn* grandmother
**damach** *m damajys* damage
**damcanep** *f damcanebow* theory (individual)
**dampnacyon** *m dampnacyons* damnation; condemnation
**dampnya** *v* damn; condemn

**danjer** *m* scruple(s); jurisdiction
**dans** *m dens* tooth
**danvon** *v* send, dispatch *Note construction* danvon nebonen a wil nampy·th = send sb to do sth
**daras** *m darajow* door
**daras gorothem** *m darajow* emergency exit
**darbar** *m darbarow* apparatus, device, gadget
**darbaror** *m darbaroryon* assistant
**darbary** *v* prepare (arrange); equip
**darbary shara** *phr* contribute (to sth)
**dargan** *f darganow* prediction, forecast
**dargana** *v* predict, forecast
**darn** *m darnow* piece, bit
**daromdak** *m daromdagow* traffic jam
**daromres** *m/v* traffic; come and go
**darsewya** *v* prosecute
**dart** *m dartys* dart
**dascafos** *v* retrieve

**dascor** *v* hand over, yield; return, give back
**dasformya** *v* reform
**daslenwel** *v* refill
**dasleuvus** *adj* second-hand
**dasleverel** *v* repeat (sth said)
**dasoberor** *m dasoberoryon* reactor
**dasqwel** (daswel) *m dasqwelow* review
**dasqweles** (dasweles) *v* review
**dasqwil** (daswil) *v* remake; restore
**dasseny** *v* echo
**dasson** *m dassonyow* echo
**dassteusadow** *adj* recyclable
**dassteusya** *v* recycle
**dastesky** *v* revise (learning)
**dastewynya** *v* reflect (light)
**dasvewa** *v* revive
**dauncya** *v* dance
**dauncyor** *m dauncyoryon* dancer

**dauns** *m dauncyow* dance
**davas** *f deves* sheep
**de** *adv* yesterday
**De Gwener** *phr* Friday
**De Lun** *phr* Monday
**De Merher** *phr* Wednesday
**De Merth** *phr* Tuesday
**De Sadorn** *phr* Saturday
**De Sul** *phr* Sunday
**De Yow** *phr* Thursday
**deantel** (diantel) *adj* precarious; hazardous
**debry** *v* eat
**debrys ha deu** *phr* all gone (food)
**decernya** *v* discern, distinguish
**declarya** *v* declare, assert; announce
**declaryans** *m declaryansow* declaration, assertion; announcement
**dëdh** (> jëdh *after* an, an keth, in, udn) *m dedhyow* day
**dedhewy** *v* promise
**dedhlyver** *m dedhlyvrow* diary

**dedhyador** *m dedhyadoryon* calendar (incl system)
**dedhyans** *m dedhyansow* date
**defendya** *v* erase; eliminate; dispel
**defia** *v* challenge (sb)
**defnyth** *m defnydhyow* subject[-matter]; ingredient
**defolya** *v* rape; pollute
**defowt** *m defowtow* defect, bug; default, failure
**defry·** *adv* indeed
**defynya** *v* define
**defynyans** *m defynyansow* definition
**degador** *m degadoryon* vehicle
**degea** *v* close, shut *Note pp* degë·s = closed, shut *adj*
**degemeres** *v* receive, accept; adopt (policy etc)
**degemeror** *m degemeroryon* recipient
**degol** *m degolyow* holiday

**degrê·** *m degrê·s* degree (rank, temperature etc)
**dehen** *m* cream
**dehen cowlys** *m* clotted cream
**dehen rew** *m* ice cream
**dehen spral** *m* sunblock
**dehesy** *v* hurl, fling
**del** *col delen* leaves
**del-codha** *adj* deciduous
**delî·t** *m delîtys* delight
**delîtya** *v* delight
**delk** *m delcow* chain (jewellery)
**dell gresa'** *phr* so far as I know
**dell hevel** *phr* apparently
**dell yw gwaitys** *phr* hopefully
**dell yw prederys** *phr* supposedly
**dell yw ûsys** *phr* as usual
**dellyon** *pl* blind people
**delow** *f delwow* statue
**delow scrin** *f delwow* icon (cinema, computer)
**delvre·sieth** *f* idealism
**delvresor** *m delvresoryon* idealist

**delvrys** *m delvresyow* ideal
**delynya** *v* draw; delineate
**delynyans** *m delynyansow* drawing
**delyvra** (delyfrya) *v* deliver (all senses); acquit
**demedhy** *v* get married (to)
**demedhyans** *m demedhyansow* wedding
**democratek** *adj* democratic
**democra·tieth** *f* democracy
**demo·nd** *m demondys* demand
**demondya** *v* demand
**den** *m tus* man; person; one (as subject of verb)
**den rescous** *m tus* rescuer
**dendyl** *v* earn; deserve
**denethy** *v* give birth (to); generate
**denewy** *v* pour; flow
**dengerenje'ek** *adj* humanitarian
**denjak** *m denjogas* hake

**densyth** *m densydhyon* dentist
**dera·y** *m* disorder, chaos
**derevel** *v* raise; rise
**derivador** *m derivadoryon* reporter; announcer
**derivadow** *m* announcement; information; statement, declaration, manifesto
**derivas** *m/v derivasow* (orth) tell, inform; report (to)
**derivas cot** *m derivasow* summary
**descador** *m descadoryon* teacher; trainer
**descor** *m descoryon* pupil, student (language class etc)
**desedha** *v* position, fit; adjust; set (device)
**desedhans** *m desedhansow* setting (device, social website)
**desedhus** *adj* appropriate
**desef** *m desevyow* assumption

**deseha** *v* wipe [up]
**desehor** *m desehoryon* wiper (on windscreen)
**desempys** *adj/adv* sudden, abrupt, immediate; instant (coffee etc); suddenly, abruptly, immediately
**desevos** *v* assume
**desî·n** *m desînyow* design
**desîna** *v* design
**desîrya** *v* desire
**dèsk** *m deskys* desk
**desky** *v* learn
**desky dhe**[2] *v* teach
**deskys brâs** *phr* learned
**desmygy** *v* guess; find out; invent; imagine
**desmygyans** *m* imagination
**desmygyansus** *adj* imaginative
**desmyk** *m desmygow* guess; invention; puzzle; riddle
**despîsya** *v* despise
**despî·t** *m despîtys* insult
**despîtya** *v* insult
**desta** *v* fixed 2$^{nd}$ state witness; certify

**destewel** *v* silence
**destna** *v* destine
**destnans** *m destnansow* destiny, fate
**devar** *m deverow* duty
**devedhek** *adj/m* future
**devedhyans** *m devedhyansow* arrival; origin
**devregh** *du* arms (two: cradling, embracing etc)
**devydnes** *v* quote
**devyn** *m devydnow* quotation
**dewana** *v* penetrate
**dewas** *m dewosow* drink
**dewdhek Cort an Gùrun** *phr* the jury (in criminal trial)
**dewdhorn** *du* handlebars
**dewedha** *v* end
**dewedhes** *adj* late (in time)
**dewetha** *adj* last
**dewfrik** (frigow) *du* nose
**dewheles** *v* come / go back, return
**dewhens** (dew'hens) *m dewhensy* dual carriageway
**dewla** *du* hands (two)

**dewlin** *du* knees (two) (especially in context of kneeling)
**dewreydhek** *adj* bisexual
**dewros** (dywros) *f dewrosow* bicycle
**dewrosa** *v* cycle
**dewrosyas** *m dewrosysy* cyclist
**dewweder** *du* binoculars
**dewyethek** *adj* bilingual
**dewyn** *m dewydnow* beam, ray
**dêwys** *m/v* choose, select; elect; choice, selection; alternative (one of a range)
**dêwys-qwartron** *m dêwys-qwartronys* constituency
**dewysel** *f dewysellow* menu (options)
**dewysyans** *m dewysyansow* election
**dhana** (nena) *adv* then, in that case
**dhe blebmyk** *phr* plainly, directly (speaking)
**dhe gafos** *phr* available
**dhe les** *phr* useful

**dhe ves** *phr* off, away *motion*
**dhe vlâmya** *phr* to blame
**dhe wir** *phr* really
**dhele·rgh** *adv* at the back
**dhe'n contrary** *phr* on the contrary
**dhe'n dor** *phr* down *motion*
**dhe'n lyha** *phr* at least
**dh'y vrës / vreus ev** *phr* in his opinion
**diadhves** *adj* immature
**diadhvetter** *m* immaturity
**dialog** *m dialogow* dialogue
**dialwhedha** *v* unlock
**diambos** *adj* unconditional; definitive
**dia·nk** *v* escape *intr*
**diankva** *f* escapism
**dianowy** *v* gape; yawn
**diegrys** *adj* shocked, appalled
**diek** *adj* lazy
**dielvednans** *m dielvenansow* analysis
**dien** *adj* complete, intact
**diencus** *adj* escapist
**dierbyna** *v* encounter

**dieth** *m diedhow* pity (cause for regret)
**dinasek** *adj* civil[ian]
**dinasy·dhieth** *f* citizenship
**dinasyth** *m dinasydhyon* citizen
**diogel** *adj* (rag) secure (against), immune (from); reliable
**diogelhe·** *v* make sure
**diogelyans flogh** *m* child protection
**dis** *m dîcyow* die (dice)
**disky** (dy'sky) *v* undress (sb); take off (clothing)
**dîvya** *v* dive (into water)
**doctour** *m doctours* doctor (PhD)
**do·cùment** *m docùmentys* document
**dôdô** *m dôdôs* dodo
**dohajë·dh** *adv/m* (in the) afternoon
**dollar** *m dollarys* dollar
**do·myno** *m do·mynôs* domino
**don** (degy) *v* carry
**don tre** *phr* harvest
**dôpyans** *m* doping
**dor** *m* ground

**dorgris** *m dorgrisyow* earthquake
**dorn** *m dornow* fist; hand; handle
**dornas** *m dornesow* handful
**dornla** *m dornleow* handle
**dorslynk** *m dorslyncow* landslide
**dorydhek** *adj* geographical
**dory·dhieth** *f* geography
**dos** (dones) *v* come; arrive
**dosbartha** *v* set (*e.g.* by ability)
**doth** *adj* discreet
**dôtya** *v* act like a fool
**dour** *adj/adv/m* care[fulness], rigour; careful(ly)
**dourwith** *m* intensive care
**doust** *m* dust
**dov** *adj* tame
**dova** *v* tame
**down** *adj* deep; profound
**downder** *m* depth
**dowr** *m dowrow* water
**dowr bian** *m* vodka

**dowr mûn** *m* mineral water
**dowr pooth** *m* hot water
**dowr tobm** *m* brandy
**dowr tobm Alban / Wordhen** *m* whisky / whiskey
**dowr tobm molâ·ss** *m* rum
**dowrergh** *m* sleet
**dowrgleth** *m* *dowrgledhyow* drain (open); canal
**dowrlam** *m* *dowrlabmow* waterfall
**dowt** *m* *dowtys* (a²) doubt; *fear (of) See also [rag] dowt
**dowtya** *v* doubt
**draggya** *v* drag
**draghtys** *pl* draughts (game)
**dragon** *f* *dragonas* dragon
**drâma** *m* *drâmas* drama
**dramatek** *adj* dramatic
**draylya** *v* drag (behind)
**dre [bùb] lycklod** *phr* probably
**dre decter** *phr* gladly
**dre gortesy** *phr* please

**dre hap** *phr* by chance
**dre / gans / in / wàr hast** *phr* hurriedly
**dre hedna** *phr* as a result
**dre rêson** *phr + noun, verb-noun, infinitive construction, na²-clause* because (of)
**dre vrâs** *phr* generally, mostly, on the whole
**drefen** *prep + noun, verb-noun, infinitive construction, na²-clause* because (of)
**drehedhes** *v* reach, attain; arrive (at)
**drehevel** *v* erect, construct
**dren** *m* *dreyn* prickle; thorn (loosely)
**dres an cûr** *phr* over the limit (drinking & driving)
**dres ehen** *phr* extremely
**dres kynda** *phr* extraordinary
**dres pùptra·** *phr* above all
**dreslebmel an lost** *phr* jump the queue
**drewyth** *m* *drewydhyon* druid

**dreys** *col* brambles
**drîvya** *v* drive (incl vehicle)
**drog** *adj (may not follow noun attributively)* bad; harmful; *dislike
**drog-gerys** *adj* notorious
**drog-goans** *m* indigestion
**drog-hanow** *m* notoriety
**drog-pës** *adj* (gans) discontented, dissatisfied (with)
**drog dens** *m* toothache
**drog pedn** *m* headache
**drogatty** *m* epilepsy
**drogdyby** *v* suspect
**drogga** *m droggys* drug
**Droglabmow ha Gorothobmow** *see* [Asran] Droglabmow ha Gorothobmow
**droglam** *m droglabmow* accident (with bad outcome)
**drogober** *m drogoberow* crime (individual)
**drogoberor** *m drogoberoryon* criminal
**drogura** *v* smear (making a mess)

**drolla** *m drollys* folktale
**dry** *v* bring
**dry** (nampy·th) **dhe gov** *phr* (nebonen) remind (sb of sth)
**dry y fog wàr**[2] *phr* focus [up]on
**du** *adj* black
**dùcheth** *m dùchethow* duchy
**dur** *m* steel
**durya** *v* (ow qwil nampy·th) last; persist (in doing sth)
**duryans** *m duryansow* duration
**dùstuny** *m dùstuniow fixed 2nd state* evidence, testimony; reference (character, past performance etc)
**duw** *m duwow* god
**duwhan** *m* sorrow, misery
**dy** *adv* there *motion*
**dyamont** *m dyamons* diamond (in cards)
**dybarow** *adj* separate; odd (number); peculiar; unparalleled

**dyba·rth** *f dybarthow* separation; departure
**dyber** *m dybrow* saddle
**dybe·rth** *v* separate; depart, leave
**dybe·rth in forgh** *phr* fork *intr* (road)
**dyberthva** *f dyberthvaow* sector; ward (hospital)
**dybla·ns** *adj* distinct; definite
**dyboo·s** *adj* unimportant
**dybrias** *adj* unmarried
**dybyta** *adj* ruthless
**dydha·n** *adj* amusing; witty
**dydhana** *v* amuse; entertain
**dydhanus** *adj* entertaining
**dydhemedhy** *v* get divorced (from)
**dydhemedhyans** *m dydhemedhyansow* divorce
**dydro·** *adj* direct
**dydrùssa** *v* unpack
**dyfen** *m/v dyfednow* forbid, prohibit(ion), ban *Note construction* dyfen orth nebonen gwil nampy·th = forbid sb to do sth
**dyfeyth** *adj/m dyfeythyow* barren; desert
**dyffra** *v* differ
**dyffrans** *adj/m dyffransow* different; difference
**dyffres** *v* defend, protect
**dyffresyans** *m dyffresyansow* defence, protection
**dyffresyas** *m dyffresysy* defender, protector
**dyfleryas** *m dyflerysy* deodorant
**dyfro·th** *adj* businesslike
**dyfudhor** *m dyfudhoryon* extinguisher
**dyfudhy** *v* extinguish
**dyfu·n** *adj* awake
**dyfuna** *v* wake [up]
**dyfunor** *m dyfunoryon* alarm clock
**dyfybrellyor** *m dyfybrelyoryon* defibrillator
**dyfygya** *v* decline; run out (sth); stall (engine)
**dyfygyans** *m* decline

**dyfyk** *m dyfygyow* shortage; deficit; eclipse
**dygabma** *v* straighten [out]
**dygelmy** *v* untie; disconnect
**dyghtya** *v* treat; manage, deal with; do (apply process to)
**dyghtyans** *m dyghtyansow* treatment (incl medical); management
**dyghtyor** *m dyghtyoryon* manager
**dyghtyor blew** *m dyghtyoryon* hairdresser
**dyglevejyas** *m dyglevejysy* disinfectant
**dyglodny** *v* discourage (sb); depress
**dyglon** *adj* downhearted; depressed
**dygompes** *adj* uneven
**dygoweth** *adj* solitary, lonely (sb)
**dygu·v** *adj* unkind
**dyharas** *m/v dyharasow* apology; apologize
**dyhaval** *adj* (orth) unlike, different (from)

**dyhepcor** *adj* indispensable, essential
**dyhow** *adj/m* right (as opposed to left)
**dyjyn** *m dyjydnow* dot (in decimal number or web address)
**dylâtya** *v* postpone
**dylâtys** *adj* delayed (flight etc)
**dylea** *v* delete; cancel
**dyle·s** *adj* useless
**dyllas** *m dyllajow* clothes
**dyllas compes-powes** *m* smart casual (dress code)
**dyllas neyja** *m dyllajow* swimsuit
**dyllasva** *f dyllasvaow* wardrobe
**dyllo** *v* emit; publish
**dyllor** *m dylloryon* publisher
**dymensyon** *m dymensyons* dimension
**dynamek** *adj* dynamic
**dynar** *m dynerow* penny
**dynargh** *m dynarhow* greeting
**dynerhy** *v* send greetings to

**dynsel** *v* bite (to eat); chew
**dynya** *v* lure, attract
**dyowl** (> jowl *after* an) *m dewolow* devil
**dyppa** *m dyppys* dip (incl edible)
**dyppya** *v* dip
**dyrêson** *adj* irrational
**dyre·wl** *adj/m* unruly; anarchy
**dyrollya** *v* unroll
**dyrusca** *v* peel
**dyruskel** *f dyruskellow* peeler
**dysabyl** *adj* disabled
**dysaby·lyta** (dysabylta) *m dysaby·lytys* disability
**dysawor** *adj* nasty, awful
**dyscarga** *v* unload; discharge (from army, custody, prosecution)
**dyscas** *m dyscosow* learning (knowledge); lesson, moral (of story etc)
**dyscle·r** *adj* blurred; vague; opaque
**dysconte·nt** *m* discontent, dissatisfaction
**dyscoo·s** *adj* vulnerable

**dyscortes** *adj* rude, impolite, discourteous
**dysco·rtesy** *m* rudeness, discourtesy
**dyscownt** *m dyscowntys* discount
**dyscrewya** *v* unscrew
**dyscryjyans** *m* disbelief
**dyscudha** *v* uncover, unveil; reveal; discover; leak (information)
**dysebylya** *v* unplug
**dyseha** *v* refresh (sb)
**dyserth** *adj* [very] steep
**dysfa·vera** *v* discriminate against
**dysfa·verans** *m* discrimination
**dyskerheth** *m* gravity (physics)
**dyskevra** *v* expose; discover; out (sexuality)
**dysle·l** *adj* disloyal; dishonest
**dyslelder** *m* disloyalty; dishonesty
**dysle·n** *adj* unfaithful
**dysmailya** *v* unwrap
**dysobeya** *v* disobey
**dysobeyans** *m* disobedience

**dysonest** *adj* indecent, improper
**dyspê·r** *m* despair
**dysplegya** *v* develop
**dysplegyans** *m dysplegyansow* development
**dysplêtya** *v* unfurl; display; deploy
**dysplêtyans** *m dyspletyansow* display; deployment
**dysqwedhes** *v* show, exhibit
**dysqwedhyans** *m dysqwedhyansow* show, exhibition
**dysqwitha** *v* relax *intr*
**dysse·nt** *m dyssentys* disagreement
**dyssentya** *v* disagree
**dysta·g** *adj* independent (person, organization)
**dystaga** *v* detach
**dystempra** *v* upset (sb)
**dysto·wgh** *adv* immediately
**dystrôwy** *v* destroy
**dystryppya** *v* strip down; dismantle
**dysty·r** *adj* insignificant

**dyswa·r** *adj* unconscious
**dyswil** *v* demolish; spoil (ruin)
**dythya** *v* dictate
**dyvarra** *v* prune
**dyvarva** *v* shave (face)
**dyvarvor** *m dyvarvoryon* shaver (for face)
**dyvedhow** *adj* sober (not drunk)
**dyvera** *v* drip, shed; pour
**dyvera goos** *phr* bleed
**dyveren** *f dyverednow* drip, drop
**dyvers** *adj* diverse, various
**dyve·th** *adj* shameless
**dyvethter** *m* shamelessness
**dyvla·s** (dyfla·s) *adj* nasty, awful
**dyvlewa** *v* shave (body hair)
**dyvlewor** *m dyvleworyon* shaver (for body hair)
**dyvroa** *v* (e)migrate
**dyvroyas** *m dyvro'ysy* migrant
**dyweth** *m dywedhow* end; outcome
**dywethyn** *adj* rigid

**dywe·yth** *adj* unemployed
**dywiryon** *adj* insincere
**dywiryonsys** *m* insincerity
**dywodhaf** *adj* unbearable, intolerable
**dywostyth** *adj* disobedient

# E

**ebost** (e-bost) *m* email (system)
**ebron** (eborn) *f* sky; weather (fine)
**Ebrow** *m* Hebrew (language)
**ebyl** *m ebylyow* peg (incl for clothes); plug (for bath etc)
**ebylya** *v* plug in
**ebylyor** *m ebylyoryon* plug (electrical)
**eco·nomy** *m eco·nomys* economy
**eco·nomyst** *m economystyon* economist
**edhen** *m ÿdhyn (edhnow)* bird
**edrek** *m* *regret

**dywredhya** *v* eradicate
**dywysyans** *m dywysyansow* industry
**dywysygneth** *m* earnestness, diligence
**dywysyk** *adj* earnest, diligent
**dywyver** *adj/m* wireless, WiFi

**efan** *adj* wide (in several dimensions)
**efander** *m* space (incl outer)
**efanhe·** *v* widen
**effeyth** *m effeythyow* effect
**effeythus** *adj* effective
**egerel** *f egerellow* opener
**egery** *v* open *Note pp* egerys = open *adj*
**eglos** *f eglosyow* church
**egor** *m egorow* opening
**egyn** *m egydnow* germ; bud
**ehel** *f ehelyow* axle; axis
**ehen** *f ehednow* kind, sort; species
**el** *m eleth* angel

**elastek** *adj/m* elastic
**electronek** *adj* electronic
**elgeth** *f elgethyow* chin
**elvednek** *adj* elementary
**elven** *f elvednow* element; factor
**elyn** *m elydnow* elbow; angle
**elyn pedrak** *m elydnow* right angle
**ema·yl** *m* enamel
**emôjy** *m emôjys* emoji
**empîr** *m empîrys* empire
**emprour** *m emprours* emperor
**empydnyon** *pl* brain(s)
**ena** *adv* there; then
**encladhva** *f encladhvaow* cemetary
**encledhyas** *m/v* bury; burial, funeral
**enef** (ena) *m enevow* soul
**enep** *m enebow* face (of object)
**enesegy** *v* insulate
**enevek** *adj* psychological
**ene·vieth** *f* psychology
**enjoya** *v* enjoy
**enor** *m enorys* honour
**enora** *v* honour

**enporth** *m enporthow* import
**enportha** *v* import
**entanus** *adj* exciting
**entanya** *v* excite (sb)
**entrans rag dysabylyon** *m* disabled access
**envies** *adj* envious, jealous
**envroans** *m* immigration
**envroyas** *m envro'ysy* immigrant
**envy** *m* envy; enmity; enemy (especially collective)
**enys** *f enesow* island
**enys'he·** *v* isolate
**eosyk** *f eosygow* nightingale
**epscop** *m epscobow* bishop
**er** *m eras* eagle
**er** *prep* by (the hand, the arm etc)
**er y varth** *phr* surprisingly
**erba** *m erbys* herb
**erbysus** *adj* thrifty, economical
**erbysy** *v* save (be sparing of)

**erbysyon** *pl* savings
**ergh** *m* snow
**erghslynk** *m erghslyncow* avalanche
**erhy** *v* order (sb or sth) *Note constructions* erhy dhe² nebonen (or infixed pronoun) gwil nampy·th *and* erhy nebonen a wil nampy·th *and* erhy may whrella / na wrella nebonen nampy·th = order sb to do / not to do sth
**erow** *f erewy* acre
**ertons** *m ertonsys* inheritance
**ervira** *v* decide [to]; conclude
**ervirans** *m erviransow* decision; conclusion
**ervirus** *adj* decisive, conclusive
**e·ryta** *v* inherit
**escar** *m eskerens* enemy
**escarus** *adj* hostile
**esedha** (sedha) *v* sit [down]
**esedhva** *f esedhvaow* lounge; siege

**esedhvos** *m esedhvosow* session; eisteddfod
**esel** *m esyly* limb; member
**esel seneth** *m esyly* member of parliament (MP)
**eseleth** *m eseledhow* membership
**eseth** *f esedhow* seat (incl in Parliament)
**eskelly grehen** *m eskelly grehyn* bat (animal)
**eskerdh** *m eskerdhow* expedition
**eskys** *f eskyjyow* shoe
**eskys sport** *f eskyjyow* trainer
**esporth** *m esporthow* export
**esportha** *v* export
**essens** *m essencys* essence
**establyshya** *v* establish
**estê·m** *m* admiration
**estêmya** *v* admire
**estrednek** *adj* foreign, alien
**estren** *m estrenyon* stranger, foreigner

**estyll** *col estyllen* shelving
**êsy** *adj* easy
**etew** *m etewy* log (for burning)
**ethedna** *v* steam; vape
**ethen** *f* steam
**eur** *f euryow* hour, time (specific, incl by the clock)
**euryador** *m euryadoryon* timetable
**euryor** *m euryoryon* watch; timer
**euth** *m* terror
**euthvil** *m euthvilas* monster
**euthwas** *m euthwesyon* terrorist
**euthweyth** *m* terrorism
**ev a garsa** *phr + verb-noun* he would like to
**ev a vydn** *phr + verb-noun* he is going to
**ev a wra** *phr + verb-noun* he will
**ev a wrug ûsya** *phr + verb-noun* he used to
**eva** *v* drink
**eva yêhes** *phr* toast (sb)
**evredhy** *v* cripple

**ewl** [boos] *f* appetite
**ewn** *adj* right, correct
**êwna** *v* correct; mend; repair
**ewnans** *m ewnansow* correction; repair
**ewnder** *m* fairness
**ewnhensek** *adj* moral, ethical
**ewnran** *f ewnradnow* ration
**êwnter** *m êwntras* uncle
**ewnyas** *m ewnysy* conditioner
**ewon** *col ewonen* foam, froth
**ewro** *m ewros* euro
**ewyn** *m ewynas* nail (anatomy); claw
**examnya** *v* examine (incl medically)
**examnyans** *m examnyansow* examination (incl medical)
**exampyl** (ensompel) *m examplys* example
**exampyl kyns** *m examplys* precedent
**excepcyon** *m excepcyons* exception

**exceptya** *v* except
**execûcyon** *m* *execûcyons* execution (death)
**execûtya** *v* execute (sb)

# F

**fakel** *f faclow* flare; inflammation
**fakel mellow** *f* arthritis
**falgh raf** *f fylghyow* strimmer
**falhas** *v* mow
**falja** *v* split
**fâls** *adj* false
**fâls** *m fâljow* split
**fancy** *m fancys* fancy, fantasy
**fara** *m* conduct
**fardel** *m fardellow* package
**fardellow** *pl* luggage, baggage
**fardellyk** *m fardelygow* packet
**fascyon** *m fascyons* fashion (fashionable)
**fascyonus** *adj* fashionable

**experyans** *m* trial and error, experience
**eylreydhek** *adj* heterosexual
**eylya** *v* alternate
**eythyn** *col* gorse

**fashyst** *m fashystyon* fascist
**fâss** *m fassow* face
**fast** *adj* firmly fixed; stable; permanent
**fastya** *v* set up (physically)
**fate·ll osta?** *phr* how are you?
**fatl'yw genes?** *phr* how are things?
**fav faven** *col* beans
**fav pebys** *col* baked beans
**fa·verus** *adj* favourable
**favour** *m favours* favour; treat
**fedna** *v* overflow
**fêkyl-jer** *m* hypocrisy
**fel** *adj* shrewd; subtle (sb)

**felder** *m felderow* shrewdness; subtlety
**felshyp** *m felshyps* staff, personnel; crew
**fe·nester** *f fe·nestry* window
**feno·menon** *m feno·mena* phenomenon
**fenten** *f fentydnyow* spring (water); fountain
**fentenva** *f fentenvaow* spa (club, hotel etc)
**fer** *m feryow* fair (fun, trade)
**ferv** *adj* firm, steady
**fèst** *adv* very
**fesya** *v* drive (sb, sth) away
**feth** *m fethyow* fact
**fetha** *v* defeat
**fevyr** *m* fever
**fia dhe'n fo** *phr* flee
**fienasow** *m* fretting, anxiety; suspense
**fin** *adj* fine (texture)
**finweth** *f finwethow* limit; final(e)
**flàm** *m flabmow* flame
**flattra gans** *v* flatter
**flerya** *v* stink
**flogh** *m flehes* child
**flogh wydn** *m flehes gwydn* grandchild
**floghgovior** *m floghgovioryon* babysitter
**floren** *f florednow* lock (inset)
**flour** *m flourys* flower; choice (as adjective)
**flourys gwëdh** *pl* blossom
**flows** *m* nonsense
**flûr** *m flûrys* deck (ship)
**flyckra** *v* flicker
**flyrtya** *v* flirt
**foesyk** *m foesygyon* refugee
**fol** *adj/m felyon* fool(ish)
**foledna** *v* leaf through
**folednyk** *f folenygow* leaflet
**folen** *f folednow* page (book)
**fong** *m fongow* fungus
**fônow pedn** *pl* headphones
**fordh** *f fordhow* way; road
**fordh adro·** *f fordhow* roundabout (traffic)
**forgh** *f ferhy* fork
**form** *f formys* form

**formya** *v* create
**forn** *f fornow* oven; stove
**fors** *m forsow* force (incl physics)
**forsâkya** *v* abandon
**forùm** *m fora* forum
**fos** *f fosow* wall
**fotografya** *v* photograph
**fowt** *m fowtow* lack; mistake
**fowt perthyans** *m* impatience
**fracsyon** *m fracsyons* fraction
**fram** *m frâmys* frame
**frâmya** *v* frame
**frank** *adj* free
**franketh** *m frankedhow* freedom, liberty
**franklondyor** *m franklondyoryon* smuggler
**frappya** *v* strike (blow)
**fraus** *m frausys* fraud
**frega** *v* tear up; shred
**fresk** *adj* fresh
**freth** *adj* vigorous, energetic
**frethter** *m* vigour, energy
**fria** *v* free
**fria** *v* fry

**frobma** *v* get excited
**frobmans** *m* excitement
**frodn** *f frodnow* bridle
**frodna** *v* bridle; curb; brake
**frodnel** *f fronellow* brake
**front** *m frontys* front (political, weather)
**frony** *v* sniff
**fros** *m frosow* flow, current, stream
**frosa** *v* stream (incl on-line)
**frosek** *adj* fluent
**frût** *m frûtys* fruit
**fug-**[2] *pref* fake, pretend, sham, imitation
**fûgen** *f fûgednow* pastry (cake)
**fùj** *m* fudge
**fùndya** *v* found
**fùndyans** *m fùndyansow* foundation, institute
**fur** *adj* wise, sensible, prudent; smart (device, motorway etc)
**furneth** *m* wisdom, prudence
**furv gùntellek** *f furvyow cùntellek* collective (grammar)

**furv liesek** *f furvyow* plural
**furv unplek** *f furvyow* singular
**furvel** *f furvellow* formula
**furvlen** *f furvlednow* form (to fill in)
**furvus** *adj* formal
**furvwir** *adj* virtual
**fusen** *f fusednow* rocket
**fusyk** *adj* lucky, fortunate
**fycsyon** *m* fiction
**fydhyador** *m fydhyadoryon* trustee
**fydhyans** *m fydhyansow* reliance; trust (legal)
**fyges** *col fygesen* figs; dried fruit
**fygùr** *m fygùrs* figure (all senses)

**fygùr a gows** *m fygùrs* figure of speech, expression
**fygùrek** *adj* figurative
**fyllel** *v* be lacking / absent
**fyllel a**² *v + verb-noun* fail to
**fyllel a weskel** *phr* miss (target)
**fyllel dhe**² *v + verb-noun* omit to
**fylmya** *v* film
**fysek** *f* medicine (remedy)
**fysla** *v* fuss; fidget
**fystena** *v* hurry
**fy·sycal** *adj* physical
**fyt** *m fyttys* match (sport)

# G

**gaja** *m gajys* wager; stake
**gal** *m galow* rascal
**gallon** *m gallons* gallon
**gallos** *m/v galosow* be able to, can, may; power; skill(s)

**gallosek** (gallojek) *adj* powerful
**galow** *m galwow* call; invitation
**galwans** *m galwansow* profession
**galwansek** *adj* professional

**gam** *m gâmys* game (for hunting, part of match)
**ganow** *m ganowow* mouth
**gans / warby·dn an howl** *phr* clockwise / anti-clockwise
**gans gorhemydnow / gor[he]mynadow a'n gwelha** *phr* best regards (at end of email etc)
**gans hebma** *phr* herewith, enclosed
**gans meur a gris** *phr* drastically
**garan** *f garanas* crane (bird, machine)
**garlont** *m garlons* garland, wreath
**garm** *f garmow* call, cry (incl of animal); slogan
**garnsy cûgol** *m garnsys* hoodie
**garow** *adj* rough; violent
**garowder** *m* violence
**garr** *f garrow* leg
**garren** *f garednow* stem, stalk
**garth gwary** *m garthow* playground

**gàs** *m gassys* gas
**gasa** *v* let; let go (of)
**gasa** (nampy·th) **dhe godha** *phr* drop
**gasa dhe goll** *phr* neglect
**gasa mes** *phr* leave out, omit
**gaulak wàr**[2] *phr* astride
**gava** *v* (nampy·th dhe[2] nebonen) forgive (sb for sth)
**gavar** *f gyfras* goat
**gay** *adj* gay (incl sexuality)
**gedya** *v* guide
**gedyor** *m gedyoryon* guide
**geler** *f gelerow* coffin
**gell** *adj* brown (light)
**gelvyn** *m gelvynas* beak
**gelwel** *v* call; invite
**genesygeth** *f genesygethow* birth
**genesyk** (genejyk) *adj* native; innate, inherent
**genydnek** *adj* genetic
**genyn** *m genydnow* gene
**ger** *m geryow* word
**ger tremena** *m geryow* password

**gerlyver** *m gerlyvrow* dictionary
**gerva** *f gervaow* vocabulary
**gerys** [**dâ**] *adj* famous
**ges** *m* joke
**geseth** *m* irony; satire
**gesya** *v* joke
**gevell** *m gevellas* twin
**gidlînen** *f gîdlinednow* guideline; directive
**gîdlyver** *m gîdlyvrow* guidebook
**giewen** *f giewednow* tendon
**gis** *m gîsyow* manner, style
**gis screfa** *m gîsyow* style (writing)
**gladn** *f gladnow* bank (river, lake etc)
**glân** *adj/adv* clean; completely
**glanhe·** *v* clean; launder (incl money); wipe (to clean)
**glanyth** *adj* neat; hygienic
**glanythter** *m* neatness; hygiene

**glas** *adj* blue, green (focus on intensity)
**glasru·dh** *adj* purple, violet
**glaswels** *m* grass (growing)
**glaw** *m* rain
**glawlen** *f glawlednow* umbrella
**glëb** *adj* wet
**glebor** *m* wet, damp
**glebya** *v* wet
**glehy** *v* soak
**glena** *v* (orth) cling (to); stick *intr* (to)
**glesyn** *m glesydnow* lawn; green (bowling, golf)
**glin** *m glinyow* knee
**glory** *m glorys* glory
**gloryùs** *adj* glorious
**glow** *m* coal
**glow predn** *m* charcoal
**glus** *m* gum; glue
**glus gwethyn** *m* latex
**glus knias** *m* chewing gum
**glusa** *v* glue
**glûth** *m* dew; condensation
**glûthglaw** *m* drizzle

**glûthvelwes** *col* *glûthvelwen* slugs
**glyttra** *v* glitter
**gnas** *f gnasow* nature, quality, character
**gober** *m gobrow* wage(s), salary; fee
**gobonya** *v* jog (run slowly)
**gobra** *v* remunerate
**gobrena** *v* hire, rent
**gocky** *adj* stupid
**gockyneth** *m* stupidity
**godhaf** (godhevel) *v* suffer; tolerate
**Godhalek** *m* Gaelic (languages: Irish, Scottish, Manx)
**godhevyans** *m* tolerance
**go'dho·r** (goodh'o·r) *f godhas dor* mole (animal)
**godhvos** *m/v* know; know how to; knowledge
**godhvos convedhes** *phr* (or convedhes *v* alone: no inflection save *pp* convedhys) perceive, realize, understand
**godn** *m godnys* gun
**godnor** *m gonoryon* gunman

**godolhyn lent'he·** *m godolhydnow* speed bump
**godra** *v* milk
**godra·bm** *m* cramp
**godrega** *v* stay (as a guest)
**godrik** *m godrigow* stay
**godros** *m/v godrosow* threat(en)
**godrosek** *adj* threatening
**godrosladrans** *m* blackmail
**godroth burm** *m* yeast extract
**gogell** *f gogellow* pulpit; cell (biology)
**goheles** *v* avoid
**gohelus** *adj* evasive
**gol** *m gôlys* goal (football etc)
**goledna** *v* claim (sth as entitlement)
**golegy** *v* edit
**goles** *m golesow* bottom (of sth)
**goleyth** *m goleythyon* roast meat
**goleyth Tùrk** *m goleythyon* kebab
**golf** *m* golf

**golghva** *f golghvaow* bathroom
**golhy** *v* wash
**golia** *v* wound
**gologhyas** *m golohysy* worshipper
**gologva** *f gologvaow* outlook
**golohy** *v* worship
**golok** *f gologow* look, glance
**golok vian** *f gologow bian* glimpse
**golow** *adj/m golowys* light; glow
**golow trafyk** *m golowys* traffic light
**golowbren** *m golowbrednyer* lamp post
**golowjy** *m golowjiow* lighthouse
**golowy** *v* light; glow
**golowyn X** *m golowydnow* X-ray
**golvan** *m golvanas* sparrow
**golweyth** *m golweythyow* festival (over several days: Edinburgh, Glastonbury etc)
**goly** *m goliow* wound

**golya** *v* celebrate (birthday, anniversary etc)
**golya** *v* sail
**gonys** *v* cultivate; work at
**gonys has** *phr* sow [seed]
**gonysegeth** *f gonysegethow* culture
**goodh** *f godhow* goose
**gool** *m golyow* day (of saint); festival
**gool** *m golyow* sail
**gool ilow** *m golyow* concert
**goon** *f gonyow* down[land], moor[land]
**goos** *m* blood
**gooth** *m* pride (usually negative), arrogance
**gora** *col* hay
**gorbeskys** *adj* obese
**gordenva** *f gordenvaow* overdraft
**gordhuwher** *adv/m* (in the) evening
**gordhya [dhe**[2]**]** *v* honour, adore
**gordhyllo** *v* fire, sack (from job)
**gorfedna** *v* finish

**gorgis** *m* suspicion (distrust)
**gorhal** *m gorholyon* ship
**gorhan** *m gorhanow* charm
**gorhana** *v* charm, enchant
**gorhanus** *adj* charming
**gorhebmyn** *m/v gorhemydnow* command, bid(ding)
**gorhebmyn medhek** *m gorhemydnow* prescription
**gorher** *m gorheryow* lid, cover
**gorhery** *v* put the lid on
**gorholeth** *m gorholedhow* requirement, requisition
**gorlywa** *v* exaggerate
**gorm** *adj* brown (dark)
**gormel** *v* praise, acclaim
**gormola** *m gormoledhow* praise, acclaim
**gorothem** *m gorothobmow* emergency
**gorour** *m gorwer* hero
**gorra** *v* put, place; apply (sth to sth)

**gorra dhe dhyscans** *phr* educate
**gorra dhe wil** *phr* apply (process, remedy etc)
**gorra gwith** *phr* (a$^2$, dhe$^2$) take care (of, to)
**gorra in arhow** *phr* deposit (money)
**gorra in charj dhe**$^2$ *phr* entrust to
**gorra in geryow** *phr* express (in words)
**gorra marth in** *phr* amaze
**gorra moy dhe**$^2$ *phr* supplement
**gorra own in** *phr* frighten
**gorra tan in** *phr* light (sth that burns)
**gorras** *m gorrasow* lift (in car)
**gorsaf** (*2$^{nd}$ state* orsaf) *m gorsavow* station
**gorsaf bùs** *m gorsavow* bus station
**gorseth** (*2$^{nd}$ state* orseth) *f gorsedhow* gorsedd
**gorth-**$^2$ *pref* anti-, counter-

**gortheby** *v* (dhe²) answer, reply, respond, react; correspond (sth to sth)
**gortheneby** *v* oppose
**gorthsaf** *m* resistance
**gorthyedho·wieth** *f* antisemitism
**gorthyp** *m* *gorthebow* answer, reply, response, reaction
**gortos** *v* wait (for)
**gorvarhas** *f* *gorvarhajow* supermarket
**gorwel** *m* *gorwelow* horizon
**goskes** *m* *goskesow* shade; shelter
**goskesy** *v* shade; shelter
**goslowes** (golsowes) *v* [orth, dhe²] listen (to)
**gosogen** *f* *gosogednow* black pudding
**gossenek** *adj* rusty
**gostyth** *adj* obedient
**goth mûn** *f* *gwythy* lode
**goth vrâs** *f* *gwythy brâs* artery
**gothen** *f* *gothnow* sole (foot, shoe); tread (tyre)

**gothys** *adj* proud (usually negative), arrogant
**goubman** *m* seaweed
**goun** *m* *gounow* gown
**gour** *m* *gwer* man (as opposed to woman); husband
**gour ambosys** *m* *gwer* fiancé
**gourow** *adj* male; masculine (grammar)
**govenek** *m* *govenegow* *hope
**gover** *m* *goverow* brook, stream
**governa** *v* govern, run (town, country)
**governans** *m* *governansow* government
**govyjyon** *pl* cares
**govyn** *m/v* *govydnow* (orth nebonen) ask, enquire (of); enquiry; ask for, request, apply for; charge (amount) *Note construction* govyn orth nebonen gwil nampy·th = ask sb to do sth
**govyn orth y honen** *phr* wonder (whether, if etc)

**govynador** *m govynadoryon* questionnaire
**govynadow** *m* enquiry; request, application
**govynva** *f govynvaow* information point
**gow** *m gowyow* lie
**gow gwir** *m gowyow* paradox
**gowdhan** *m gowdhanas* moth
**gowek** *adj/m gowygyon* mendacious; liar
**gowleverel** *v* [tell a] lie
**gôy** *v* digest
**gradh** *m gradhow* grade; degree (academic)
**gradhva** *f gradhvaow* scale (size)
**grahell** *f grahellow* heap, pile
**grahella** *v* heap, pile
**gràm** *m gramow* gram
**gramer** *m gramers* grammar
**grappa** *m grappys* grape
**grâss** *m grassow* (a$^2$) thanks (for)
**grassyùs** *adj* gracious
**grastal** *m grastallow* tip (gratuity)
**grava** *m gravathow* stretcher
**grava ros** *m gravathow* wheelbarrow
**gravyans** *m gravyansow* sculpture
**gre** *f greyow* herd, flock (pasturing animals)
**gre sodhogyl** *m* offical status
**grêf** *m grêvys* grief
**greun** *col greunen* grains; berries
**greun olew** *col greunen* olives
**greunvos** *m greunvosow* cereal (incl for breakfast)
**grevya dhe**$^2$ *v* afflict, harm (sb)
**grolyak** *adj/m grolyogyon* grumbling; grumbler
**gromercy** (mercy) [**dhis / dhywgh why**] *phr* thank you
**gromyal** *v* growl
**grônd** *m grôndow* ground (especially figuratively)

**grôndya** *v* base (argument, assumption etc)
**growedha** (*2nd state* wrowedha) *v* lie [down]
**growyn** *col* grit; gravel
**grug** *col* heather
**grugys** (*2nd state* wrugys) *m grugysow* belt; zone
**grugys sawder** *m grugysow* safety belt
**grugys sawya** *m grugysow* lifebelt
**gùhy** *col gùhien* wasps
**gùstel** *m gùstlow* riot
**gùsygen** *f gùsygednow* bladder; blister
**gwacter** *m gwacterow* emptiness; vacuum; void
**gwadn** *adj* weak; dim (light)
**gwag** *adj* empty, vacant; hungry (between meals)
**gwain** *m gwainys* win; gain, profit; income
**gwainya** *v* win; gain, obtain
**gwainyor** *m gwainyoryon* winner
**gwaityans** *m gwaityansow* expectation

**gwakhe·** *v* empty
**gwall** *m gwallow* accident (with good or bad outcome)
**gwana** *v* pierce
**gwandra** *v* wander; ramble
**gwaneth** *col* wheat
**gwanhe·** *v* weaken; dim (light)
**gwara** *col* goods (bought and sold)
**gwarak** *f gwaregow* bow; arch
**gwarak an glaw** *f gwaregow* rainbow
**gwarak wysk** *f gwaregow gwysk* coat-hanger
**gwardya** *v* guard
**gwariel** *f gwariellow* toy, plaything
**gwarior** *m gwarioryon* player (incl device); actor
**gwarnya** *v* warn
**gwarnyans** *m gwarnyansow* warning; notice (upcoming event)
**gwarr** *f gwarrow* neck (nape); shoulders (loosely)

**gwarsagh** *m gwarseghyer* rucksack
**gwartha** *m gwarthavyow* top
**gwarthek** *col* cattle
**gwarthevyans** *m* supremacy; predominance
**gwarthowl** *f gwarthowlow* stirrup
**gwary** *m/v gwariow* play (incl in theatre); game; act (drama)
**gwary dall** *m gwariow* raffle
**gwary dauns** *m gwariow* dance (event)
**gwary fol** *m gwariow* farce
**gwary ger** *m gwariow* pun
**gwary ilow** *m gwariow* musical (West End etc)
**gwary kenys** *m gwariow* opera
**gwary mildam** *m gwariow* jigsaw puzzle
**gwary mir** *m gwariow* spectacle
**gwaryjy** *m gwaryjiow* theatre
**gwaryva** *f gwaryvaow* stage
**gwas** *m gwesyon* fellow, chap, guy
**gwasca** *v* press
**gwascas** *m gwascasow* pressure (incl media)
**gwask** *f gwascow* press
**gwastas** *adj* level
**gwâv** *m gwavow* winter
**gwavgùsca** *v* hibernate
**gway** *m gwayow* move
**gwaya** *v* move (physically)
**gwaynten** *m gwayntenyow* spring (season)
**gweder** *m gwedrow* glass (material, optical instrument)
**gweder aspia** *m gwedrow* telescope
**gweder lyw** *m* stained glass
**gweder meras** *m gwedrow* mirror (for looking at reflection)
**gwëdh** *col gwedhen* trees
**gwëdhboll** *m* chess

**gwedhen-ven** *m gwedhen-venow* [tree] trunk
**gwedhow** *adj* widowed
**gwedhra** *v* wither
**gwedren** *f gwedrednow* glass (for drinking)
**gwel** *m gwelow* sight; scene
**gwel** *m gwelyow* field; pitch (sport)
**gwelen** *f gwelyny* stick, rod; cue (for pool etc)
**gwelen debry** *f gwelyny* chopstick
**gwelen eva** *f gwelyny* straw (for drinking)
**gweles** *v* see
**gweljow bian** *pl* scissors
**gwell** *adj* better; *prefer
**gwellhe·** *v* improve; get better (from illness)
**gwely** *m gweliow* bed; layer (beneath sth)
**gwely dêdh** *m gweliow* sofa, settee, couch
**gwenogen** *f gwenogednow* wart
**gwenogen troos** *f gwenogednow* verruca
**gwenol** *f gwenyly* swallow (bird); shuttle[cock]
**gwenyn** *col gwenenen* bees
**gwer** (gwerdh) *adj* green (contrasted with blue)
**Gwer** (Gwesyon, Mebyon) *pl* Gents (toilet)
**gweras** *m gweresow* soil
**gweres** *m/v* (orth) help (with); aid, assist(ance) *Note construction* gweres [dhe[2]] nebonen ow qwil nampy·th = help sb to do sth
**gweres mona** *m* subsidy
**gweresor** *m gweresoryon* helper, aide
**gwerghsys** *m* virginity
**gwern** *f gwernow* mast (incl for communication)
**gwerrya** *v* fight a war
**gwerryans** *m* warfare
**gwers** *f gwersyow* verse
**gwerth** *f gwerthow* sale
**gwertha** *v* sell
**gwerthor** *m gwerthoryon* seller; salesman
**gwerthveurhe·** *v* appreciate (sb or sth)

**gweryn** *f* folk
**gwerynor** *m gwerynoryon* peasant; worker (proletarian); pawn
**gweskel** *v* beat (strike); hit (target, website)
**gwest** *f* accommodation
**gwesty** *m gwestiow* guesthouse
**gwesty** *v* host
**gwetha** (gwitha) *v* (rag) keep, preserve, protect (from)
**gwetha** *v* deteriorate
**gwethhe·** *v* aggravate
**gwethyas** *m gwethysy* guard; carer
**gwethyas âlsyow** *m* coastguard
**gwethyas cres** *m gwethysy* police officer
**gwethyas sawder** *m gwethysy* security guard
**gwethyas train** *m gwethysy* conductor
**gwethyas treth** *m gwethysy* lifeguard (on beach)
**gwethyn** *adj* supple; tough (meat)
**gwetyas** *v* expect; hope (expectantly)
**gweus** *f gwessyow* lip (anatomy)
**gwewen** *f gwewednow* heel
**gweyth** *m gweythyow* work (concept, finished product)
**gweytha** *v* operate (sth)
**gweytha orth** *v* work at, exploit
**gweythor** *m gweythoryon* worker
**gweythres** *m gweythresow* action; function; app
**gweythresa** *v* action, implement; function
**gweythresek** *adj* active
**gweythresor** *m gweythresoryon* activist; executive (business)
**gweythva** *f gweythvaow* works, factory, plant
**gwia** *v* weave; knit; wind (river, road etc)
**gwias** *m gwiasow* textile; web
**gwiasva** *f gwiasvaow* website

**gwîhal** *v* squeak, squeal; creak
**gwil** (gul) *v* make; do See also ev a wra
**gwil defnyth a**$^2$ *phr* make use of, utilize
**gwil dhe**$^2$ (nebonen / nampy·th) *phr* + *verb-noun* make sb / sth (do sth)
**gwil ergh** *phr* snow
**gwil ges a**$^2$ *phr* make fun of
**gwil glaw** *phr* rain
**gwil marthùjyon** *phr* wonder (be amazed; also, idiomatically, whether, if etc)
**gwil mencyon a**$^2$ *phr* mention
**gwil môcyon** *phr* gesture
**gwil powes** *phr* have a rest
**gwil revrons dhe**$^2$ *phr* respect (sb)
**gwil vry a**$^2$ *phr* heed; respect (sb, sth)
**gwil warle·rgh** *v* imitate
**gwil y welha** *phr* do one's best
**gwin** *m* wine

**gwir** *adj/m gwiryow* true, authentic; real; right (to sth)
**gwir pryntya** *m gwiryow* copyright
**gwirhaval** *adj* probable; plausible
**gwiryon** *adj* innocent; sincere
**gwiryonsys** *m* innocence; sincerity
**gwith** *m* custody; supervision, care
**gwithty** *m gwithtiow* museum
**gwithva** *f gwithvaow* store (incl for sales)
**gwlân** *m* wool
**gwlân coton** *m* cotton wool
**gwlanek** *adj/m gwlanegow* woolly; jumper, sweater, pullover
**gwlas** *f gwlasow* country, land (political)
**gwlasegeth** *f* politics (national, local)
**gwlasegor** *m gwlasegoryon* politician
**gwlasek** *adj* political (national, local)

**gwragh** *f gwrahas* witch; woodlouse
**gwreck** *m gwreckys* wreck
**gwrëdh** *col gwredhen* root
**gwredhek** *adj* original
**gwreg** *f gwrageth* wife
**gwres** *f* heat(ing); temperature; fervour, ardour
**gwres cresednek** *f* central heating
**gwresak** *adj* fervent, ardent
**gwresel** *f gwresellow* thermometer
**gwrians** *m gwriansow* activity; manufacturing
**gwrias** *v* sew
**gwrîhon** *col gwrîhonen* sparks
**gwrionedhek** *adj* actual
**gwrioneth** (gwiryoneth) *m gwrionedhow* truth; reality
**gwrith** *f* deeds, actions, performance
**gwrydnya** *v* (orth; in) grapple (with); squeeze, squash (into)

**gwybes** *col gwybesen* gnats, midges, mosquitos
**gwycor** *m gwycoryon* trader, dealer (legal or illegal)
**gwydn** *adj* white
**gwydnyk** *adj* pale
**gwylan** *f gwylanas* [sea]gull
**gwylanel** *f gwylanellow* glider
**gwylcos** *m gwylcosow* jungle
**gwylfos** *m* wilderness
**gwyls** *adj* wild
**gwynder** *m* whiteness; paleness
**gwynkya** *v* wink
**gwynru·dh** *adj* pink
**gwyns** *m gwynsow* wind
**gwynsak** *adj* windy
**gwynvÿs** *adj* lucky, fortunate *Note optional construction* gwydn y vÿs
**gwysca** *v* dress; put on (clothing)
**gwyscas** *m gwyscosow* layer (on top of sth); coat (paint)
**gwysk** *m gwyscow* costume, attire

**gwyskva** *f gwyskvaow* dressing room
**gwyskys ha deu** *phr* worn out (clothing)
**gwystel** *m gwystlow* hostage; bet
**gwystla** *v* bet
**gwythien** *f gwythy* vein
**gwyver** *m gwyvrow* wire (material, individual)
**gwyw** *adj* suitable
**gwywder** *m* suitability
**gwywer** *m gwyweras* squirrel
**gyga-**[1] *pref* giga-
**gyttern** *m gytterns* guitar
**gyvyans** *m* forgiveness

# H

**ha browsyon in y gerhyn** *phr* in breadcrumbs
**ha +** *noun* **intredhans** *phr* including
**ha kestew in y gerhyn** *phr* in batter
**ha ny ow côwsel** *phr* by the way, incidentally
**ha pelha** *phr* what's more, furthermore, moreover
**hacter** *m* ugliness; cruelty
**hag erel** *phr* et cetera (etc)
**hager** *adj* ugly
**hager-**[2] *pref* nasty
**halô·** *interj* hello (answering phone)
**hanaf** *m hanavow* cup
**Hanaf an Bÿs** *m* The World Cup
**hanaja** *v* sigh; groan; murmur
**hanajen** *f hanajednow* sigh; groan; murmur
**handla** *v* touch (with hand); handle, manipulate
**haneth** *adv* tonight; this evening
**hanow** *m henwyn* name; reputation
**hanow crev** *m henwyn* noun

**hanow dâ** *m* fame
**hanow gwadn** *m henwyn* adjective
**hanter-dëdh** *m* midday
**hanter-nos** *f* midnight
**hanter-our** *m* half an hour
**hanvos** *m/v* exist(ence)
**hanwans** *m hanwansow* nomination
**harber** *m harberys* refuge
**hardh** *adj* bold, audacious
**hardha** *v* bark
**hardhva** *f* bark[ing]
**harp** *m harpys* harp
**has** *col hasen* seed; sperm
**hâtya** *v* hate
**haunsel** *m haunsels* breakfast
**hâv** *m havow* summer
**haval** *adj* (dhe², orth) like, similar (to)
**havyas** *m havysy* summer visitor
**havyas campya** *m havysy* camper
**heb awhe·r** *phr* happily, willingly

**heb bry** *phr* invalid
**heb confort** *phr* uncomfortable (sth)
**heb côwsel a²** *phr* not to mention
**heb danjer** *phr* without hesitation
**heb drog** *phr* innocent
**heb gàs** *phr* still (bottled water)
**heb glûten** *phr* gluten-free
**heb hedhy** *phr* constant(ly)
**heb kespar** *phr* single (status)
**heb let** *phr* immediately
**heb mar [na martesen]** *phr* without doubt, of course
**heb nàm** *phr* flawless(ly)
**heb othem** *phr* unnecessary, unnecessarily
**heb prevyans** *phr* inexperienced
**heb rekna** *phr* excluding
**heb teythy specyal** *phr* mediocre
**heblek** *adj* flexible

**hedhes** *v* reach [as far as]; fetch, bring, hand over
**hedhon** *adj* portable
**hedhy** *v* stop, pause (action, motion)
**hedhyw** *adv* today
**hedor** *adj* fragile
**hegar dhe ûsya** *phr* user-friendly
**hel** *m helow* hall
**helgh an tyller** *m* the local hunt
**helghya** *v* hunt
**hèn yw** *phr* that is (i.e.)
**hèn yw dhe leverel** *phr* that is to say
**hèn yw dhe styrya** *phr* namely
**hen-whedhel** *m hen-whedhlow* legend
**hendra** *f hendraow* antique
**hens** *m hensy* track; lane (on carriageway)
**hens horn** *m hensy* railway
**hens tira** *m hensy* runway
**hensador [lorednek]** *m hensadoryon* satnav

**henwel** *v* name
**hepcor** *v* forgo, do without
**herdhwyns** *m herdhwynsow* hurricane
**herdhya** *v* thrust, shove; blow (wind)
**hern** *col hernen* pilchards
**hern gwydn** *col hernen wydn* herrings
**hern opyn** *col hernen* kippers
**hernes** *m hernessow* harness; equipment
**hernessya** *v* harness; equip
**herôt** *m herôs* herald
**herwyth** *prep + noun* according to
**herwyth lojyk** *phr* logical(ly)
**herwyth sians** *phr* arbitrary, arbitrarily
**hës** *m hesow* length
**hes** *f hesow* flock (birds); swarm; shoal (fish)
**heskedna** *v* saw
**hesken** *f heskednow* saw
**hesp cregys** *m hespow* padlock

**hesres** *m hesresow* longitude
**hevelepter** *m* (dhe², orth) similarity (to)
**hevelly** *v* seem
**hevleny** *adv* this year
**heyl** *m heylyow* estuary
**hil** *m hilyow* race (ethnic)
**hile·gieth** *f* racism
**hir** *adj* long
**hirbedrak** *adj/m hirbedrogow* oblong; rectangle, rectangular
**hireth** *m* longing; loneliness; nostalgia; blues (mood, music)
**hirethek** *adj* lonely (sb); nostalgic
**hirgorn** *m hirgern* trumpet
**hirgren** *adj* oval
**hirhe·** *v* lengthen
**hobba** *m hobbys* hobby
**hockya** *v* hesitate
**hockya in y gows** *phr* stutter, stammer
**hockyans** *m hockyansow* hesitation
**hôk** *m hôkys* hawk
**hôk caryn** *m hôkys* vulture

**holan** *m* salt
**holanek** *adj* salty
**holergh** *adj* late (after due time)
**holya** (folya) *v* follow (sb)
**honensys** *m honensesow* identity
**honenus** *adj* selfish
**honenuster** *m* selfishness
**hôra** *f hôrys* prostitute
**hormôn** *m hormônow* hormone
**horn** *m* iron
**hornel** *f hornellow* iron (for clothes)
**ho·roscôp** *m horoscôpow* horoscope
**hos** *adj* hoarse
**hos** *m heyjy* duck
**hot** *m hottys* hat
**howl** *m* sun[light]
**howl-leskys** *adj* sunburnt
**howlek** *adj* sunny
**howllen** *f howllednow* sun umbrella
**howlsedhas** *m* sunset
**hùbbadùllya** *m* din, racket (noise)
**hudor** *m hudoryon* magician (entertainer)

**hùmbronk** *v* lead, escort
**hùmbrynkyas** *m hùmbrynkysy* leader
**hùmor** *m* humour
**hunlef** *m hunlevow* nightmare
**hunros** *m hunrosow* dream
**hunrosa** *v* dream

# I

**idhyow** *col* ivy
**idn** *adj* narrow (in several dimensions)
**iffarn** *m* hell
**iffarnak** *adj* hell of a
**igam-ogam** *adv* zigzag
**ilyn** *adj* clear (water); net[t]
**in bàn** *phr* up *motion*; upstairs *motion*
**[in] chy** *phr* at home
**in cres** *prep* in the middle of
**in dadn gel** *phr* secret(ly)
**in dadn scoos** *prep* under the auspices of
**in dadn veugh** *prep* sponsored by

**hùrtya** *v* hurt (sb or *intr*)
**hyga** *v* cheat
**hyk** *m hycow* hiccup
**hylgeth** *m* soot
**hympna** *m hympnys* hymn
**Hyndou** *adj/m Hyndous* Hindu
**Hyndou·ieth** *f* Hinduism

**in danjer** *prep* addicted to
**in spit / in despî·t** *prep* + *noun* **in spit dhe**[2] / **in despî·t dhe**[2] *prep* + *pronoun* in spite of, despite
**in ewn angùs** *phr* in agony
**in gwir** *phr* indeed
**in gwrioneth** *phr* in fact, actually
**in hans dhe**[2] *prep* beyond *position*
**in herwyth** *prep* + *possessive pronoun* according to
**in kerdh / in kergh** *phr* away *motion*

**in kerhyn** *prep + possessive pronoun* all around
**in kever** *prep + possessive pronoun* in relation to, concerning, about
**in le** *prep + noun, demonstrative / possessive pronoun* **in le a**[2] *prep + verb-noun* instead of
[**in**] **mes** *phr* out[side] *motion*
[**in**] **mes a**[2] *prep* out of *motion*
**in mesk** *prep* among
**in neb câss** *phr* in any case, anyway
[**in**] (**wàr**) **neb fordh** *phr* somehow
[**in**] **neb le** *phr* somewhere
[**in**] **neb maner** *phr* somehow
**in nebes geryow** *phr* concise(ly)
**in ogas** *phr* nearby
**in ogas** *prep + possessive pronoun*
[**in**] **ogas dhe**[2] *prep* near *position*
**in oll an bÿs** *phr* in the world (reinforcing negative or superlative)
**in poynt dâ** *phr* fit, in good shape
**in prës dâ** *phr* opportune(ly)
**in pùb le** *phr* everywhere
**in rag** *phr* forwards; fast (clock)
**in tre** *phr* at home
**in vain** *phr* in vain
**i'n contrary part** *phr* on the contrary
**i'n côstys-ma** *phr* in these parts, around here
**i'n dallath** *phr* at first
**i'n eur-ma** *phr* now
**i'n eur-na** (**nena**) *phr* then
**i'n fordh ûsys** *phr* as usual
**i'n gwelha prës** *phr* fortunately
**i'n gwetha prës** *phr* unfortunately
**i'n kettermyn** *phr* (**gans**) at the same time; in time (with - music)

**i'n mên-termyn** *phr* meanwhile
**i'n tor'-ma** *phr* at the moment
**inclynya pedn** *phr* nod
**indella** *adv* like that
**indelma** *adv* like this
**inia** *v* (wàr nebonen) insist; urge, incite (sb)
**iniadow** *m* insistence
**injynor** *m injynoryon* engineer
**injyno·rieth** *f* engineering
**ink** *m* ink
**installya** *v* instal
**interpretya** *v* interpret
**inwe·dh** *adv* also, too, as well
**iredy** (aredy) *adv* readily; surely
**is-**[1] *pref* sub-, vice-
**is-carg** *m is-cargow* download
**is-carga** *v* download

**is-dewysyans** *m is-dewysyansow* by-election
**isel** *adj* low
**iselbrîs** *adj* cheap
**iselhe·** *v* lower
**iskydna** *v* mount (horse etc)
**iskydnor** *m iskynoryon* lift (elevator)
**iskynva** *f iskynvaow* ramp
**Islâ·m** *m* Islam
**Islâmek** *adj* Islamic
**islînya** *v* underline
**ispan** *m ispadnow* lining
**ispoynt** *m ispoyntys* minimum
**ispoyntek** *adj* minimum; minimal
**i·story** *m i·storys* history
**istydna** *v* extend; pass (to sb)
**istydnans** *m istynansow* extension

# J

**jàm** *m* jam
**jaunt** *m jauntys* ride (at funfair)

**jèl** *m jelys* gel
**jenevra** *m* gin

**jentyl** *adj* graceful, elegant
**je·ntylys** *m* grace[fulness], elegance
**jerkyn** *m jerkynys* jacket
**jerkyn sawder** *m jerkynys* life jacket
**Jesu Crist** *m* Jesus Christ
**jîns** *pl* jeans
**jôker** *m jôkers* joker (in cards)
**jolyf** *adj* merry, lively
**jolyfta** (jolyfter) *m* merry-making
**jorna** *m jornys* day (as frame for events)
**jornalyst** *m jornalystyon* journalist
**jorryk** *m jorrygow* beer mug
**jowal** *m jewelys* jewel
**joy** *m* joy
**jùbylê·** *m jùbylê·s* jubilee
**jùglya** *v* juggle
**jùj** *m jùjys* judge
**jùjment** *m jùjmentys* judgement
**jùjya** *v* judge
**jùnya** *v* join, connect (sth [to sth])
**jùst** *adj* just
**jùstyfia** *v* justify
**jùstys** *m* justice; magistrate
**jy·lofer** *m jy·lofers* carnation
**jyn** *m jynys* machine; engine, motor
**jyn dewros** *m jynys* motorbike
**jyn ebron** *m jynys* aircraft
**jyn ethen** *m jynys* steam engine
**jyn falhas** *m jynys* lawn mower
**jyn kemysky** *m jynys* mixer
**jyn tedna** *m jynys* tractor
**jyn whelas** *m jynys* search engine
**jyn-dewrosyas** *m jyn-dewrosysy* motorcyclist, biker
**jynjy** *m jynjiow* engine house
**jy·njyber** *m* ginger
**jynweyth** *m jynweythyow* mechanism

**jynweythek** *adj* mechanical

# K

**ke** *m keow* fence; hedge
**keas fe·nester** *m keasow* shutter
**keber** *f kebryow* beam (timber)
**kedhow** *m* mustard
**kedna** *v* coat
**kednen** *f kenednow* film (incl cinema etc); coating; cataract (eye)
**kedry·dn** *f kedrydnow* row (quarrel)
**kef** *m kefyon* stump (tree)
**kefeth owravallow** *m* marmalade (orange)
**kefnys** *col kefnysen* spiders
**kefrë·s** *adv* also, too, as well; even
**kefrë·s ha** *prep* as well as, in addition to
**kefrysek** *adj* federal
**kefrysyans** *m kefrysyansow* (con)federation; alliance
**kegy** *v* cook

**jynweythor** *m jynweythoryon* mechanic

**kegyn** *f kegynow* kitchen
**kegy·nieth** *f* cooking; cuisine
**kegynor** *m kegynoryon* chef
**kehaval** *adj* equal
**keher** *m keherow* muscle
**keles** *v* hide, conceal
**kelgh** *m kelhow* circle, ring; hoop; circuit
**kelghlyther** *m kelghlytherow* circular, newsletter
**kelghres** *m kelghresow* cycle
**kelghrester** *f kelghrestry* rota
**kell** *f kellow* cell (for prisoner etc)
**kelly** *v* lose; miss (bus etc)
**kellyn** *m* scum
**kelmy** *v* tie, bind
**kelmys ganso** *phr* related, connected

**kelorn** *m kelornow* bucket
**Kelt** *m Keltyon* Celt
**Keltek** *adj* Celtic
**kelyn** *col* holly
**kelyon** *col kelyonen* flies
**Kembrek** *m* Welsh (language)
**kemenessa** *v no inflection* communicate
**kemeneth** (keme·nieth) *f kemenethow* community; commonwealth
**kemeres** *v* take
**kemeres dhyworth** *v* subtract from
**kemeres in bàn** *phr* get up (from table)
**kemeres in prest** *phr* borrow (money)
**kemeres les in** *phr* be interested in
**kemeres meth** *phr* ($a^2$) be ashamed (of) / embarrassed (by)
**kemeres preder** $a^2$ *phr* consider
**kemeres radn** *phr* (in) take part / participate (in)
**kemeres trueth** $a^2$ *phr* pity
**kemeres with** *phr* ($a^2$) take care (of)
**kempedna** *v* tidy
**kempen** *adj* tidy
**kempensys** *m* tidiness
**kemusur** *adj/m kemusurow* proportion; proportional; proportionate
**kemyn** *adj* common; ordinary; general
**kemysk** *m kemyskow* mix[ture], blend; miscellany
**kemysky** *v* mix, blend; confuse (sth)
**ken** *adj/adv* another; else; otherwise
**ken** *m* cause (incl legal proceedings)
**ken fordh** *f fordhow* alternative
**ke·nderow** *m kendyrewy* cousin
**kendon** *f kendonyow* debt; obligation; liability (legal, financial)
**ke·nedhel** *f kenedhlow* generation; nation
**kenedhlek** *adj* national

**kenegen** *f kenegednow* bog
**kenertha** *v* boost; encourage (sth)
**kenseth** *m kensedhow* lobby
**kenter** *f kentrow* nail; spike
**kentra** *v* nail
**kentrevak** *adj/m kentrevogyon* neighbour(ing)
**kentrevogeth** *m kentrevogedhow* neighbourhood
**kenwerth** *m kenwerthow* trade, commerce
**kenwertha** *v* trade
**kenwes** *m kenwesow* feast
**kenyn ewynek** *col kenynen* garlic
**keny·therow** *f kenythyrewy* cousin (female)
**kepa·r** (peca·r) **ha** *prep* like
**ker** *adj* dear, expensive
**kerdh** *m kerdhow* walk
**kerdhes** *v* walk
**kerdhes i'n dowr** *phr* paddle
**kerdhfôn** *m kerdhfônow* mobile [phone]
**kerdhor** *m kerdhoryon* walker
**keredhy** *v* reproach
**kerenje'ek** *adj* affectionate
**kerens** *pl* relatives; parents (where context clear)
**kerensa** *f* love, affection
**kerensa gans an bobel** *f* popularity
**keres** *col keresen* cherries
**kereth** *f* reproach
**kergh** *col* oats
**kerhes** *v* fetch, get
**kerhydna** *v* surround; besiege
**kerhydneth** *m kerhynedhow* environment
**Kernow** *m Kernowyon* Cornishman
**Kernowek** *m* Cornish (language)
**kert** *m kertys* cart; lorry, truck (road)

**kert adrë·v** *m kertys* trailer (vehicle)
**kertyk** *m kertygow* trolley (supermarket, airport, hospital etc)
**kervya** *v* carve
**kesassoylyans** *m kesassoylyansow* compromise
**keschaunj** *m keschaunjys* exchange; swap
**keschaunjya** *v* exchange, swap
**kescorra** *v* assemble (sth)
**kescowetha** *f* companionship, company
**kescowethyans** *m kescowethyansow* partnership; relationship (social)
**kescows** *m kescowsow* conversation; talks (diplomacy)
**kescôwsel** *v* have a conversation
**kescruny** *v* amass, concentrate
**kescùssulyans** *m kescùssulyansow* conference
**keser** *col keseren* hail
**kesgwlasek** *adj* international
**kes'hens** *m kes'hensy* junction (motorway etc)
**keskerdh** *m keskerdhow* procession; march
**keskerdhes** *v* move in procession; march
**keskians** *m keskiansow* conscience
**keslînek** *adj* parallel
**keslowenhe·** *v* congratulate
**kesobery** *v* co-operate, collaborate
**kespar** *m & f kesparow* partner (in relationship)
**kesparthek** *adj* reciprocal, mutual
**kespos** *m* equilibrium
**kesposa** *v* balance (sth)
**kesres** *adj* current, up to date
**kesres'he·** *v* update
**kesscrefa** *v* (gans) correspond (with sb)
**kessedhek** *m kessedhegow* committee
**kessenyans** *m* harmony

**kesson** *adj kessonyow* harmonious; consistent
**kesstrif** *m kesstrîvow* competition
**kesstrîvya** *v* compete
**kesstrîvyor** *m kestrivyoryon* competitor
**kessydhyans** *m* sanction(s)
**kestaf** *m kestavow* contact
**kesten** *col kestenen* chestnuts
**kestrevna** *v* co-ordinate
**kestrevnek** *adj* co-ordinated
**kesunya** *v* combine
**kesunyans** *m kesunyansow* combination
**kesunyans lavur** *m kesunyansow* [trade] union
**kesva** *f kesvaow* board (organization)
**kethneth** *m* slavery
**kethreydhecter** *m* homosexuality
**kethreydhek** *adj* homosexual
**keus** *m* cheese

**kevalaf** *f* capital (finance)
**kevalavo·rieth** *f* capitalism
**kevals** *m kevalsyow* joint (incl meat)
**kevambos** *m kevambosow* (orth) contract, pact (with)
**kevambos kesgwlasek** *m kevambosow* (orth) treaty (with)
**kevarhewy** *v* invest
**kevarwedha** *v* direct
**kevarwedhor** *m kevarwedhoryon* director (company etc)
**kevarweth** *f* information
**kevelsys** *adj* articulated
**keveryans** *m keveryansow* direction; orientation
**keveryans brës** *m keveryansow* mindset
**keveryans reydhek** *m keveryansow* sexual orientation
**keveylya** *v* accompany (musically)
**keveylyth** *m keveylydhyon* accompanist

**kevosek** *adj/m kevosogyon* contemporary
**kevradna** *v* (in) share, participate (in); allot *Note pp* kevrydnys
**kevradnak** *m kevranogyon* participant
**kevradnor** *m kevranoryon* shareholder
**kevran** *f kevradnow* share (incl in company)
**kevrath** *m kevradhow* rate
**kevren** *f kevrednow* link (incl to website); coupling; conjunction
**kevres** *m kevresow* series (objects, events); serial (TV etc)
**kevresek** *adj* serial
**kevreth** *f kevrethyow* system
**kevrethek** *adj* systematic
**kevrin** *m kevrinyow* mystery; secret
**kevrinek** *adj* mysterious; secret
**kevrol** *f kevrolyow* volume (book)

**kewar** *adj* precise; precisely right
**kewarhen** *f* cannabis, marijuana
**kewerder** *m* precision
**keweyth** *m keweythyow* project (concerted action)
**kewny** *col* moss; lichen; mildew
**keworra** *v* (dhe$^2$) add (to)
**keworrans** *m keworransow* addition; supplement; annex(e)
**keworransyn** *m keworransydnow* additive
**keybal** *m keybalow* ferry (boat)
**keyfordh** *f keyfordhow* tunnel
**keyn** *m keynow* back (anatomical or 'quasi-anatomical' – *e.g.* of chair); keel; ridge
**keynsagh** *m keynseghyer* backpack
**keynsaghyor** *m keynsaghyoryon* backpacker
**keynvÿs** *m keynvysow* universe
**kibya** *v* snatch

**kig** *m* flesh; meat
**kig an dens** *m* gum(s)
[**kig**] **bowyn** *m* beef
**kig leugh** *m* veal
**kig ôn** *m* lamb
**kig porhel** *m* pork
**kig yar** *m* chicken (meat)
**kigsconyor** *m kigsconyoryon* vegetarian
**kil** *m kilyow* back (of sth); recess; bay (hospital)
**kildedna** *v* pull back; retreat
**kildro** *f kildroyow* recession (economic)
**kilva** *f kilvaow* background
**knack** *adv + adverb or preposition of position* just, right
**knâva** *m knâvys* knave; jack (in cards)
**knoukya** *v* knock
**know** *col knofen* nuts (incl for screws)
**know côco** *col knofen gôco* coconuts
**know dor** *col knofen dhor* peanuts
**know toos** *col knofen* doughnuts

**ky** *m keun* dog
**kybell** *f kybellow* tub
**kybell atal** *f kybellow* skip
**kydnyaf** *m kynyavow* autumn
**kydnyow** *m kynyewow* dinner
**kyffewy** *m kyffewyow* party (celebration)
**kyffewya** *v* party
**kyfy dhe**[2] *v* confide in
**kyjya** *v* fuck
**kylo-**[1] *pref* kilo-
**kynda** *m kyndys* kind, sort; genus
**kyns** *adv* previously; rather
**kyns** (kyn) *prep + noun, verb-noun* before
**kyns ès** *prep + noun, non-personal pronoun, verb-noun, infinitive construction* before
**kyns nape·ll** *phr* before long
**kyns oll** *phr* above all, principally, especially
**kyns pedn** *prep* within (time)

97

**kyny** *v* lament, grieve, mourn

# L

**label** *m labelyow* label
**labm** *m labmow* jump, leap
**lacka** *adj* worse
**lader** *m ladron* thief
**ladha** *v* kill; slaughter; douse (light)
**ladhva** *f ladhvaow* slaughter; massacre; cull (badgers etc)
**ladra** *v* steal
**ladrans** *m ladransow* theft
**lafyl** *adj* legal
**lagas** *m lagasow* eye
**lagen** *f lagednow* pond; puddle
**lagya** *v* splash (make splashes)
**laha** *m lahys* law
**lamlen** *f lamlednow* parachute
**lamwely** *m lamweliow* trampoline
**larj** *adj* generous
**larjes** *m* generosity

**kyttryn** *m kyttrynyow* bus

**laser** *m laserow* laser
**lash in rag** *m lashys* forward slash
**lash wàr dhele·rgh** *m lashys* backslash
**lâss** *m lâcys* lace, tie
**lath** *f lathow* yard (length)
**la·tymer** *m la·tymers* interpreter
**Latyn** *m* Latin
**laun** *m launow* blade
**launchya** *v* launch
**lavar** *m lavarow* remark; sentence
**lavar coth** *m lavarow* proverb
**lavaren** *f lavarednow* phrase
**lavasos** *v* venture, dare
**lavrak** *m lavrogow* trousers
**lavrak bian** *m lavrogow* [under]pants
**lavrak cot** *m lavrogow* shorts

**lavrak neyja** *m lavrogow* swimshorts
**lavregyn** *m lavregydnow* panties, knickers
**lavur** *m* toil, labour (incl childbirth); work
**lavurya** *v* toil, labour; work; walk (considerable distance)
**le** *adj/adv* less
**lebma** *v* sharpen
**lebmel** (labma) *v* jump, leap
**lebmyn** *adv* now
**lebmyn hag arta** *phr* [every] now and then, occasionally
**lecher** *m lecherow* frying-pan
**ledan** *adj* broad, wide
**ledanhe·** *v* broaden, widen
**leder** *f ledrow* slope, slant; bias
**ledn** *f lednow* sheet
**ledn baby** *f lednow* nappy
**ledn dewl** *f lednow tewl* blind (for window)
**ledry** *v* slope, slant
**lêdya** *v* lead

**lêdyor** *m ledyoryon* leader
**leftenant** *m leftenans* lieutenant
**legest** *m legesty* lobster
**legestyk** *m legestygow* prawn
**legestyk Bay Dûlyn** *m legestygow* scampi
**legh** *f lehow* slab
**legh fe·nester** *f lehow* window sill
**lehe·** *v* reduce
**lehen** *f lehednow* slate (roofing, writing); tile (loosely); tablet (device)
**lel** *adj* loyal; honest
**lelder** *m* loyalty; honesty
**lemygya** *v* sip
**len** *adj* faithful
**le·ndùry** *m* faithfulness
**lendya** (lêna) *v* lend (sth specific)
**lenky** *v* swallow
**lent** *adj* slow
**lenwel** *v* (a$^2$) fill (with)
**les** *m* breadth, width; gauge (railway)
**les** *m* interest; welfare
**lêsa** *v* spread
**lesca** *v* swing; rock

**lêsha** *m lêshys* leash, lead
**lesk** *m lescow* swing (motion); cradle
**lesk lovan** *m lescow* swing (playground)
**lesky** *v* burn
**leslen** *f leslednow* spreadsheet
**lesres** *m lesresow* latitude
**lesson** *m lessons* lesson (incl bible reading)
**lester** *m lestry* vessel (incl ship); vase
**lester sedhy** *m lestry* submarine
**let** *m lettys* obstacle, hindrance; setback
**leth** *m* milk
**leth shakys** *m* milkshake
**lether** *m* leather
**lettya** *v* block, prevent, stop
**letys** *col letysen* lettuce(s)
**leun** *adj* (a$^2$) full (of)
**leun a dhedhewadow** *phr* promising
**leun a frobmans** *phr* exciting

**leungara** *v* adore
**leur** *m leuryow* floor; storey
**leurlen** *f leurlednow* carpet
**leurweth** *adj* horizontal
**lev** *m levow* voice
**level** *m levelyow* level
**Level A** *m Levelyow* A Level
**leven** *adj* smooth, even (incl number)
**levender** *m* smoothness, evenness
**levenhe·** *v* level
**leverel** *v* (dhe$^2$, orth) say (to)
**leveryans** *m leveryansow* pronunciation
**leveryas** *m leverysy* spokesman
**levna** *v* smooth; iron, press
**lewyador** *m lewyadoryon* pilot
**lewyans** *m* steering; driving
**lewyas** *v* steer; drive (vehicle)

**lewyor** *m lewyoryon* driver
**lewyth** *m lewydhyon* governor (school etc)
**leyth** *adj* damp; humid
**leythter** *m* dampness; humidity
**lia** (tia) *v* swear (oath)
**lien** *m* literature
**lien** *m lienyow* fabric, cloth (cotton, linen)
**lien bord** *m lienyow* tablecloth
**lien codna** *m lienyow* scarf
**lien dewla** *m lienyow* napkin, serviette
**lien dorn** *m lienyow* handkerchief
**lien gwely** *m lienyow* bedsheet
**lien seha lestry** *m lienyow* tea towel
**lien-ladrans** *m lien-ladransow* plagiarism
**lies** *adj + singular or collective noun* many, numerous
**lies-leur** *adj* multi-storey
**lies'he·** *v* multiply

**lin cales** *m lînow* hard shoulder (motorway)
**linedna** *v* rule line(s); outline
**linednor** *m linenoryon* ruler (for lines)
**lînen** *f linednow* line; stripe; rail (track)
**lion** *m lions* lion
**lis** *m* mud
**lisak** *adj* muddy
**lîter** *m lîtrow* litre
**lith** *f lithas* plaice
**liv** *m livow* flood
**lo** *f loyow* spoon
**loas** *m loesow* spoonful; scoop (of ice cream)
**lobm** *adj* bare (place)
**lobmen pis** *f* mushy peas
**loder** *m lodrow* stocking
**lodryk** *m lodrygow* sock
**logas** *col logosen* mice
**logas brâs** *col logosen vrâs* rats
**lojyk** *m* logic
**londer** *m londrys* gutter (roof)
**londya** *v* land (especially from boat)
**loneth** *f lonethy* kidney

**longus** *adj* relevant
**longya** *v* (dhe²) belong (to)
**loor** *f lorow* moon
**loos** *adj* grey; mouldy
**loren** *f lorednow* satellite (artificial)
**lorgh** *m lorhow* staff, stick
**losk pengasen** *m* heartburn
**loskveneth** *m loskvenydhyow* volcano
**losow** *col losowen* plants, vegetation
**losow debry** *col losowen* vegetables
**losowek** *adj* vegetable
**lost** *m lostow* tail; queue
**losten** *f lostednow* skirt
**lovan** *f lovonow* rope
**lowarn** *m lewern* fox
**lowarth** *m lowarthow* garden
**lowarthor** *m lowarthoryon* gardener
**lowen** *adj* happy
**lowender** *m* happiness, joy; merriment
**lowenhe·** *v* rejoice

**lower** *adj + singular or collective noun* quite a few
**lowr** *adj/adv* sufficient, enough; quite
**lowr a²** *phr* enough; lots of
**lows** *adj* loose, slack; careless
**lowsel** *v* loosen
**lu** *m luyow* host (great number); army
**lûbergh** *m* slush
**lùck** *m* luck
**lugarn** *m lugern* lamp
**luhes** *col luhesen* lightning; flashes
**luhesy** *v* flash
**lùll ha lay** *m* lullaby
**lùlla** *v* lull
**lus** *col lusen* bilberries; blueberries
**lus rudh** *col lusen* cranberries
**lusow** *col lusowen* embers; ash[es]
**lust** *m lustys* lust
**lybm** *adj* sharp; acute
**lybm y skians** *phr* on the ball

**lybral** *adj/m lybrals* liberal
**lyckya** *v* lick
**lydn** *m lydnow* liquid
**lydn** *f lydnow* lake
**lyfrêson** *m lyfrêsons* delivery
**lyftya** *v* lift
**lyha** *adj/adv* least
**lyly** *col lylien* lilies
**lyly Corawys** *col lilien* daffodils
**lymder** *m* sharpness; acuteness
**lymna** *v* paint (art); illustrate
**lymnans** *m lymnansow* painting; illustration
**lymnor** *m lymnoryon* painter (art); illustrator
**lymon** *m lymons* lemon

# M

**mab** *m mebyon* son
**mab den** (mabde·n) *m mebyon tus* mankind; human being
**mab y dhama** *phr* what's-his-name
**mabm** *f mabmow* mother

**lymytya** *v* limit
**lyn** *m* flax; linen
**lynas** *col lynasen* nettles
**lystedna** *v* bandage
**lysten** *f lystednow* bandage
**lyther** *m lytherow* letter
**lyther kebmyn** *m lytherow* will (testament)
**lytherdoll** *f* postage
**lytheren** *f lytherednow* letter (alphabet)
**lyver** (lever) *m lyvrow* book
**lyver termyn** *m lyvrow* magazine
**lyverjy** *m lyverjiow* library
**lyvryk** *m lyvrygow* booklet, brochure
**lyw howl** *m* [sun]tan
**lywa** *v* dye

**Mabmyk** *f* Mum[my]
**madâma** *f madâmys* lady; madam (addressing sb)
**maga** *v* feed, nourish; bring up, rear; breed

**maga tâ** (magata·) *phr* also, too, as well
**maghteth** *f meghtythyon* maid[en]; lass
**maglen** *f maglednow* mesh; grid; trap; gear
**magor** *f magoryow* old walls, ruin
**mailya** *v* wrap
**mailyans** *m mailyansow* wrap[per]
**mailyer** *m mailyers* envelope
**main** *m mainys* medium; means
**mainor** *m mainoryon* agent; broker
**maino·rieth** *f mainoriethow* agency (concept, organization)
**màl** *m literally* 'eagerness': *be eager / looking forward to
**mala** *v* grind
**mamscrif** *m mamscrifow* original (document)
**mamyeth** *f mamyethow* mother-tongue
**màn** *m literally* 'nil'*: with express negative* at all, *with implied negative* not at all
**managh** *m menegh* monk
**mandât** *m mandâtys* mandate (political)
**manek** *f manegow* glove
**maner** *f manerow* manner
**ma·nerlych** *adv* appropriately
**mango** *m mangôs* mango
**mantol** (montol) *f mantolyow* scales (for weighing)
**mantolly** *v* weigh (sth)
**ma·nykyn** *m ma·nykyns* model (fashion)
**manylyon** *pl* details
**mappa** *m mappys* map
**mar pleg** *phr* please
**marchont** *m marchons* merchant
**margh** *m mergh* horse
**margh horn** *m mergh* bicycle
**margh tan** *m mergh* locomotive
**marghredyk** *m* horseradish

**marhak** *m marhogyon* horseman, rider; knight
**marhas** *f marhajow* market
**marhas stockys** *f marhajow* stock market
**marhogeth** *v* ride
**marhogieth** *f marhogiethow* knighthood
**marnas** *prep + noun, pronoun (independent if personal)* except *with express negative See also 'Grammar Words'*
**marner** *m marners* sailor
**marow** *adj* dead; out (fire) *Note construction* ev a veu marow = he died
**mars yw res** *phr* if necessary
**mars yw taclow indelma** *phr* in that case
**martesen** (martejen) *adv* perhaps, maybe
**marth** *m* wonder; *be surprised
**marthys** *adj/adv* wonderful[(ly)
**ma's** *prep literally* 'except': *with express or implied negative* only

**mason** *m masons* mason (incl freemason)
**maso·nieth** *f* freemasonry
**mass** *m massys* mass (physics)
**mâta** *m mâtys* pal, mate
**mater** *m* matter (incl physics), affair
**maw** *m mebyon* boy, lad
**mayonê·s** *m* mayonnaise
**mebla** *v* furnish (with furniture)
**mebyl** *m meblys* furniture
**meder** *m medrow* aim
**medhegieth** *f* medicine (science)
**medhegva** *f medhegvaow* surgery (GP; MP figuratively)
**medhek** *m medhygyon* doctor
**medhek meyny** *m medhygyon veyny* general practitioner (GP)
**medhel** *adj* soft; tender
**medhelder** *m* softness; tenderness
**medhelhe·** *v* soften
**medhelweyth** *m* software

**medhow** *adj* drunk
**medhowynjy** *m* drunkenness
**medras** *m medrasow* objective
**mega-**[1] *pref* mega-
**megy** *v* smoke; smother; muffle (sound)
**mel** *m* honey
**meleganes** *f meleganesow* blonde
**melen** *adj* yellow
**melen y vlew** *phr* blond
**mellya** *v* (orth) interfere (with)
**melwhes** *col melwhen* snails
**melyn wyns** *f melynyow gwyns* windmill; wind turbine
**melys ha wherow** *phr* sweet and sour
**melysor** *m melysoryon* sweetener
**men** *m meyn* stone (incl weight and in fruit)
**mencyon** *m mencyons* mention
**meneges** *v* indicate; state

**menegva** *v menegvaow* index
**menegyans** *m menegyansow* indication; statement
**menegyans resek** *m menegyansow* commentary
**menestrouthy** *m* instrumental music; band
**meneth** *m menydhyow* mountain
**mengleth** *m mengledhyow* quarry
**menowgh** *adj* frequent
**menta** *m* mint (plant)
**mentêna** *v* uphold, maintain
**mênyng** *m* meaning
**menyster** *m menystrys* minister
**menystra** *v* administer, manage
**menystror** *m menystroryon* administrator, manager
**menystry** *m menystrys* ministry
**mer** *m mêras* mayor
**meras** (miras) *v* (orth, wàr) look (at)

**merhyk** *m merhygas* pony
**Meriasek** *m* St Meriadoc
**merk** *m merkys* mark; brand, make
**merkya** *v* notice
**mernans** *m mernansow* death
**meror** *m meroryon* onlooker, spectator
**merther** *m mertheryon* martyr
**merwel** *v* die
**meryt** *m me·rytys* merit
**mes** *see* [in] mes
**mes a²** *see* [in] mes a²
**meschau·ns** *m meschauncys* disaster, catastrophe
**messach** *m messajys* message
**mêster** *m mestrysy* master (**Mêster** *title* Mr)
**mêstres** *f mestresow* mistress (**Mêstres** *title* Mrs, Ms)
**Mestresyk** *title* Miss
**mestrynsys** *m mestrynsesow* mastery; regime (political)
**mesva** *f mesvaow* inch

**mesya** *v* hitch[-hike]
**me·tafor** *m metaforow* metaphor
**mêter** *m mêtrow* metre
**meth** *m* shame; embarrassment; shyness; *be ashamed / embarrassed / shy
**method** *m methodys* method
**Me·thodyst** *m Methodystyon* Methodist
**methus** *adj* shameful, disgraceful
**metya** *v* [gans] meet
**metyans** *m metyansow* meeting (informal)
**meugh** *m meughyow* bail; sponsorship
**meur** *adj/adv* great; much
**meur a²** *phr* lots of
**meur a bonvos** *phr* a real pain (nuisance)
**meur attê·s** *phr* luxurious, luxury
**meur ras [dhis / dhywgh why]** *phr* (a²) thank you (for)
**meur y berthyans** *phr* patient

**meur y deythy** *phr* gifted
**meur y dros** *phr* noisy
**meur y hanow** *phr* famous
**meur y nell** *phr* forceful
**meur y vern** *phr* concerned; important
**meur yw y les in** *phr* he is interested in
**meureth** *m* greatness
**meurgerys** *adj* popular
**meyny** *m meynys* household
**meyny cabyn** *m meynys* cabin crew
**meythrynva** *f meythrynvaow* nursery, crèche
**meythy** *v* feed (baby)
**mil dov** *m milas* pet
**mildi·r** *f mildiryow* mile
**milva** *f milvaow* zoo
**milvedhek** *m milvedhygyon* vet
**min** *m minyon* edge; brim
**minfron** *f minfrodnow* muzzle (for dog)
**minlyw** *m minlywyow* lipstick
**minvlew** *col* moustache; whiskers (cat etc)

**minwharth** *m* smile
**minwherthyn** *v* smile
**mis** *m misyow* month
**mis Du** *m* November
**mis Ebrel** (**Ebr**) *m* April
**mis Est** *m* August
**mis Genver** (**Gen**) *m* January
**mis Gortheren** (**Gor**) *m* July
**mis Gwyngala** (**Gwn**) *m* September
**mis Hedra** (**Hed**) *m* October
**mis Kevardhu** (**Kev**) *m* December
**mis Me** *m* May
**mis Merth** (**Mer**) *m* March
**mis Metheven** (**Mvn**) *m* June
**mis Whevrel** (**Whe**) *m* February
**mockya** *v* mock
**môcyon** *m môcyons* motion, movement; gesture
**model** *m modelys* model (of / for sth)
**modrewy** *f modrewyow* bracelet

**modryp** *f modrebeth* aunt
**mog** *m* smoke
**moghhe·** *v* enlarge; increase
**mol** *adj* bald; bare (hill)
**moldra** *v* murder, massacre, assassinate
**molgh dhu** *f molhas du* blackbird
**momentùm** *m* momentum
**mona** *m monies* money; currency
**mona munys** *m* small change
**mona parys** *m* cash
**monhe·** *v* slim
**moon** *adj* slender, slim
**mor** *m morow* sea
**mor du** *col moren dhu* blackberries
**mora·lyta** *m* morality (good or bad)
**mordardh** *m* surf
**mordhardha** *v* surf
**mordhos** [hogh] *f* ham
**mordrik** *m mordrigow* low tide
**morethek** *adj* unhappy, miserable (subjectively)

**morgaja** *m morgajys* mortgage
**morhogh** *m morhohas* porpoise
**morlanow** *m morlanowyow* high tide
**morlu** *m morluyow* navy
**morrep** *m morrebow* seashore
**mortal** *adj* mortal; fatal, lethal
**morthol** *m mortholow* hammer
**mortholya** *v* hammer
**mortîd** *m mortîdys* tide
**morvil** *m morvilas* whale
**morvil ladha** *m morvilas* killer whale
**morvleyth** *m morvleydhas* shark
**mos** (mones) *v* go
**mos a wel** *phr* disappear
**mos adro·** *phr* circulate
**mos dhe**[2] *v* attend
**mos dhe goll** *phr* get lost; perish
**mos i'n ewn fordh** *phr* go straight (ahead, to somewhere)
**mos in rag** *phr* proceed

**mos wàr bedn dewlin** *phr* kneel [down]
**mòsk** *m moskys* mosque
**most** *m* dirt
**mostya** *v* contaminate
**mothow** *pl* failure
**môtorfordh** *f môtorfordhow* motorway
**mousak** *adj* smelly
**mowes** *f mowysy* girl
**moy** *adj/adv* more *Note constructions* moy + *uncountable noun,* moy a$^2$ + *plural or collective*
**moy ha moy** *phr* more and more, increasingly
**moy pò le** *phr* more or less
**moyha** *adj/adv* most
**Mùhamad** *m* Muhammad
**mùllyon** *col mùllyonen* clover; clubs (in cards)
**mûn** *m mûnyow* mineral
**mûndalas** *m mûndalasow* royalty
**munys** *adj* tiny
**mùryon** *col mùryonen* ant
**muscok** *adj* mad
**muscotter** *m* madness

**Mùslym** *adj/m Mùslyms* Muslim
**musura** *v* measure
**musurans** *m musuransow* measurement
**mûsycyan** *m mûsycyans* musician
**mûsyk** *m* music
**mûtya** *v* sulk
**muvya** (môvya) *v* move (emotionally)
**muvyans** *m muvyansow* emotion; movement (political, symphony etc)
**muvyansek** *adj* emotional
**my a'th / a'gas pës** *phr* please
**mycro-**$^1$ *pref* micro-
**my·crofôn** *m mycrofônow* microphone
**mydnas** *m* will, intention *See also* ev a vydn
**mygla** *v* cool (sth)
**mygyl** *adj* lukewarm
**Myhal Sans** *m* St Michael
**mylly-**$^1$ *pref* milli-
**my·lytant** *adj/m mylytantyon* militant

**myns** *m* size
**mynsek** *adj* sizeable, considerable
**mynys** *col mynysen* minutes (time)
**myowal** *v* miaow
**myrgh** *f myrhas* daughter; girl
**myrgh hy dama** *phr* what's-her-name

**myshevya** *v* mess up, ruin
**myssyon** *m myssyons* mission
**myte·rn** *m myterneth* king
**myternes** *f myternesow* queen
**myttyn** *adv/m* (in the) morning

# N

**na felha** *phr with express negative* any longer, *with implied negative* no longer
**na fors** *phr + question word* no matter
**na gyk na myk** *phr* not a squeak (no sound at all)
**nabma** *v* stain (incl figuratively)
**nacyon** *m nacyons* nation
**Nadelyk** *m* Christmas
**nader** *f nedras* adder, viper
**nagh** *m nahow* denial; refusal
**naha** *v* deny; refuse

**nahe·n** *adj/adv with express negative* any other; in any other way, *with implied negative* no other; in no other way
**najeth** *f najedhow* needle
**nàm** *m nabmow* blemish, stain (incl figuratively)
**namenowgh** *adv with express or implied negative* rarely, seldom
**nameu·r** *adv with express negative* much; often, *with implied negative* not much; not often, *with express or implied negative* hardly, scarcely

111

**namnyge·n** *adv* just [now]
**namo·y** *adv with express negative* any more, *with implied negative* no more
**nane·yl** *adv with express negative* either, *with implied negative* neither
**nano-**[1] *pref* nano-
**nans yw pell** *phr* long ago
**nappya** *v* have a nap; sleep (computer)
**nas** *f nasow* nature (personal), character (personal); feature (of sth)
**natur** *f naturyow* nature
**naturek** *adj* natural
**neb fordh** *see* [in] neb fordh
**neb ken** *phr* for some reason
**neb le** *see* [in] neb le
**neb maner** *see* [in] neb maner
**neb sort a**[2] *phr* some sort of
**nedh** *col nedhen* nits
**nefra** *adv with express negative* ever, *with implied negative* never (present or future reference)
**nefra namo·y** *phr with express negative* ever again, *with implied negative* never again (future reference)
**negedhek** *adj* negative
**negesyth** *m negesydhyon* commissioner
**negesyth golyas** *m negesydhyon* ombudsman
**negys** *m negysyow* (orth) affair; business (with)
**nell** *m* might, power
**nèn** *m nednow* ceiling
**nepprë·s** *adv* sometime
**nerth** *m* might, power; energy (physics)
**nerth nowedhadow** *m* renewable [energy]
**nerth y vydnas** *phr* willpower
**nerv** *f nervow* nerve
**nervus** *adj* nervous (anxious)
**nes** *adj* nearer

**nes'he·** *v* bring near[er]; come near[er], approach
**nessa** *adj* nearest; next; second (in a sequence)
**neus** *col neujen* threads
**nev** *m nevow* heaven
**new** *f newyow* sink
**newher** *adv* last night; yesterday evening
**neyj** *m neyjow* flight
**neyja** *v* [**i'n air** / **ebron**] fly; float
**neyja** *v* [**i'n dowr**] swim; float
**neyth** *m neythow* nest
**neythy** *v* nest
**nith** *f nithow* niece
**normal** *adj* normal
**Norman** *adj/m Normans* Norman
**north** *adj/m* north(ern)
**nos** *f nosow* night
**nosweth** *f noswedhow* characteristic
**nôten** *f notednow* note
**noth** *adj* bare, naked, nude
**notha** *f* nudity
**nôtya** *v* note; remark; announce

**nôtyans** *m notyansow* note; announcement
**noudel** *m noudels* noodle
**novel** *m novelys* novel
**now** *interj* now
**nowedhy** *v* renew
**nowethhe·** *v* renovate
**nown** *m* hunger
**nownek** *adj* hungry (for lack of food)
**nowodhow** *pl* news
**nowyth** *adj* new; just
**nowyth flàm** *phr* brand new
**noy** *m noyens* nephew
**nùmber** *m nùmbers* number (countable quantity)
**nùmbra** *v* number (assign number(s) to, be counted among)
**ny +** *verb* **malbew dàm** *phr* be damned if
**ny spêdyas** (nampy·th) *phr* (sth) failed
**ny syns ev oy a**[2] *phr* he has no time for (dislikes)
**ny vern** *phr* it doesn't matter

**ny wrug** (nebonen)
**soweny** *phr + present participle* (sb) failed (to)
**nylon** *m* nylon
**ny'n deur** *phr* he doesn't care
**nyver** *m nyverow* number (for specific purpose)
**nyver aswonvos [personek]** *m* personal identificaton number (PIN)
**nyver Surynjy Kenedhlek** *m* National Insurance number
**nyvera** *v* count (1, 2, 3)
**nyveren** *f nyverednow* numeral
**nywl** *m nywlow* fog, mist
**nywlek** *adj* foggy, misty

# O

**ober** *m oberow* work (specific); deed; effort
**oberen** *f oberednow* task, job
**oberwas** *m oberwesyon* workman
**obery** *v* achieve; act (take action)
**oberyans medhek** *m oberyansow* operation (surgery)
**obeya** *v* obey
**obeyans** *m* obedience
**objeta** *m objetys* object (grammar)
**obma** *adv* here
**obsessys** *adj* (gans) obsessed (with)
**ocasyon** *m ocasyons* occasion
**ocûpya** *v* occupy
**odour** *m odours* smell (individual)
**oferen** *f oferednow* mass (Catholic)
**offendya** *v* offend (all senses)
**offe·ns** *m offencys* offence (all senses)
**offra** *v* offer
**offrydna** *v* sacrifice (especially figuratively)
**ogas** *adj/adv* (dhe[2]) near, close (to) *position*; intimate; *+ adjective* almost

**ogas ha** *prep + noun* almost
**ogas lowr** *phr* approximate(ly)
**ogasty·** (ogatty·) *adv* almost
**ogh** *interj* oh
**ôker** *m* interest (on deposit or loan)
**ol** *m olow* footprint; trace, vestige
**ola** *v* weep, cry
**olas** *f olasow* hearth, fireplace; home
**olcan** *m olcanyow* metal
**olew** *m* olive oil
**[oll] a'y anvoth** *phr* reluctantly
**[oll] a'y vodh** *phr* gladly
**olyfans** *m olyfansow* elephant
**omassaya** *v* (ow qwil nampy·th) practise (doing sth)
**omassayans** *m omassayansow* exercise, practice
**omberthy** *v* balance *intr*
**omborth** *m* balance
**omborthus** *adj* wobbly; ambivalent; ambiguous

**ombredery** *v* (a$^2$) meditate, reflect (on)
**ombrofya** *v* (rag) apply (for)
**ombrofyor** *m ombrofyoryon* candidate
**omdava gans** *v* contact (sb)
**omdedha** *v* dissolve *intr*
**omdedna** *v* retire; shrink; log off
**omden** *m* retirement
**omdhal** *v* quarrel
**omdhehesy warby·dn** *v* collide with
**omdhevas** *adj/m omdhevasow* orphan
**omdhiscores** (omdhy'scores) *f omdhiscoresow* stripper (entertainer)
**omdhisky** (omdhy'sky) *v* get undressed
**omdho·n** *m/v* behaviour; behave
**omdhysodha** *v* resign
**omdhysqwedhes** *v* appear (come into sight)
**omdhysqwedhyans** *m omdhysqwedhyansow* appearance

**omdowl** *m* wrestling
**omdôwlel** *v* wrestle
**omdrailyans** *m* *omdrailyansow* revolution (turn)
**omfydhyans** *m* confidence
**omgelmy** *v* (gans) engage (with); log on
**omgemeres** *v* undertake (task, venture)
**omgemeres rag** *v* take responsibility for (sth to be done)
**omgemeryans** *m* *omgemeryansow* undertaking (venture); responsibility, portfolio
**omglowans** *m* *omglowansow* feeling (physical or emotional)
**omgùntell** *v* gather, assemble *intr*
**omgùssulya** *v* (gans) consult, discuss (with)
**omhevelly** *v* (dhe$^2$) simulate
**omhevellyans** *m* *omhevelyansow* simulation; calque

**omjùnya** *v* (dhe$^2$) join (group, association)
**omladha** *v* *no inflection* commit suicide
**omlath** *m/v* *omladhow* (gans) fight
**omlêsa** *v* spread *intr*
**omoffrydnans** *m* self-sacrifice
**omrôlya** *v* check in *intr*
**omry** *v* (dhe$^2$) give up; devote oneself (to)
**omsettya** *v* (wàr$^2$) attack
**omsettyans** *m* *omsettyansow* attack
**omsewya** *v* result
**omunya gans** *v* identify with
**omvagly** *v* (in) get involved (in)
**omvetya** *v* (gans) rendezvous (with)
**omwel** *m* *omwelow* interview
**omwenel** *v* squirm
**omweres** *v* cope
**omwheles** *v* overturn, upset (sth)
**omwolhy** *v* wash *intr*
**ôn** *m* *ên* lamb

**onen a'n vrâsyon** *phr* VIP
**onest** *adj* decent, proper
**only** *adv* only
**onyon** *col onyonen* onions
**oos** *m osow* age
**ôp** *m ôpys* ope[way]
**oportûnyst** *m oportûnystyon* opportunist
**opyn** *adj* open
**opynwelys** *adj* evident
**opynyon** *m opynyons* opinion
**or** *f oryon* border, frontier
**o·rchestra** *m o·rchestras* orchestra
**ordna** *v* set in order
**ordyr** *m ordrys* order (good order, sequence)
**organ** *m organow* organ (all senses)
**organek** *adj* organic
**ors** *m orsas* bear
**orth y vrës / vreus** *phr* in his opinion
**orthodontyth** *m orthodontydhyon* orthodontist

**orthopedek** *adj* orthopaedic
**oryel** *m oryels* gallery (art)
**ost** *m ôstys* host; landlord (pub)
**ostel** *f ostelyow* hotel
**ôstyas** *m ostysy* guest
**osweyth** *m osweythyow* era
**ot obma** (otobma) *phr* here is / are
**othem** *m* *need
**othomva** *f othomvaow* services (motorway etc)
**our** *m ourys* hour
**outra·y** *m outrayow* outrage; atrocity
**outrayus** *adj* outrageous; atrocious
**overcùmya** *v* beat, overcome
**ow cortos yn parys** *phr* on standby (sb)
**ow kelly** *phr* slow (clock)
**ow kemeres pêmons socyal** *phr* on benefits
**[ow] tùchya** *prep* relating to, concerning, about
**ow tyseha [yn] teg** *phr* refreshing

**own** *m* (a²) *fear (of)
**owr** *m* gold
**owraval** *m owravallow* orange (fruit)
**owrbysk** *m owrbùscas* goldfish

**owrek** *adj* golden
**owrlyn** *m* silk
**oy** *m oyow* egg
**oyl** *m* oil
**oylya** *v* oil

# P

**pab** *m pabow* pope
**padel** *f padellow* pan
**padel dhorn** *f padellow dorn* saucepan
**padellyk** *f padelygow* saucer
**padn** *m padnow* fabric, cloth
**pain** *m painys* pain
**paint** *m paintys* paint
**paintya** *v* paint
**pal** *f palyow* spade (incl in cards)
**palas** *v* dig; excavate
**paljia** *v* paralyse
**palm** *m palmys* palm (plant)
**palores** *f paloresow* chough
**pals** *adj* + *plural* abundant, plenty of

**palv** *f palvow* palm (hand)
**palva** *v* stroke (with hand)
**palvala** *v* feel for, grope
**paly** *m* velvet
**palys** *m palycys* palace
**pana brow?** *phr* (mar) what's the use? (of)
**panel** *m panellow* panel
**panes** *col panesen* parsnips
**pans** *m pansow* dell
**paper** *m paperyow* paper
**paper gwal** *m* wallpaper
**paper nowodhow** *m paperyow* newspaper
**par hap** *phr* perhaps
**para** *m parys* team
**pa·radhys** *f* paradise
**pa·ranoyd** *adj* paranoid

**park** *m parcow* field (especially for grazing, also of force); pitch (sport)
**park ca·ravan** *m parcow* caravan site
**park kerry** *m parcow* car park
**parkya** *v* park
**part** *m partys* part (mechanical, dramatic, in any joint action)
**parth** *f parthow* side (especially left, right)
**party** *m partys* party (legal, political)
**Party an Gemynwer** *m* The Communist Party
**Party an Gonservegoryon** *m* The Conservative Party
**Party an Lavur** *m* The Labour Party
**paruster** *m* readiness
**parusy** (parujy) *v* get ready, prepare
**parys** *adj* (dhe²) ready (to)
**pas** *m pasow* cough
**pasa** *v* cough
**pasbord** *m* cardboard

**Pask** *m* Easter
**passya** *v* pass; overtake
**passyon** *m passyons* passion
**pasta** *m* pasta
**pastel dir** *f pastellow tir* smallholding; allotment
**pasty** *m pastys* pasty; pie
**patâta** *m patâtys* potato
**patron** *m patronys* pattern
**paw** *m pawyow* paw; claw (crab, lobster)
**pawgen** *m pawgednow* slipper
**payon** *m payonas* peacock
**pê** *v* pay [out]
**pedn** *m pednow* head; top; end (extremity)
**pedn an colodhyon** *m pednow* appendix (anatomy)
**pedn an hens** *m pednow hens* destination
**pedn bloodh** *m pednow* birthday
**pedn** *m* **cales** stubborn [person]
**pedn pùsorn** *m pednow* refrain (of song)

**pedn-cyta** *f pedn-cytys* capital
**pedrak** *adj/m pedrogow* square
**pedren** *f pedrednow* buttock
**pedrevan** *f pedrevanas* lizard
**pedry** *v* rot; corrupt
**pedrys** *adj* corrupt
**pega·ns** *m* means (financial)
**peha** *v* sin
**pehador** *m pehadoryon* sinner
**pehadow** *m* sin
**pejadow** *m* prayer
**pejy** (pesy) *v* pray (for sth) *Note constructions* pejy gans nebonen = pray for sb *and* pejy wàr nebonen = pray to sb *and* pejy orth nebonen (or infixed pronoun) a wil / na wrella nampy·th = ask sb to do / not to do sth
**pel** *f pelyow* ball
**pel droos** *f* football (game)
**peldrosyas** *m peldrosysy* footballer
**pelednyk** *f pelenygow* pill
**pell** *adj/adv* distant; far
**pellder** *m pellderow* distance
**pellen** *f pelednow* ball (of sth)
**pellgôwsel** *v* (orth) telephone
**pellgowsor** *m pellgowsoryon* telephone
**pellwolok** *f* television
**pellwolok realeth** *f* reality TV
**pelour** *m pelours* fur (for wearing)
**pêmont** *m pêmons* payment
**Pencast** *m* Pentecost, Whitsun
**pendom** *adj* extremist
**peneglos** *f peneglosyow* cathedral
**penfenten** *f penfentydnyow* source
**pengasen** *f pengasednow* stomach
**penrewl** *f penrewlys* principle
**penscol** *f penscolyow* university

**penscrefor** *m penscreforyon* editor (of periodical)
**penser** *m pensery* architect
**pensevyges** *f pensevygesow* princess
**pensevyk** *m pensevygyon* prince
**penseythen** *f penseythednow* weekend
**pensyon** *m pensyons* pension
**per** *col peren* pears
**Peran** *m* St Piran
**perfeth** *adj* perfect
**perfethter** *m* perfection
**perfethyth** *m perfethydhyon* perfectionist
**perhedna** *v* possess; own
**perhednek** *m perhenogyon* proprietor; landlord (of tenant)
**perhen** *m perhednow* owner
**perl** *m perlys* pearl
**persecûtya** *v* persecute
**person** *m persons* person

**perswâdya** *v* persuade *Note construction* perswâdya may whrella / na wrella nebonen nampy·th persuade sb to do / not to do sth
**perthy** *v* tolerate, put up with
**perthy awhe·r** *phr* be anxious
**perthy cov** *phr* ($a^2$) remember
**perthy danjer** *phr* be hesitant
**perthy dowt / own** *phr* ($a^2$) fear, be afraid (of)
**perthy envy** *phr* ($a^2$) envy, be jealous (of)
**perthy grêvons** *phr* (orth) bear a grudge (against)
**perthyans** *m* patience
**perthyn dhe**[2] *v* relate to
**perthynas** *m perthynasow* relation[ship] (abstract)
**perthynecter** *m* relativity
**perthynek** *adj* relative
**peryl** *m peryllow* danger, risk
**peryllya** *v* endanger

**peryllys** *adj* dangerous
**pës dâ** *phr* (gans) content, satisfied, pleased (with)
**peswar torn** *phr* crossroads
**pêsya** (pêjya) *v* (ow qwil nampy·th) continue (to do sth)
**pêsyans** *m pesyansow* continuation
**pëth yw dha** (children only) / **agas hanow?** *phr* what's your name?
**pethow** *pl* assets, possessions
**petrol** *m* petrol
**petrolva** *f petrolvaow* filling station
**petycyon** *m petycyons* petition
**peul** *m peulyow* post (in ground)
**pewas** *m pewasow* prize, award
**pib** *f pibow* pipe (incl for smoking)
**pibel** *f pibellow* pipe (especially plumbing)
**piben** *f pibednow* tube
**pibow sagh** *pl* bagpipes

**piga** *v* prick; excite
**pigvon** *adj* pointed
**pînaval** *m pinavallow* pineapple
**pis** *col pisen* peas
**pith** *adj* mean, stingy
**pith** *m pithow* well
**pithneth** *m* meanness, stinginess
**pîtsa** *m pîtsas* pizza
**pla** *m plaow* plague
**plain** *adj/m plainys* plain; square (in town)
**plain an gwary** *m plainys* theatre (open-air)
**planet** *m planettys* planet
**plans** *m plansow* plant (specifically planted)
**plansa** *v* plant
**plâss** *m plassow* place (incl at table)
**plastek** (plastyk) *m plastygyon* plastic
**plaster** *m* plaster (material)
**plastyfia** *v* laminate
**plat** *adj* flat
**plât** *m plâtys* plate
**platten** [**rivednek**] **liesdefnyth** *f platednow*

digital versatile disc (DVD)
**platten gompact** *f platednow compact* compact disc (CD)
**platten vînyl** *f platednow* vinyl [record]
**plattya** *v* flatten; crouch
**plaudya** *v* applaud
**pleg** *m plegow* bend; fold
**plegel** *f plegellow* folder
**plegya** *v* bend; fold
**plegya dhe**[2] / **gans** *v* please
**plegya tâl** *phr* frown
**plesont** *adj* pleasant
**plesour** *m plesours* pleasure
**plestryn** *m plestrydnow* plaster (for minor cut)
**pleth** *f plethow* plait
**plethy** *v* plait
**plit** *m plîtys* situation; state, condition
**plobm** *m* lead (metal)
**plobmor** *m plomoryon* plumber
**plos** *adj* dirty
**plos y davas** *phr* foul-mouthed

**plot** *m plottys* plot (conspiracy or of story)
**plu** (pluw) *f pluyow* parish
**plùmen** *f plùmednow* plum
**pluv** *col pluven* feathers *Note that* pluven *also used in sense of 'pen'*
**pluvak** *f pluvogow* pillow; cushion
**pluven belvleyn** *f pluvednow pelvleyn* biro
**pluven blobm** *f pluvednow plobm* pencil
**pobas** *v* bake
**pobel** *f poblow* people
**poblans** *m poblansow* population
**poblegeth** *f poblegethow* republic
**poblegy** *v* publicize
**poblek** *adj* public
**pock** *m pockyow* poke, prod; push
**pocket** *m pockettys* pocket
**pockya** *v* poke, prod; push
**poder** *adj/m* rotten; rot; corruption

**podradow** *adj* biodegradable
**podrek** *adj* decayed; depraved, perverted
**podrethes** *m* rot, decay; pus; sleaze
**podyk** *m podygow* jug
**poll** *m pollow* pool; pit (hollow)
**poll atal** *m pollow* dump
**poll neyja** *m pollow* swimming pool
**poll pry** *m pollow* claypit
**pollat** *m pollatys* fellow, lad
**pollgor** *m pollgorow* committee (incl of Parliament)
**pollgreun** *m polgreunyow* reservoir
**pols** *adv/m polsys* pulse; beat (musical); some way; [for] some while
**pols bian** *phr* a little way; [for] a little while
**pols dâ** (polta) *phr* a good [long] way; [for] a good [long] while
**polsor** *m polsoryon* pendulum
**polsya** *v* polish

**polter** *m polteryow* powder
**polter godn** *m* gunpowder
**po·lycy** *m po·lycys* policy (political, insurance)
**po·lytek** *f* politics (generally or within organization)
**poly·tycal** *adj* political (generally or within organization)
**pompyon** *m pompyons* pumpkin
**pompyon wheg** *m pompyons* melon
**pompyonyk gwer** *m pompyonygow* courgette
**pons** *m ponsow* bridge
**pons cregys** *m ponsow* suspension bridge
**pons kerdh** *m ponsow* footbridge
**ponvos** *m* trouble, vexation, misery
**ponya** *v* run *intr* (sb or sth animate)
**poos** *adj/m posow* heavy; bad (breath); pound (weight); *be reluctant

**popet** *m popettys* doll; puppet
**po·pynjay** *m po·pynjays* parrot
**pòr**[2] *adv* very
**pora·n** *adv* exactly
**porhel** *m porhelly* pig
**pornografek** *adj* pornographic
**porpos** *m porposys* purpose; intention
**pors** *m porsys* purse; pouch (incl of marsupial)
**portal** *m portalys* porch; portal (incl internet)
**porth** *m porthow* gateway; harbour, port; cove
**portraya** *v* portray
**portwîn** *m* port (drink)
**pory** *v* graze; browse (internet, shops etc)
**posa** *v* weigh (so many pounds etc); lean *intr*
**poslef** *m poslevow* stress, emphasis
**posleva** *v* stress, emphasize
**posnya** *v* poison
**po·ssybyl** *adj* possible

**post** *m pôstow* post (pillar, postal service)
**pôstcôd** *m pôstcôdys* postcode
**pôsten** *f postednow* post (on-line)
**poster** *m posters* poster
**po·sytyf** *adj* positive
**pot** *m pottow* pot; jar
**pot tê** *m pottow* teapot
**pôtya** *v* kick
**pow** *m powyow* country (geographical)
**powdir** *m powdiryow* countryside
**powes** *m/v powesow* pause; rest; interval (theatre)
**powes wàr**[2] *v* depend on
**pows** *f powsyow* dress; robe
**pows nos** *f powsyow* nightie
**poynt** *m poyntys* point; *with express negative* at all
**poynt a brow** *m poyntys* advantage
**poynt a skians** *m poyntys* maxim

**poyntyans** *m poyntyansow* appointment
**poyntyor** *m poyntyoryon* pointer
**poyson** *m poysons* poison
**pra·ctycal** *adj* practical
**practycya** *v* practise (all senses)
**practys** *m pra·ctycys* practice (all senses)
**pras** *m prasow* meadow
**prat** *m prattys* trick; stunt
**preder** *m prederow* thought; worry, care
**prederus** *adj* worried, anxious
**predery** *v* think (consider); worry
**predn** *m prednyer* wood; bar; spar
**predna** *v* bar, bolt (a door)
**prena** (perna) *v* buy, purchase
**prenas** *m prenasow* purchase
**prenassa** *v no inflection* shop
**prenor** *m prenoryon* buyer, purchaser
**prentys** *m prentycys* apprentice
**prës** *m pryjyow* time (specific, actual)
**prës boos** *m pryjyow* meal
**prës ly** *m pryjyow* lunch
**prës parys** *m pryjyow* ready meal
**prës yw** *phr + verb-noun* it is time to
**present** *adj/m* present (time)
**presentya** *v* present; introduce (programme etc)
**presentyans** *m presentyansow* presentation
**prèst** *adv* all the time
**prest** *m prestow* loan (money)
**prestya** *v* lend (money)
**pre·sydent** *m pre·sydens* president
**pretendya** *v* claim (that sth is so)
**prëv** *m prevas* creepy-crawly

**prëv del** *m prevas* caterpillar
**prevy** *v* prove; test
**prevyans** *m prevyansow* experience
**prias** *adj/m priosow* married; spouse
**pris** *m prisyow* prize; price
**problem** *m problemow* problem (to be solved)
**professour** *m professours* professor
**profet** *m profettys* prophet
**profya** *v* propose, suggest; offer, bid; dedicate (book etc)
**profyans** *m profyansow* proposal, suggestion; offer, bid
**profyt** *m profyttys* profit (especially commercial)
**progeth** *m/v progowthow* sermon; preach
**program** *m programow* programme (action)
**promys** *m promysyow* promise
**pronter** *m prontyryon* priest

**pros** *m* prose
**Pro·testant** *adj/m Pro·testans* Protestant
**protestya** *v* protest
**protestyans** *m protestyansow* protest
**prov** *m provow* proof; test
**prov lewyas** *m provow* driving test
**prov menystry** *m provow* MOT [test]
**provia** *v* provide (all senses); supply
**provians** *m proviansow* provision (all senses); supply
**provior** *m provioryon* supplier
**provôkya** *v* provoke
**prow** *m* benefit, advantage
**pry** *m* clay; earthenware
**pry gwydn** *m* china clay
**pryck** *m pryckys* degree (circle)
**prydy·dhieth** *f* poetry
**prydyth** *m prydydhyon* poet
**pryjweyth** *m pryjweythyow* moment

**pryl** *m prylyon* lump
**prylehen** *f prylehednow* tile
**prynt** *m pryntys* print
**pryntya** *v* print
**prysner** *m prysners* prisoner
**pryson** *m prysonyow* prison
**prysonya** *v* imprison
**pryva** *adj* private, confidential
**pryvedhyow** *pl* toilet(s)
**pryvetter** *m* privacy
**pùb** + *noun* **a'y honen** *phr* each individual
**pùb termyn** *phr* always
**pùb wàr y dorn** *phr* [each] in turn
**puber** *m* pepper
**pubryn** *m pubrydnow* bell pepper
**pùdyn** *m pùdyns* pudding
**pùmp** *m pùmpys* pump
**pùmpya** *v* pump
**puns** *m punsow* pound (sterling)
**pùnsya** *v* punish
**pù·nyshment** *m pù·nyshmens* punishment
**pùpprë·s** *adv* always

**pur** *adj* pure
**pùrrya** *v* purr
**pùscador** *m pùscadoryon* fisherman
**pùscas crogednek** *pl* shellfish
**pùsorn** *m pùsernow* bale; bundle
**py eur yw?** *phr* what's the time?
**pyâno** *m pyânôs* piano
**pyck** *m pyckys* pick[-axe]
**pyckel** *m pyckels* pickle
**pyckla** *v* pickle
**pyctour** *m pyctours* picture
**pydna** *v* pin
**pyffyor** *m pyffyoryon* dolphin
**pyjamas** *pl* pyjamas
**pykern** *m pykernow* cone
**pyllen** *f pylednow* rag; fringe
**pyn** *m pydnys* pin
**pyncel** *m pyncels* brush (art, make-up); pencil (especially for make-up)
**pynch** *m pynchys* pinch
**pynchya** *v* pinch
**pynt** *m pyntys* pint
**pysa** *v* piss, urinate

**pysas** *m* piss, urine
**pysk** *m pùscas* fish
**pyskessa** *v no inflection* fish
**pyskva** *f pyskvaow* aquarium
**pystrior** *m pystrioryon* wizard
**pystry** *m* magic; mumbo-jumbo
**pystyga** *v* injure
**pystyk** *m pystygow* injury
**pyt** *m pyttys* pit (typically narrow and/or deep)

# Q

**qwa·lyta** *m qwa·lytys* quality
**qwarel** *m qwarels* pane
**qwestyon** *m qwestyonow* question
**qwôrùm** *m qwôra* quorum
**qwylkyn** *m qwylkynas* frog
**qwyz** *m qwyzys* quiz

# R

**rach** *m* care, caution
**radn** *f radnow* part; fate
**radna** *v* divide *Note pp* rydnys
**radna in mes** *phr* distribute
**ra·dycal** *adj* radical
**radyo** *m radyôs* radio
**rafna** *v* rob
**rafnans** *m rafnansow* robbery
**rafnor** *m rafnoryon* robber
**rag an present termyn** *phr* for the time being
**rag exampyl** *phr* for example (e.g.)
**rag hedna** *phr* therefore
**rag kerensa** *prep* for the sake of
**rag tecken** *phr* [for] a moment
**rag tro** *phr* temporary, temporarily
**ragêr** *m rageryow* preposition

**ragerhy** *v* reserve, book
**raghanow** *m raghenwyn* pronoun
**raglen** *f raglednow* programme (TV, radio, theatre)
**ragpren** *m ragprenow* subscription
**ragprena** *v* subscribe (to periodical)
**ragprena eseleth in** *phr* subscribe to (association)
**ragresor** *m ragresoryon* pioneer
**ragvreus** *f ragvreusow* prejudice
**randir** *m randiryow* region, district
**randirek** *adj* regional
**ranjy** *m ranjiow* flat, apartment
**ranles** *m ranlesow* commission (fee)
**rastel** *f rastellow* rack (incl for torture); grill
**rastella** *v* grill (cook)
**re**[2] *adv* (a[2]) too [much] *For 'too many' use* re aga nùmber
**realeth** *m realedhow* reality
**realeth furvwir** *m realedhow* virtual reality
**rebellya** *v* rebel
**Rebellyans Lyver Pejadow** *m* The Prayer Book Rebellion
**recepcyon** *m recepcyons* reception (arrival point, event)
**recêva** *v* receive; adopt (policy etc)
**rece·yt** *m receytys* recipe
**recken** *m reknys* calculation; invoice
**re·ckenva** *f reckenvaow* checkout
**record** *m recordys* record (sport etc)
**recordya** *v* record (incl music etc)
**reden** *col redenen* bracken, ferns
**redya** *v* read
**redyk** *m redygow* radish
**referendùm** *m referenda* referendum
**re·jyment** *m re·jymens* regiment
**rekna** *v* calculate
**rekna cowlsùm** *phr* total [up]

**rekna ogas lowr** *phr* estimate
**rekna termyn** *phr* time (sth)
**rekna warba·rth** *phr* include
**reknans** *m reknansow* calculation
**reknel** *f reknellow* calculator
**remainya** *v* stay, remain
**remembra** *v* remember
**remôcyon** *m remôcyons* move (to new address); promotion (career)
**remuvya** (remôvya) *v* remove
**rencas** *m rencasow* class (social)
**rencas cres** *m* middle class
**rencas lavur** *m* working class
**renk** *m renkyow* rank (military etc)
**renky** *v* snore; snort; croak; gurgle; rasp
**rent** *m rentys* revenue; rent
**repentons** *m* repentance
**repentya** *v* repent

**representya** *v* represent
**reqwîrya** *v* require
**res** *f resyow* row, sequence
**res adro·** *m resow* carousel
**res [porre·s] yw dhodho** *phr + verb-noun* he [really] must (obligation)
**res yw** *phr + infinitive construction* he must [have] (inferential)
**res yw avowa** *phr* admittedly
**rescous air ha mor** *m* air-sea rescue
**resegva** *f resegvaow* race (contest); career
**resegva bêwnans** *f resegvaow* curriculum vitae
**resek** *v* run *intr* (sth inanimate)
**rêson** *m* reason (rationality)
**resonek** *adj* rational
**resonus** *adj* reasonable
**rester** *f restry* arrangement, scheme
**restry** *v* sort out, arrange

**restryn** (restren) *m restrydnow* file (documents, incl on computer)
**reswysk** *m reswyscow* tracksuit
**reth** *f rethyow* law (especially as concept or subject of study)
**reun** *m reunas* seal (animal)
**rev** *f revow* oar, paddle; shovel
**revrons** *m* respect
**revya** *v* row, paddle; shovel
**rew** *m* frost; ice
**rewardya** *v* reward
**rewl** *f rewlys* rule; control
**rewl boos** *f rewlys* diet
**rêwlya** *v* rule; regulate
**rewlyans** *m rewlyansow* regulation
**rewor** *m reworyon* freezer
**rewy** *v* freeze
**rewys** *adj* icy
**reydh** *f reydhow* sex, gender
**rial** *adj* royal; splendid
**rim** *m rîmys* rhyme

**ris** *col* rice
**rivednek** *adj* digital
**ro** *m royow* gift, present
**robot** *m robotow* robot
**rol** *f rôlyow* roll; list
**rol vytel** *f rôlyow* menu (food)
**rôlbren** *m rolbrednyer* roller; reel
**rollya** *v* roll; taxi (aircraft)
**rom** *m rômys* room (all senses)
**rom esedha** *m rômys* sitting room
**rom kydnyow** *m rômys* dining room
**rom studhya** *m rômys* study (room)
**Roman** *adj/m Romans* Roman
**romantek** *adj* romantic
**rônd** *adj* round
**ronk** *adj/m roncow* snore; snort; croak; gurgle; rasp; raucous, rasping
**roos** *f rosow* net
**ros** *col rosen* roses
**ros** *f rosow* wheel
**rôstya** *v* roast

**rosva** *f rosvaow* avenue; driveway (in front of house)
**rosweyth** *m rosweythyow* network
**rôsya** *v* stroll; surf (internet)
**roweth** *m* prestige, standing
**rowtor** *m rowtoryon* director (film etc); air traffic controller; router (internet)
**rowtya** *v* rule the roost; direct; route
**rùber** *m* rubber (material)
**rudh** *adj* red
**rudhak** *m rudhogas* robin
**rudhvelen** *adj* orange (colour)
**rudhya** *v* blush
**rùgby** *m* rugby
**rugla** *v* rattle

**rusk** *col* rind; bark (tree)
**rùstla** *v* rustle
**rûth** *f rûthyow* crowd
**rùttya** *v* rub
**ry** *v* give
**ry brodn dhe**[2] *phr* breastfeed
**ry colon dhe**[2] *phr* encourage (sb)
**ry cubmyas rag** *phr* permit (sth)
**ry gweres dhe**[2] *phr* help, assist
**rybyn** *m rybyns* ribbon; streak
**rych** *adj* rich
**rychys** *pl* wealth, riches
**rygol** *m rygolyow* rut; groove
**rythym** *m rythmow* rhythm
**ryver** *m ryvers* river

# S

**sacrys** *adj* sacred
**sàd** *adj* sober, serious, grave (sb)
**sagh** *m seghyer* bag; sack

**sagh cùsca** *m seghyer* sleeping bag
**sagh dorn** *m seghyer* handbag
**salad** *m saladys* salad

**sans** *adj* holy
**sant** *m santys* course (meal)
**sant melys** *m santys* dessert
**sarcastek** *adj* sarcastic
**sarfven** *m* serpentine
**savla** *m savleow* position
**savla bùs** *m savleow* bus stop
**savyour** *m savyours* saviour
**saw** *adj* safe, secure; *prep + noun, pronoun (independent if personal)* except for; in the absence of; *with express negative* except See also 'Grammar Words'
**sawder** *m* safety, security
**sawor** *m saworyow* smell, fragrance (specifically pleasant or unpleasant)
**sa·woren** *f saworednow* aroma; flavour (particularly associated with food)
**sawory** *v* smell (sth); taste (sth)

**sawya** *v* save, rescue; recover (from illness)
**Saxon** *adj/m Saxons* Saxon
**scaffa gyllyn / gylta** *phr* as quick as I could / you can
**scaffotys** *pl* scaffolding
**scafhe·** *v* lighten
**scala** *m scalys* bowl (shallow)
**scant** *adj/adv* scarce; *+ optional negative* hardly, scarcely
**scant** *col scanten* scales (fish, reptile); flakes
**scantlyn** *m scantlyns* measure (length and figuratively)
**scanya** *v* scan
**scanyor** *m scanyoryon* scanner
**scappya** *v* escape, get away
**scath** *f scathow* boat
**scath sawya** *f scathow* lifeboat
**scav** *adj* light (weight); swift
**scavel** *f scavellow* stool; bench

**scavel an gow** *f*
the rumour mill
**scavel cronak** *f scavellow* mushroom, toadstool
**scent** *m scentys* scent, perfume
**sciens** *m sciencys* science
**sciensek** *adj* scientific
**sciensyth** *m sciensydhyon* scientist
**sclander** *m sclanders* scandal (general or specific)
**sclandrus** *adj* scandalous
**scobmyn** *m scobmow* chip (chocolate, computer etc)
**scochfordh** *f scochfordhow* alley[way]; shortcut
**scodhya** *v* support
**scodhya wàr**[2] *v* rely on
**scodhyans** *m scodhyansow* support
**scodhyor** *m scodhyoryon* supporter
**scol** *f scolyow* school
**scol elvednek** *f scolyow* primary school
**scol nessa** *f scolyow* secondary school
**scol veythryn** *f scolyow meythryn* nursery school
**scolor** *m scoloryon* pupil (school)
**scon** *see* [yn] scon
**scons** *col sconsen* scones
**sconya** *v* reject
**sconya dhe**[2] *v + verb-noun* forbid (sb to do sth)
**scoodh** *f scodhow* shoulder
**scoos** *m scojow* shield; safeguard
**scor** *m scorys* score; rating
**scornya** *v* scorn; satirize
**scorr** *col scorren* branches
**scoske** *m scoskeow* crash barrier
**scot** *m scottys* bill (in restaurant etc)
**scovarn** *f scovornow* ear; handle (of cup etc)
**scovarnak** *m scovarnogas* hare

**scovarnygow** *pl* earphones
**scovva** *f scovvaow* shelter; booth
**scrambla** *v* scramble (eggs, message etc)
**screfa** (scrifa) *v* write
**screfor** *m screforyon* writer
**screw** *m screwys* screw
**scrif** *m scrifow* writing (specific); work (of author)
**scrij** *m scrijow* shriek
**scrija** *v* shriek
**scrin** *f scrînyon* shrine
**scrin** *f scrînyow* screen (for viewing)
**scriven** *f scrivednow* script (examination etc)
**scrivynyas** *m scrivynysy* secretary
**scruth** *m scruthow* horror; shock
**scruthus** *adj* horrible; shocking
**scryp** *m scryppys* hand luggage
**scrypt** *m scryptys* script (dramatic)

**scubel** *f scubellow* broom
**scubel sùgna** *f scubellow* vacuum cleaner
**scubel wolhy** *f scubellow golhy* mop
**scubya** *v* brush, sweep
**scubylen** *f scubylednow* brush
**scubylen dens** *f scubylednow* toothbrush
**scudel** *f scudellow* dish
**scùllya** *v* spill; squander, waste
**scùllyak** *adj* wasteful; extravagant
**scùllyans** *m scùllyansow* spill; waste; extravagance
**seban** *m* soap
**secùnd** *m secùndys* second (time)
**sedhek brusy** *m sedhegow* tribunal
**sedhy** *v* sink *intr*; submerge; set (sun)
**sëgh** *adj* dry; barren
**seha** *v* dry
**sehes** *m* thirst; *be thirsty
**selder** *m selders* cellar; basement

**selsygen** *f selsygednow* sausage (for frying, grilling)
**selven** *m selveyn* foundation; basis
**selvenegor** *m selvenegoryon* fundamentalist
**selvenek** *adj* fundamental, basic
**semlant** *m semlans* look, appearance
**sempel** *adj* simple
**sempelhe·** *v* simplify
**seneth** *m senedhow* parliament, synod (both loosely); senate (US etc)
**sens** *m sencys* sense ('five' senses)
**sens a dhydha·n** *m* sense of humour
**sens a spral** *m* frustration (emotion)
**sensor** *m sensoryon* holder; compartment (*e.g.* for 'gloves'); stand (*e.g.* for sheet music); container (for lorry, ship)
**sensy** *v* hold; keep, retain; detain; contain; think (estimation)
**sensy in y breder** *phr* concentrate on
**se·nsytyf** *adj* sensitive
**sensyty·vyta** *m sensyty·vytys* sensitivity
**sentry** *m sentrys* sanctuary
**seny** *v* sound, ring
**ser predn** *m sery* carpenter
**sera** *m serys* sir (addressing sb)
**serhak** *adj/m serhogyon* (dhe²) dependent, contingent (upon); dependant
**serpont** *m serpons* snake, serpent
**serry** *v* irritate, annoy; be annoyed, be indignant
**serrys** *adj* irritated, annoyed, indignant, angry
**serth** *adj* upright, vertical, straight; stiff
**servont** *m servons* servant
**servya** *v* serve; do (be sufficient)
**servyas** *m servysy* waiter; server

(incl computer)
**servyour** *m servyours* tray
**servys** *m servysyow* service (all senses)
**sêson** *m sêsons* season
**seth** *f sethow* arrow
**sethor** *m sethoryon* gannet; remote control (for device)
**settya** *v* set, station
**settya prës** *phr* make an appointment
**settya wor'gobren** *phr* hire out, rent out, let (to tenant)
**sevel** *v* stand [up]; get up (from bed); stop (stand still)
**sevel orth** *v* resist; refrain from
**sevel orth aswon** *phr* ignore
**sevur** *adj* serious, strict (sb or sth)
**sevureth** *m* seriousness, strictness
**sewt** *m sewtys* suit (incl cards)
**sewt staunch** *m sewtys* wetsuit

**sewya** *v* follow (all senses)
**sewyans** *m sewyansow* consequence; result
**sexy·stieth** *f* sexism
**seythen** *f seythednow* week
**shafta** *m shaftys* shaft (in ground)
**shakya** *v* shake
**shal** *m* shale
**sham** *m* shame
**shampou·** *m* shampoo
**shâmya** *v* shame
**shâp** *m shâpys* shape
**shâpya** *v* shape
**shara** *m sharys* share, portion; contribution
**sherp** *adj* sharp (bend, tone of voice etc)
**sherys** *m* sherry
**Shiek** *adj* Shia
**Shiyas** *m Shiysy* Shia
**shoppa** *m shoppys* shop
**shôra** *m shôrys* attack (heart); fit (epileptic)
**show** *m showys* show (entertainment or to impress)
**shùgra** *m* sugar
**shùgra leth** *m* lactose

**shyndya** *v* damage, harm (sb or sth)
**sia** *v* hum
**sians** *m siansow* whim
**siansus** *adj* capricious
**Sik** *adj/m Sîkas* Sikh
**Sî·kieth** *f* Sikhism
**sin** *m sînys* sign, signal
**sîna** *v* sign (incl with signature); signal
**sînans** *m sinansow* signature
**skech** *m skechys* sketch (comic playlet)
**skentyl** *adj* intelligent
**ske·ptycal** *adj* sceptical
**sketh** *m skethow* strip (of sth)
**skethry** *v* chop (wood)
**skethryk** *m skethrygow* splinter (under skin)
**skeul** *f skeulyow* ladder; scale (music)
**skeul scappya** *f skeulyow* fire escape
**skeus** *m skeusow* shadow; suspicion
**skeus lugarn** *m skeusow* lampshade
**skeuse·dnieth** *f* photography

**skeusednor** *m skeusenoryon* photographer
**skeusek** *adj* shady; suspicious
**skeusen** *f skeusednow* photo[graph]
**skevens** *pl* lungs
**skew** *f skewyow* screen (from sight, wind etc)
**skewwyns** *f skewwynsow* windscreen
**skia** *v* ski
**skians** *m* intellect, intelligence; knowledge
**skiansek** *adj/m skiansegyon* intellectual
**skit** *m skîtys* squirt; diarrhoea
**skîtel** *f skitellow* syringe; epipen
**skîtya** *v* squirt; inject
**skîtyans** *m skityansow* injection
**sky** *m skîs* ski
**skyber** *f skyberyow* barn
**skydnya** *v* descend; get off, alight (from)
**skyla** *m skylys* (rag) reason, cause
**sley** *adj* skilful; astute

**sleyneth** *m* skilfulness; astuteness
**slynkfordh** *f slynkfordhow* slip road
**slynkva** *f slynkvaow* slide (playground)
**slynkya** *v* slide, slip
**slyppya** *v* slip (while walking); skid
**smellyng** *m* smell (generally)
**snèl** *adj/adv* speedy, speedily
**snod** *m snôdys* hairband; tape (audio, video)
**snod clos** *m snôdys* cassette
**snouker** *m* snooker
**socour trobm** *m* first aid
**socyalyth** *m socyalydhyon* socialist
**sodhak** *m sodhogyon* officer; official
**sodhogyl** *adj* official
**sodhva** *f sodhvaow* office (place)
**sodhva bost** *f sodhvaow post* post office
**sogh** *adj* blunt
**sojeta** *m sojetys* subject (grammar)

**sol** *m solyow* base
**solabrë·s** *adv* already
**solempna** *adj* solemn
**solempnya** *v* celebrate (with ceremony)
**sole·mpnyta** *m sole·mpnytys* ceremony
**soler** *m soleryow* landing, gallery
**solyd** *adj/m solydow* solid
**solyda·ryta** *m* solidarity
**son** *m sonyow* sound
**soodh** *f sodhow* office, post, position, job
**soposya** *v* suppose
**sordya** *v* arouse; initiate, originate; trigger; start (system)
**sorr** *m* anger, indignation
**sort** *m sortas* hedgehog
**sort** *m sortys* sort, kind, variety
**sos** *m* guy(s) (addressing sb/s)
**sotel** *adj* cunning (sb); subtle (sth)
**sotelneth** *m* cunning; subtlety
**soth** *adj/m* south(ern)

**soudor** *m soudoryon* soldier
**sowena** *f* prosperity
**soweny** *v* prosper; + *present participle* succeed (in doing sth)
**soweth** *interj* unfortunately
**sowman** *m sowmens* salmon
**sowndya** *v* sound (all senses)
**sowndyans** *m sowndyansow* opinion poll
**sows** *m sowsow* sauce; gravy
**sows cogh** *m* ketchup
**Sowsnek** *m* English (language)
**sowthan** *m* bewilderment; surprise
**sowthanas** *v* bewilder; surprise
**spagetty** *m* spaghetti
**spal** *m spalyow* fine (penalty)
**spâss** *m spâcys* space, room; opportunity
**specyal** *adj* special
**specyfyk** *adj* specific

**spe·cymen** *m spe·cymens* specimen
**spêda** *f* success
**spêdya** *v* succeed (sb or sth)
**spellya** *v* spell
**spêna** (spendya) *v* spend; use up
**spenser** *m spensers* dispenser
**spessly** *adv* especially, particularly
**spis** *m spisow* interval (between events)
**spîsek** *adj* spicy
**spit** *m* spite, malice
**spîtys** *adj* spiteful, malicious
**spladn** *adj* bright, brilliant, splendid
**spladna** *v* shine
**splander** *m* brightness, brilliance, splendour
**splat** *m splattys* plot (land)
**sponj** *m sponjow* sponge (incl cake)
**sport** *m sportys* sport; fun
**sportyas** *m sportysy* sportsman

**spot** *m spottys* spot (speck)
**spot a**[2] *phr* a little
**spralla** *v* hamper, impede
**spredya** *v* spread (incl on bread)
**spredyas** *m spredyasow* spread (for bread)
**sprusek** *adj* nuclear, atomic
**spynach** *m* spinach
**spyrys** *m spyryjyon* spirit
**sqward** *m sqwardyow* tear (torn)
**sqwardya** *v* tear, rip
**sqwash** *m* squash (game)
**sqwat** (scat) *adv/m sqwattow* blow, slap; with a bang / crash
**sqwattya** *v* hit, slap; swat; break
**sqwir** *m sqwîrys* standard (norm)
**sqwith** *adj* tired; bored
**sqwitha** *v* tire; bore
**sqwithus** *adj* tiring; boring
**sqwychel** *f sqwychellow* switch (device)

**sqwychel gwres** *f sqwychellow* thermostat
**sqwychya mes / rag** *phr* switch off / on
**sqwychys dhe barys** *phr* on standby (device)
**stâbel** *m stablys* stable
**stadyùm** *m stadya* stadium
**stag** *adj* fixed
**staga** *v* tether; fix; attach (incl to email)
**stagell** *f stagellow* tether; appendix (to document); attachment (to email)
**stairys** *pl* stairs
**stalla** *m stallys* stall (market, stable); cubicle (toilet)
**stallyon** *m stallyons* stallion
**stampdoll** *f* stamp duty
**stampen** *f stampednow* stamp (postage)
**stampya** *v* stamp
**stankya** *v* stamp (on), trample
**stap** *m stappys* step (all senses); stage
**stap ha stap** *phr* step by step

**starnedhek** *adj* structural
**starneth** *m starnedhow* structure
**stât** *m stâtys* estate; state (all senses)
**staunch** *adj* sealed (tight)
**staunchya** *v* seal (container etc)
**stauns** *m stauncys* stance, position
**stêk** *m stêkys* steak
**sten** *m* tin (metal)
**stenor** *m stenoryon* tinner
**steppyow** *pl* stepladder
**ster** *col steren* stars (incl celebrities)
**steus** *f steusow* series (medication, talks, TV etc)
**stêvya** *v* rush, dash; swoop
**stock** *m stockys* block (of sth); stock (goods, finance); stump (cricket)
**stoff** *m stoffys* stuff; substance (chemical)
**stoffya** *v* stock (goods); stockpile; stuff (sth); cram (for examination)

**stoffyas** *m* stuffing (bird, furniture)
**stoppya** *v* block [up]
**stordy** *adj* sturdy
**strait** *adj* straight (incl sexuality)
**stranj** *adj* strange
**stranjnes** *m* strangeness
**strayl** *m straylyow* mat
**straylyk** *m straylygow* place mat; beer mat, coaster
**strech** *m strechys* delay
**strechya** *v* delay
**strêt** *m strêtys* street
**strew** *m strewyow* sneeze
**strewy** *v* sneeze
**strîfwerth** *m strifwerthow* auction
**strîvya** *v* strive, make every effort
**strîvyans** *m strivyansow* effort
**strocas** *m strocosow* blow; stroke (incl medical)
**stroll** *m* litter, mess
**strolla** *v* make a mess (of)

**strollargh** *f strollarhow* litter bin
**stroth** *adj/m strothow* tight; strict; brace (teeth); clamp (wheel)
**strotha** *v* tighten; squeeze; restrict; clamp (wheel)
**strus** *m strusyow* ostrich
**stryppya** *v* strip
**stubm** *m stubmow* curve; inclination; position
**stubma** *v* curve, bend
**studh** (stuth) *m studhow* state, condition
**studhva** *f studhvaow* study (investigation)
**studhya** *v* study
**studhyor** *m studhyoryon* student
**styf** *f styvow* jet (of sth)
**styfa** *v* spray
**styr** *m styryow* sense, meaning
**styrya** *v* mean; account for, explain
**sùbstans** *m* substance (incl wealth)
**sùdron** *col sùdronen* drones (incl device)
**sugal** *col* rye

**sùgan** *m* juice
**sùgna** *v* suck
**sùgnek** *adj* juicy
**sùm** *m sùmys* sum (calculation, amount)
**sùmya** *v* add up
**Sùnek** *adj* Sunni
**Sùnyas** *m Sùnysy* Sunni
**sur** *adj* sure
**surhe·** *v* ensure; insure
**sùrreal** *adj* surreal
**surynjy** *m* insurance
**swàn** *m swadnys* swan
**sygen** *f sygednow* tag
**sygen hash** *f sygednow* hashtag
**sygera** *v* seep, ooze; leak out; smoulder; idle (engine)
**syght** *m syghtys* sight; look
**sylly** *m syllias* eel
**sylwans** *m sylwansow* save (incl in goal)
**sylwel** *v* save
**sym** *m symas* monkey
**Syndrom an Imûndyfyk [Aqwîrys] (SIDA)** *m* Acquired Immune Deficiency Syndrome (AIDS)

**syrop** *m syropys* syrup
**sythel** *m sythlow* strainer; filter

# T

**tâbel** *m tablys* table (all senses)
**tabm** *m tybmyn* bit, piece
**tabm a**² *phr* a little
**tabm dainty** *m tybmyn* delicacy
**tabm ha tabm** *phr* little by little, gradually
**tabour** *m tabours* drum
**tackya dewla** *phr* clap
**tact** *m* tact
**taga** *v* choke, suffocate, strangle; clog
**tagus** *adj* choking, suffocating
**tâl** *m tâlyow* forehead, brow (incl hill)
**talenep** *m talenebow* façade
**talent** *m talens* talent
**talveja** *v* value (all senses)
**talvesek** *adj* valuable
**talyk** *m talygow* garret, attic

**sythla** *v* strain; filter
**syvy** *col syvien* strawberries

**tan** *m tanow* fire
**tan creft** *m tanow* firework
**tanbeledna** *v* bomb; shell
**tanbellen** *f tanbelednow* bomb; shell
**tanbren** *m tanbrednyer* match (for flame)
**tangasor** *m tangasoryon* firefighter (incl figuratively)
**tank** *m tancow* tank (incl military)
**tanow** *adj* thin; scarce, rare
**tanowhe·** (tanow'he·) *v* thin [out]
**tansys** *m tansesow* blaze; bonfire
**tanya** *v* start (engine)
**tap** *m tappys* tap
**tâpa** *m tâpys* tape
**taran** *f tarednow* thunder[bolt]
**tardar** *m terder* drill

**tardh** *m tardhow* burst; explosion
**tardha** *v* burst, explode; erupt
**tardhans** *m tardhansow* eruption
**tardra** *v* drill
**tarosvan** *m tarosvanow* ghost; illusion
**tarosvanus** *adj* ghostly; illusory
**tarow** *m te·rewy* bull
**tart** *m tartys* tart (food)
**tas** *m tasow* father
**tas gwydn** *m tasow* grandfather
**tasek** *m tasygyon* patron; godfather (Mafia)
**Tasyk** *m* Daddy
**taunt** *adj* cheeky, impertinent
**tava** *v* touch
**tavas** *m tavosow* tongue; language
**tavasa** *v* scold
**tavern** *m tavernyow* pub
**taw** *m* silence
**tawesek** *adj* silent
**taxy** *m taxys* taxi
**tê** *m* tea
**tê erba** *m* herbal tea

**tebel-**[2] (tebel-[1] before d g) *pref* evil, wicked
**tebel-dyghtya** *v* abuse
**technegor** *m technegoryon* technician
**technegyl** *adj* technical
**technolo·gieth** *f* technology
**technyk** *m technygow* technique
**tecter** *m* beauty
**tedha** *v* melt; thaw
**tedn** *m tednow* draw, pull, tug; shot; sketch (drawing)
**tedna** *v* draw, pull, tug; attract; stretch; (dhe[2]) shoot
**tedna dowr in** *phr* flush (toilet)
**teg** *adj/adv* beautiful, pretty; fair (incl play); quite (completely)
**teg y dhysqwithans** *phr* relaxing
**tegednek** *adj* ornamental
**tegen** *f tegednow* ornament; trinket
**tegen telly** *f tegednow* piercing (jewellery)

**telly** *v* make a hole / holes in; pierce (ear etc)
**templa** (tempel) *m templys* temple (place of worship)
**tempra** *v* moderate
**temprys** *adj* moderate
**temptacyon** *m temptacyons* temptation
**temptya** *v* tempt
**tenewen** *m tenwednow* flank, side
**tent** *m tentys* tent
**tenva** *f tenvaow* tension; stress
**tenva kyns mislif** *f* pre-menstrual tension (PMT)
**tenys** *m* tennis
**ter** *adj* vehement
**tera-**[1] *pref* tera-
**terghya in** *v* hack (computer etc)
**termyn** *m termynyow* time (concept, period, past or future, right time to do sth); term (school, university)
**termyn keas** *m termynyow* deadline
**terras** *m terracys* terrace (for sitting)

**terry** *v* break
**terry an jëdh** *m* dawn
**terstuth** *m terstudhow* crisis
**tervans** *m* turmoil
**tervus** *adj* tumultuous
**tesak** *adj* sultry
**tesen** *f tesednow* cake
**tesen gales** *f tesednow cales* biscuit (usually sweet)
**tesen vian** *f tesednow bian* fairy cake
**Test Jehôva** *m Testow* Jehova's Witness
**testen** *f testednow* topic
**testscrif** *m testscrifow* certificate
**Testscrif Ollkemyn [Adhyscans Nessa]** *m* General Certificate of Secondary Education (GCSE)
**tesyans bÿs-efan** *m* global warming
**tethen** *f tethednow* nipple
**tevy** *v* grow
**tevyans** *m tevyansow* growth; tumour
**tevysak** *adj/m tevysogyon* adult

**tew** *adj* thick; dense; fat
**tewas** *col* sand (material)
**tewel** *v* fall silent
**teweth** *m tewedhow* storm
**teweth ergh** *m tewedhow* snowstorm, blizzard
**tewhe·** (tew'he·) *v* thicken; fatten
**tewl** *adj* dark
**tewl hy blew** *phr* brunette
**tewlder** *m* darkness
**tewlhe·** *v* darken; obscure (argument etc)
**tewlwolow** *m* twilight, dusk
**te·wolgow** *m* dark[ness] (lack of light)
**text** *m textys* text (incl message)
**textya** *v* text
**teyl** *m* manure; compost
**teylu** *m teyluyow* clan; family
**teythiak** *adj* idiomatic
**teythy** *pl* attributes
**them** *m thêmow* theme
**tiak** *m tiogyon* farmer
**tîger** *m tîgras* tiger

**tin** *f tinyon* tail-end; bottom (anatomy), arse
**tîp** *m tîpow* type
**tîpek** (tîpyk) *adj* typical
**tir** *m tiryow* land
**tira** *v* land (especially aircraft)
**tireth** *m tiredhow* terrain; territory
**to** *m tohow* roof; umbrella (figuratively)
**tobm** *adj* hot, warm
**tobma** *v* heat
**tobmor** *m tomoryon* heater; radiator
**todn** *f todnow* wave
**tôkyn** *m toknys* token; ticket; label (on goods)
**tôkyn mos ha dewheles** *m toknys* return ticket
**tôkyn mos only** *m toknys* single ticket
**tokynador** *m tokynadoryon* ticket machine
**toll** *m tell* hole
**toll** *f tollow* toll; tax
**toll adneth** *f* rates
**toll daswerth** *f* value added tax (VAT)

**tollva** *f tollvaow* toll booth; customs
**tolly** *v* tax
**ton** *m tônyow* tone; tune
**ton seny** *m tônyow* ringtone
**tona** *m tonys* ton
**tônya** *v* tune
**toos** *m* dough; paste
**toos dens** *m* toothpaste
**top** *m topyow* top (of head, of object, also clothing)
**torchen** *f torchednow* torch (burning or electric)
**torgh coos** *m torhas* wild boar
**torment** *m tormens* torment, torture
**torment tin** *m* pain in the arse (nuisance)
**tormentya** *v* torment, torture
**torn** *m tornow* turn (show); bout (flu, wrestling etc)
**torn dâ** *m tornow* favour, good turn
**torr** *f torrow* belly, abdomen
**torrva** *f torvaow* break; breach, infringement; breakdown; shipwreck; cut (power); hernia
**torth** *f torthow* loaf
**torthen** *f torthednow* bun
**torthen tê** *f torthednow* teacake
**tos** (toos) *m tosow* tuft
**tosa** *v* knead; massage
**toth** (tooth) *m* speed
**toth men** *phr* at full speed, pretty damn quick
**toul** *m toulys* tool, implement
**tour** *m tourow* tower, steeple
**tournay** *m tournays* tournament
**touryst** *m tourystyon* tourist
**toury·stieth** *f* tourism
**towal** *m towellow* towel
**towan** *m tewednow* dune
**towl** *m towlow* throw; plan
**towladow** *adj* disposable
**towlcost** *m towlcostow* estimate (of cost)

**towledna** *v* program, schedule; plan (development)
**tôwlel** *v* throw; plan
**tôwlel golok wàr**² *phr* glance at
**tôwlel predn** *phr* draw lots
**towlen** *f towlednow* program (incl computer), schedule; plan (development)
**tra** *f taclow* thing, object
**tradycyon** *m tradycyons* tradition
**trady·cyonal** *adj* traditional
**trailya** *v* (dhe²) turn; translate (into)
**trailya adenewen** *phr* turn aside; distract
**trailyans** *m trailyansow* translation
**train** *m trainow* train
**traita** *v* betray
**traitour** *m traitours* traitor
**tra·jedy** *m tra·jedys* tragedy
**tràm** *m tramyow* tram
**trauma** *m traumas* trauma

**traweythyow** *adv* sometimes
**tre** *adv/f trevow* town; home (adjectivally); home *motion*; back (returning)
**trebuchya** *v* trip, stumble
**tredan** *m* electricity
**tredanek** *adj* electric[al]
**tregereth** *f* sympathy
**tregh** *m trehow* slice
**trehor** *m trehoryon* tailor
**trehy** *v* cut
**tremena** *v* pass; pass away (die)
**tremencubmyas** *m tremencumyasow* passport
**tremenva** *f tremenvaow* passage, corridor; aisle
**tremenyas** *m tremenysy* passenger
**tremlyw** *m tremlywyow* make-up
**tremyn** *m tremydnow* look, expression (on face); aspect
**treneyja** *v* flutter
**trenk** *adj* sour, acid
**trenken** *f trenkednow* acid
**tres ledan** *m* broadband

**tresour** *m tresours* treasure
**trespasseth** *m* crime (generally)
**trespassor** *m trespassoryon* offender
**trèst** *m* *trust
**trester** *m tresters* cross-bar; sleeper
**trestya dhe**² *v* trust
**treth** *m trethow* beach; sand (on beach)
**treth** *m trethyow* ferry (crossing)
**treuscorra** *v* transmit (communication)
**treusfurvyor** *m treusfurvyoryon* transformer (electricity)
**treusperthy** *v* transfer
**treusreydhek** *adj* transgender
**treusva** *f treusvaow* crossing (level, zebra etc)
**treuthow** *m* threshold
**trevas** *f trevasow* crop, harvest; vintage
**treveglos** *f trevow eglos* village

**trevesygeth** *f trevesygethow* settlement, colony
**treveth** *f trevethyow* time (occasion – especially with ordinal numeral)
**trevna** *v* organize
**trewa** *v* spit (saliva)
**trial** *m trials* trial
**trielyn** *m trielydnow* triangle
**trigva** *f trigvaow* address
**trist** *adj* sad
**tro** *f troyow* turn (incl in game etc); round (in pub)
**tro ha** *prep* towards
**tro in** *f troyow* excursion to
**tro kerdhes** *f troyow* stroll
**tro-askel** *f tro-eskelly* helicopter
**trobel** *m troblys* trouble, bother, worry
**trobla** *v* trouble, bother, worry; haunt
**troen** *f troednow* twist, twirl
**trog** (trock) *m tregys* case (luggage); boot (car)

**trog dogvednow** *m tregys* briefcase
**trog dyllas** *m tregys* suitcase
**trog tedna** *m tregys* drawer (storage)
**trogentrel** *f trogentrellow* screwdriver
**trogh** *adj/m trohow* cut; section; issue (periodical); cracked, broken (incl figuratively)
**troghya** *v* dunk
**troll** *m trollyon* troll
**tron** *m tronow* snout; trunk (elephant); nozzle
**troos** *m treys* foot; leg (of object); pedestal
**tros** *m trosow* noise (loud)
**trosel** *f trosellow* pedal
**trosella** *v* pedal
**tros'hes** *m tros'hesow* foot (length)
**trosvedhek** *m trosvedhygyon* podiatrist
**trouvya** *v* find (especially after search)
**trouvyans** *m trouvyansow* find

**troyll** *f troyllyow* spin, whirl; spiral; lap (pitch, track)
**troyllya** *v* spin, whirl; twist, twirl
**truan** *adj* poor, miserable (objectively)
**trueth** *m truedhow* pity, compassion; sad state of affairs
**trufyl** *adj/m truflys* trifle; trifling
**trûlergh** *m trûlerhow* [foot]path
**trùmp** *m trùmpys* trump
**trùssa** *v* pack
**trustrùm** *m* bait
**truth** *m truthas* trout
**tryck** *m tryckys* trick (in cards)
**trygger** *m tryggers* trigger
**tu** *m tuyow* side
**tu arâg** *m tuyow* front (of sth)
**tu warle·rgh** *m tuyow* back (of sth)
**tùch** *adv/m tùchys* touch; [for] a moment
**tùchya** *v* touch [on]; light (cigarette, pipe etc)

**tuedhyans** *m tuedhyansow* inclination, tendency
**tùll** *m* deceit; disappointment
**tùlla** *v* deceive; disappoint
**tùllwysk** *m tùllwyscow* disguise; fancy dress
**tù·lyfant** *m tù·lyfans* turban
**tûna** *m tûnas* tuna
**turont** *m turons* tyrant
**turya** *v* burrow; rummage
**tus dâ** *pl* in-laws
**tyby** *v* think (have ideas or opinions)
**tybyans** *m tybyansow* thought; idea; opinion

# U

**udn làm** *phr* [for] a moment
**udnyk** *adj* unique
**ufer** *adj* futile
**ufern** *m ufernyow* ankle
**ughboynt** *m ughboyntys* maximum
**ughboyntek** *adj* maximum

**tyckly** *adj* delicate, tricky
**tycky-Duw** *m tycky-Duwas* butterfly
**tydn** *adj* tight, taut; stressful; tender (painful)
**tydnyow** *pl* tights
**tygen mona** *f tygednow* wallet
**tyller** (teller) *m tyleryow* place, position, location; room (space)
**tylly** *v* pay (what is due)
**tylly heb tùchya** *phr* contactless payment
**tysk flourys** *m tyscow* bouquet
**tytel** *m tytlys* title (all senses)
**tythus** *adj* fizzy, sparkling

**ugh-carg** *m ugh-cargow* upload
**ugh-carga** *v* upload
**ughson** *m* ultrasound
**uhel** *adj* high; loud
**uhelder** *m* height; volume
**uheldir** *m uheldiryow* high ground

**uhelwhans** *m uhelwhansow* ambition
**uhelwhansek** *adj* ambitious
**uj** *m ujow* scream; howl; yell; roar
**uja** *v* scream; howl; yell; roar
**ûla** *m ûlys* owl
**ùncoth** (ancoth) *adj* weird
**ùnderstondya** *v* understand
**ùnderstondyng** *m* understanding
**ùnlafyl** *adj* illegal
**ùnpo·ssybyl** (impo·ssybyl) *adj* impossible
**unsys** *m unsesow* unit[y]; module
**unweyth arta** *phr* once again
**unwos** *adj* related (by blood); cognate
**unwysk** *m unwyscow* uniform
**unya** *v* unify; unite
**uras** *m urasow* lubricant
**ûsadow** *m* custom
**uskys** *adj* fast, quick
**uskys'he·** *v* accelerate, speed up
**ûsya** *v* use *See also* ev a wrug ûsya
**ûsyans ha sqwardyans teg** *phr* fair wear and tear
**uthyk** *adj* terrible, dreadful
**uvel** *adj* humble, modest
**uvelder** *m* humility, modesty
**uvelhe·** *v* humble; humiliate

# V

**valew** *m valewys* value
**valy** *m valys* valley
**vansya** *v* vanish, disappear
**vansyans** *m vansyansow* disappearance
**vanylla** *m* vanilla
**varia** *v* vary
**varies** *adj* frantic, manic
**varies gans fevyr** *phr* delirious

**vas** *adj* good, useful; convenient
**venjyans** *m* revenge
**verb** *m verbys* verb
**vernsya** *v* varnish
**vernysh** *m vernyshys* varnish
**vertû** *m vertûs* virtue; power (inherent)
**very nebes** *phr* very little / few
**veyl** *m veylys* veil
**viaj** *m viajys* journey; ride; voyage
**viajya** *v* travel
**vil** *adj* obscene
**vôta** *m vôtys* vote
**vôtya** *v* vote
**voward** *m vowardys* front[line]
**vu** *m vuys* view
**vy·ctory** *m vy·ctorys* victory
**vyctym** *m vyctyms* (a²) victim (of)
**vyral** *adj* viral
**vyrùs an imûndyfyk denyl (VID)** *m* human immune deficiency virus (HIV)
**vysour** *m vysours* mask
**vysyt** *m vysytys* visit
**vysytya** *v* visit

# W

**war** *adj* careful, cautious; aware
**wàr / dhywar dûta** *phr* on / off duty
**wàr / dhywar lînen** *phr* on / off line
**wàr an dyweth** *phr* at last, finally
**wàr an tu aral** *phr* on the other hand
**wàr dhele·rgh** *phr* backwards
**wàr eyl tu ... wàr y gela** *phr* on the one hand ... on the other [hand]
**wàr nans** *phr* down *motion*
**wàr neb cor** *phr* in any case, anyway
**wàr vainys cowethasek** *phr* on social media

**wàr vàn** *phr* above *position*; upstairs *position*
**warba·rth** *adv* together
**warleny** *adv* last year
**warle·rgh an abecedary** *phr* in theory
**warrant** *m warrantys* warrant(y); guarantee
**warrantya** *v* guarantee, warrant; authenticate
**wast** *m wâstys* waist
**wèl** *interj* well
**we·ryson** *m we·rysons* reward
**wèst** *adj/m* west(ern)
**whaf** *m whaffys* whack, wallop
**whans** *m whansow* wish, desire; *want (sth)
**whansa** *v* wish, want *(if construction with* whans *would be very awkward)*
**whar** *adj* meek, mild; humane; civilized
**whare·** *adv* presently, anon
**wharheans** *m wharheansow* civilization
**wharth** *m* laugh(ter)

**wharthus** *adj* funny; ridiculous
**wharvos** *m/v wharvosow* occurrence, event; happen, occur
**whath** *adv* still, yet
**whecter** *m* sweetness; niceness, pleasantness
**whedh** *m whedhow* swelling
**whedhel** *m whedhlow* story, tale, anecdote; rumour
**whedhy** *v* swell
**wheg** *adj* sweet; nice, pleasant; dear (in salutation)
**whegen** *f whegednow* darling (female)
**whegrew** *m* icing
**whegyjyon** *pl* sprinkles
**whegyn** *m whegydnow* darling (male); sweet
**wheja** *v* vomit, be sick
**whejus** *adj* sick (nausea)
**whejuster** *m* nausea
**whel** *m whelyow* work (on-going)
**whel bal** *m whelyow* mine

**whelas** (whilas) *v* seek, look for; + *verb-noun* try to
**wheldro** *f wheldroyow* revolution (political, industrial etc)
**whensys dhe wodhvos** *phr* curious
**wherow** *adj* bitter; harsh, severe
**wherowder** *m* bitterness; harshness, severity
**wherthyn** *v* laugh
**whës** *m* sweat, perspiration
**whesa** *v* sweat, perspire
**whesker** *col wheskeren* insects
**wheth air** *m whethow* draught
**whetha** *v* blow
**whethfy** *v* inflate; amplify (sound)
**whethfyans** *m* inflation (incl prices rising); amplification
**whor** *f wheryth* sister
**whyban** *m* whistle, whistling
**whybana** *v* whistle; wheeze
**whybonel** *f whybonolow* flute
**whydn** *col whadnen* fleas
**whyl** *m whylas* beetle
**whyl tan** *m whylas* moped
**whystra** *v* whisper
**whystrans** *m whystransow* whisper
**whytel** *m whytlow* shawl, wrap
**whythell** *f whythellow* whistle (instrument)
**whythra** *v* [orth] explore; (re)search; investigate
**whythrans** *m whythransow* exploration; [re]search; investigation; inquiry; inquest
**wolcùbma** *v* welcome
**wolcùm** *adj/m wolcùbmys* welcome
**wordhy** *adj* (a$^2$) worthy (of); respectable; admirable
**wor'tu ha** *prep* towards
**wortyweth** (oteweth) *adv* in the end
**wosa** (woja) *prep + noun, non-personal pronoun,*

157

*verb-noun, infinitive construction* after
**wosa pùptra·** *phr* after all

# Y

**y coodh / codhvia dhodho** *phr + verb-noun* he ought to [have] / should [have]
**y honen oll** *phr* alone
**y'n jeves** *phr* he has / gets
**y'n jeves an gwir** (**dhe**[2]) *phr* he is right; he is entitled to
**y tal / talvia [dhodho]** *phr + verb-noun* it would be / have been worth
**yagh** *adj* healthy (sb and figuratively)
**yaghhe·** *v* heal, cure (sb)
**yahus** *adj* healthy (sth)
**yar** *f yer* hen
**yar gyny** *f yer* turkey
**Yêdhow** *m Yedhewon* Jew
**yêhes** *m* health
**yet** *m yettys* gate
**yêth** *f yêthow* language (phenomenon, usage)

**wosa termyn** *phr* after a while
**yêwny** *v* yearn for
**yêyn** *adj* cold
**yeynder** *m* cold(ness), chill
**yeynor** *m yeynoryon* refrigerator
**yma· odour** *m + noun / adjective* **wàr**[2] *phr* smell (have a particular smell)
**yma· sa·woren** *f + noun / adjective* **wàr**[2] *phr* taste (have a particular taste)
**yma· syght** *m + noun / adjective* **wàr**[2] *phr* look (have a particular look)
**yn fen** *phr* firmly, strongly
**yn fenowgh** *phr* often
**yn keverek** *phr* relatively
**[yn] scon** *phr* soon
**yn udnyk** *phr* only
**yogùrt** *m* yoghurt
**yonk** (**yowynk**) *adj* young
**yorgh** *m yorhas* roe-deer
**yos kergh** *m* porridge

**yowynkes** *m* youth (incl young people collectively)
**ÿs crack** *col* popcorn
**ÿs wheg** *col* maize, sweetcorn

**ÿst** *adj/m* east(ern)

# Z

**zyp** *m zyppys* zip

## A few notes on spelling

The consonant groups dhv vl vn vr are sometimes spelled thv fl fn fr, reflecting the likely pronunciation in Middle Cornish. Where such a spelling is common in the literature published in Standard Cornish, it is also accepted here (*e.g.* defnyth, kefnys, lyfrêson). But the option of writing a devoiced consonant before suffix -va (*e.g.* 'medhekva' instead of medhegva) has not been taken in this dictionary.

One may find j substituted for some intervocalic d where that had resisted assibilation in Middle Cornish ('descajor', 'pùscajor' etc); but in this dictionary d is preserved.

Occasionally there is an argument for respelling th as dh when comparison is made with Breton or Welsh. Where such a respelling has already appeared in published traditional Cornish, this dictionary generally adopts it, sometimes keeping the spelling with th as an alternative: *e.g.* studh. But elsewhere th alone has been retained: *e.g.* garth. There is certainly no good reason why the change should be made in a loan-word like brykethen.

The vowel now written oo was for many years represented by simple o. A few instances of oo are still controversial, and o is sometimes written instead.

The circumflex has been used on the letter i where stressed in loan-words with several syllables; but this has not been extended to native words. You may prefer to write the accent wherever you give a long pronunciation to this vowel in a word of more than one syllable. The circumflex and grave accents operate as markers of end-stress in a few words: notably agè·s, and disyllabic cognates with prefixed a-[2] such as mes / avê·s, pàn / abà·n. This accent is sometimes omitted.

# GRAMMAR WORDS

Here you will find many words that are best learned as grammar. The list includes particles, pronouns and other 'pronominals', inflecting prepositions, conjunctions, and question words. Some technical language has been used in order to describe them in a small compass. Consult your textbook if in doubt, or check with your teacher. Note that initial û counts as a vowel even when pronounced 'yoo'.

## *Particles*

**a$^2$**
links subject or object of relative clause to clause verb; links subject of nominal sentence to its inflected verb (particle is dropped before vowel of inflected form of bos / mos); introduces inflected verb of question beginning with question word or phrase in subject or object relationship

**a$^2$**
introduces inflected verb of 'yes/no' question (particle is dropped before vowel of inflected form of bos / mos)

**a$^2$**
optionally used before noun of address (no mutation if proper name)

**ass**
replaces *assa$^2$* before vowel of inflected form of bos / mos and also before w (< gw) of gwil

**assa$^2$**
introduces inflected verb to express wonder / admiration

**ma**
replaces *may$^5$* before na$^2$

**-ma**
'this' (demonstrative – attaches to last word of noun 'string')

**may**[5]
introduces relative clause for antecedent that is neither subject nor object of that clause; introduces result clause; introduces purpose clause with subjunctive verb (frequently gallos)

**mayth**
replaces *may*[5] before vowel / h *pre-mutation*

**na**[2]
negates imperative verb; negates inflected verb of causal, concessive, purpose, result, or temporal clause; negates inflected verb echoing verb of question, or command, or assertion; introduces negative indirect statement with inflected verb; replaces *y*[5] to negate prag-question; replaces *a*[2] to link subject or object of negative relative clause to clause verb; replaces *a*[4] (*mar*[4]) to negate protasis of unreal conditional sentence

**nag**
replaces *na*[2] before vowel of inflected form of bos / mos

**-na**
'that' (demonstrative – attaches to last word of noun 'string')

**namna**[2]
before inflected verb: 'almost' (namnag replaces *namna*[2] before vowel of inflected form of bos / mos)

**nans** (nanj)
used before yw and o with sense 'by now, ago' / 'by then'

**ny**[2]
negates inflected verb of verbal sentence; in conditional sentence negates inflected verb of protasis and/or apodosis; precedes unpropped infixed pronoun in negative subordinate

clause where affirmative version of clause would require $y^5$ *only* to prop infixed pronoun

**nyns** (nynj)
replaces $ny^2$ before vowel of inflected form of bos / mos

**ow⁴**
precedes verb-noun to form present participle

**owth**
replaces $ow^4$ before vowel / h

**re²** (b of inflected form of bos resists mutation)
replaces $a^2$ to link subject or object of relative clause to its preterite clause verb yielding present perfect sense; replaces $a^2$ to link subject of nominal sentence to its preterite verb yielding present perfect sense; replaces $a^2$ as default particle introducing inflected verb of question beginning with question word or phrase yielding present perfect sense; introduces preterite verb of question beginning with *ple⁵*, *py⁵*, *peur⁵*, *prag*, *pes termyn* or other adverbial phrase, yielding present perfect sense (and replacing $y^5$ where it occurs); replaces $y^5$ to introduce affirmative direct or indirect statement with preterite verb yielding present perfect sense; used optatively to introduce present subjunctive of bos expressing a wish

**res**
replaces $re^2$ before preterite form of mos

**y⁵**
introduces inflected verb of affirmative verbal sentence (2nd state substituted for particle when simple complement fronted without particular emphasis); introduces inflected verb of question beginning with *prag*, *pes termyn* or other adverbial phrase; introduces affirmative indirect statement with inflected verb; precedes unpropped infixed pronoun in subordinate clause not otherwise requiring a particle

**yn**[5]
converts adjective into adverb

**yth** (th')
replaces *y*[5] before vowel / h *pre-mutation*

## *Particle phrases*

**a ny**[2]
introduces inflected verb of interrogative negative verbal sentence (nyns replaces *ny*[2] before vowel of inflected form of bos / mos)

**an pëth a**[2]
'what' (relative – sometimes extended to indirect question)

**bys may**[5]
'until' (mayth replaces *may*[5] before vowel / h *pre-mutation*

**hag a**[2]
replaces *a*[2] to link subject or object of relative clause to clause verb with clearer distinction from nominal sentence (a[2] is dropped before vowel of inflected form of bos / mos)

**in udn**[2]
precedes verb-noun to form adverbial present participle (collateral action regarded as manner in which main action is performed)

**kenyver a**[2]
'as many as' (a[2] is dropped before vowel of inflected form of bos / mos)

**le may**[5]
'where' (relative when no specific antecedent of place)

**myns a**[2]
before inflected verb: 'all who / that' (a[2] is dropped before vowel of inflected form of bos / mos)

**neb a²**
functions as a proxy-phrase for 'who(m)' (and even occasionally for 'which' referring to an inanimate antecedent) in relative construction probably influenced by English grammar (a² is dropped before vowel of inflected form of bos / mos)

**neb may⁵**
functions as a proxy-phrase for 'to whom' (*see* neb a² – mayth replaces *may⁵* before vowel / h *pre-mutation*)

**peskytter** (pyskytter) **may⁵**
before subjunctive verb: 'as soon as [ever]' (mayth replaces *may⁵* before vowel / h *pre-mutation*)

**pesqweyth [oll] [ma]y⁵**
before subjunctive verb: 'whenever' ([may]th replaces *[ma]y⁵* before vowel / h *pre-mutation*)

**pëth a²**
'which' (relative when whole proposition is antecedent)

**ple pyna·g [ma]y⁵**
before subjunctive verb: 'wherever' ([ma]yth replaces *[ma]y⁵* before vowel / h *pre-mutation*)

**[pùp]pyna·g [oll] a²**
before subjunctive verb: 'whoever', 'whatever' (a² is dropped before inflected form of mos)

**rag may⁵**
introduces purpose clause with subjunctive verb (frequently gallos – mayth replaces *may⁵* before vowel / h *pre-mutation*)

**rag na²**
introduces negative purpose clause with subjunctive verb (nag replaces *na²* before vowel of inflected form of bos / mos)

**seul a²**
before inflected verb: 'all who' (a² is dropped before vowel of inflected form of bos / mos)

## Personal pronouns

*First person singular*

**avy·**
optionally replaces *vy* as subject after certain preterites lacking a personal ending (*e.g.* deuth, gwrug), or when reinforcing for greater emphasis

**'m**
'me' (infixed)

**-ma**
'I' (suffixed as subject after verb; fusion causes sound / spelling changes)

**mavy·** (-ma vy)
replaces *-ma* or *vy* as subject after verb for added emphasis

**me**
optionally replaces *my* as subject of nominal sentence / infinitive construction or after non-inflecting preposition

**my**
'I', 'me' (independent)

**vy**
'I', 'me' (as subject after verb, as object after verb where grammar permits, or reinforcing)

*Second person singular*

**dhejy·** (tejy·)
replaces *jy* when reinforcing for added emphasis

**jy**
'you' *one person familiar* (as subject after verb, as object after verb where grammar permits, or reinforcing)

**sy**
optionally replaces *jy* when reinforcing

**-ta**
'you' *one person familiar* (suffixed as subject after verb; fusion causes sound / spelling changes)

**tejy·** (-ta jy)
replaces *-ta* or *jy* as subject after verb for added emphasis

**te**
optionally replaces *ty* as subject of nominal sentence / infinitive construction or after non-inflecting preposition

**'th**[5]
'you' *one person familiar* (infixed)

**ty**
'you' *one person familiar* (independent)

*Third person singular*

**e**
replaces *ev* as grammatical object after imperative; optionally replaces *ev* as logical object after forms of *y'm beus*

**ee·v**
replaces *ev* when reinforcing for added emphasis

**ev**
'he', 'him'; 'it' *masculine reference* + tra + *fact, verbal action, result of action* (independent, as subject after verb, as object after verb where grammar permits, or reinforcing)

**hy**
'she', 'her'; 'it' *feminine reference* + time, weather, circumstance, condition (independent, as subject after verb, as object after verb where grammar permits, or reinforcing)

**hyhy·**
replaces *hy* for added emphasis

**'n**
'him'; 'it' *masculine reference* + tra + *fact, verbal action, result of action* (infixed)

**'s**
'her'; 'it' *feminine reference + time, weather, circumstance, condition* (infixed)

**va**
optionally replaces *ev* as subject after verb

**vae·v**
replaces *ev or va* as subject after verb for added emphasis

*First person plural*

**'gan**
'us' (infixed)

**ny**
'we', 'us' (independent, as subject after verb, as object after verb where grammar permits, or reinforcing)

**nyny·**
replaces *ny* for added emphasis

*Second person plural*

**'gas**
'you' *one person polite / more than one person* (infixed)

**why**
'you' *one person polite / more than one person* (independent, as subject after verb, as object after verb where grammar permits, or reinforcing)

**whywhy·**
replaces *why* for added emphasis

*Third person plural*

**anjy·** (this is a late form)
'they', 'them' (independent, as object after verb where grammar permits)

**'s**
'them' (infixed)

**y**
'they', 'them' (independent, as subject after verb, as object after verb where grammar permits, or reinforcing)

**ynsy·**
replaces *y* for added emphasis

## *Possessive pronouns*

*First person singular*

**ow**³
'my'

*Second person singular*

**dha**²
'your' *one person familiar*

*Third person singular*

**y**²
'his'; its *masculine reference* + tra + *fact, verbal action, result of action*

**hy**³
'her'; 'its' *feminine reference* + *time, weather, circumstance, condition*

*First person plural*

**agan** (gàn)
'our'

*Second person plural*

**agas** (gàs)
'your' *one person polite / more than one person*

*Third person plural*

**aga**³ (gà³)
'their'

*Contracted forms with a² 'from'/ 'of', dhe² 'to', in 'in'; ha 'and / as / with', na 'nor'*

*First person singular*
**a'm, dhe'm, i'm; ha'm, na'm**

*Second person singular*
**a'th⁵, dhe'th⁵, i'th⁵; ha'th⁵, na'th⁵**

*Third person singular (masculine)*
**a'y², dh'y²; ha'y², na'y²**

*Third person singular (feminine)*
**a'y³, dh'y³; ha'y³, na'y³**

*First person plural*
**a'gan, dh'agan, i'gan; ha'gan, na'gan**

*Second person plural*
**a'gas, dh'agas, i'gas; ha'gas, na'gas**

*Third person plural*
**a'ga³, dh'aga³, i'ga³; ha'ga³, na'ga³**

The personal and possessive pronouns are quite complex. Please bear in mind that basic forms given in the English-Cornish section are meant as a springboard only.

## *Other pronominals*

**an aral** the other [one]
**an eyl** the latter
**an eyl** + *noun* the one (as opposed to the other)

**an eyl ... y gela** the one ... the other
**an holl²** + *noun* the whole

**an keth** + *noun* (ha) the same (as): contact mutation as for definite article an (excluding c, d, k, p, q, t)
**an keth hedna** the same thing
**an re** the ones
**an re erel** the others / other ones
**an re-ma** these [ones]
**an re-na** those [ones]
**den vëth** *with express negative* anyone, *with implied negative* no one
**hebma** (**hobma** *feminine*) this [one]
**hedna** (**hodna** *feminine*) that [one]
**hèm** replaces *hebma* before yw / o
**hèn** replaces *hedna* before yw / o
**hòm** replaces *hobma* before yw / o
**hòn** replaces *hodna* before yw / o
**honen** + *possessive pronoun* self; + *possessive pronoun,* *which also precedes noun* own
**honen-**[2] *pref* self-
**kebmys** so much / many
**ken onen** another one
**kenyver** every [one], each [one]
**kettep huny** every one
**lies huny** many [a one]
**lower onen** (a[2] + *personal pronoun*) many
**nagonen** *with express negative* anyone, *with implied negative* no one
**nampy·th** (neppy·th) something; anything (in non-negative question)
**neb** some; any (in non-negative question)
**nebes** some, a little, a few *See also* very nebes
**neb[onen]** someone; anyone (in non-negative question)
**neptra·** something; anything (in non-negative question)
**oll** all
**onen** one (indefinite)
**pùb** every, each
**pùb huny [oll]** every one

**pùb[onen]** everyone
**pùptra·** everything
**re** (a$^2$) some *Only people, things, not uncountable quantity*

**tra vëth** *with express negative* anything, *with implied negative* nothing
**vëth [oll]** *with express negative* any, *with implied negative* no
**y gela** the former

## Inflecting prepositions

Where *seven* inflected forms are specified, they are *1* first person singular, *2* second person singular, *3* third person singular (masculine), *4* third person singular (feminine), *5* first person plural, *6* second person plural, *7* third person plural. Where *three* inflected forms are given, they are *1* third person singular (masculine), *2* third person singular (feminine), *3* third person plural.

Basic meanings are given here. Prepositions are also used idiomatically, especially a$^2$, dhe$^2$, orth, wàr$^2$.

**a**$^2$ from; of (but not simple possession); about
**ahanaf, ahanas, anodho, anedhy, ahanan** (also = from here), **ahanowgh, anodhans**

**adha·dn**$^2$ from beneath / under
**adhadnof, adhadnos, adhadno, adhadny, adhadnon, adhadnowgh, adhadnans**

**agè·s** than (note also agè·s dell$^2$ + *verb*)
**agesof, agesos, agesso, agessy, ageson, agesowgh, agessans**

**a-ugh** (a-ught) above, over
**a-uhof, a-uhos, a-uho, a-ughty, a-uhon, a-uhowgh, a-ughtans**

**ave·ll** as
**avellof, avellos, avello, avelly, avellon, avellowgh, avellans**

**dhe**[2] to, for (destination), at (point in time)
**dhybm** (also **dhybmo** *slight emphasis*), **dhis** (**dhys**) (also **dhyso** *slight emphasis*), **dhodho, dhedhy, dhyn, dhywgh, dhedhans** (**dhodhans**)

**dhia**[2] from (place); since
**dhianodho, dhianedhy, dhianodhans**

**dhyra·g** in front of; + *noun, pronoun* before
**dhyragof, dhyragos, dhyragtho, dhyrygthy, dhyragon, dhyragowgh, dhyragthans**

**dhywar**[2] off
**dhywarnaf, dhywarnas, dhywarnodho, dhywarnedhy, dhywarnan, dhywarnowgh, dhywarnodhans**

**dhyworth** from (person, position)
**dhyworthyf, dhyworthys, dhyworto, dhyworty, dhyworthyn, dhyworthowgh, dhywortans**

**dre**[2] (usually der before vowel, but note dre'n alongside der an) through; by (instrumentality)
**dredhof, dredhos, dredho, dredhy** (also = thereby), **dredhon, dredhowgh, dredhans**

**dres** across, over; past; during
**drestof, drestos, dresto, dresty, dreston, drestowgh, drestans**

**ès** than (note also ès dell[2] + *verb*)
**esof, esos, esso, essy, eson, esowgh, essans**

**gans** with (accompaniment); by (agency)
**genef** (ge·nama), **genes, ganso, gensy, genen, genowgh, gansans**

**heb** without; not counting
**hebof, hebos, heptho, hepthy, hebon, hebowgh, hepthans**

**in** in, at (= inside); *with verb of motion* into; *+ noun predicatively after verb* as
**inof, inos, ino, inhy, inon, inowgh, inans**

**in dadn**² (in dàn²) beneath, under; precedes verb-noun to form adverbial present participle (action simultaneous with that of main verb)
**in dadnof, in dadnos, in dadno, in dadny, in dadnon, in dadnowgh, in dadnans**

**inter** (intra) between; among (agreement, fixed idioms)
**intredhof, intredhos, intredho, intredhy, intredhon, intredhowgh, intredhans**

**orth** (worth) [up] against; at (when not inside); according to (some measure); replaces *ow*⁴ */ owth* when possessive pronoun used with verb-noun
**orthyf, orthys, orto, orty, orthyn, orthowgh, ortans**

**rag** *+ noun, pronoun* for; from (barrier / protection); *+ verb-noun* in order to; *+ infinitive construction, na²-clause* for (reason)
**ragof, ragos, ragtho, rygthy, ragon, ragowgh, ragthans**

**ryb** beside
**rybof, rybos, ryptho, rypthy, rybon** (also = nearby), **rybowgh, rypthans**

**wàr**[2] [up]on; on to *with verb of motion*
**warnaf, warnas, warnodho, warnedhy, warnan, warnowgh, warnodhans**

**warby·dn** against (motion, opposition); by (specific time)
**wàr ow fydn, wàr dha bydn, wàr y bydn, wàr hy fydn, wàr agan pydn, wàr agas pydn, wàr aga fydn**

**warle·rgh** behind *with verb of motion*; according to; + *noun, pronoun, verb-noun, infinitive construction* after
**wàr ow lergh, wàr dha lergh, wàr y lergh, wàr hy lergh, wàr agan lergh, wàr agas lergh, wàr aga lergh**

## *Co-ordinating conjunctions*

| | |
|---|---|
| **ada·r** | 'not' (contrastive) |
| **bone·yl ... bò** | 'either ... or' |
| **ha** | 'and' |
| | *also with prepositional force:* |
| | 'as' (equality) + *noun, pronoun (independent if personal)* |
| ; | 'with' (attribute) + *possessive pronoun + noun* |
| **ha ... ha** | 'both ... and' |
| **hag** | replaces *ha* before vowel |
| **kefrë·s ... ha** | 'both ... and' |
| **mès** | 'but' (sharper contrast than saw) |
| **na** | 'nor' |
| **na ... na** | 'neither ... nor' |
| **nag** | replaces *na* 'nor' before vowel |
| **nane·yl ... na** | 'neither ... nor' |
| **pò (bò)** | 'or' |
| **pò ... pò** | 'either ... or' |

| | |
|---|---|
| **poke·n** (boke·n) | '[or] [otherwise]' |
| **rag** | 'for' |
| **saw** | 'but' (more common than mès) |
| **ytho·** | '[and] so' (also adverbially of consequence 'then') |

## Subordinating conjunctions

| | |
|---|---|
| **a**[4] | 'if' (unreal / improbable / impossible – with [imperfect] subjunctive verb) |
| **abà·n**[2] | 'now that', 'since' (temporal, causal) |
| **bys pàn**[2] | 'until' |
| **bÿth pàn**[2] | 'whenever' (with subjunctive verb) |
| **dell**[2] | 'as' (all senses); 'that' (indirect statement) |
| **erna·**[2] | 'until' |
| **erna·g** | replaces *erna·*[2] before vowel |
| **fate·ll**[2] | 'that' (indirect statement) |
| **ha** | + *noun / pronoun + adjectival or adverbial complement* attendant circumstances |
| **[ha] kyn**[5] | even though (with [imperfect] subjunctive verb) |
| **hadre·**[2] | before forms of bewa and subjunctive of bos only: 'so long as' |
| **hag** | replaces *ha* before vowel |
| **kepa·r ha pàn**[2] | '[just] as if' (with [imperfect] subjunctive verb) |
| **kettel**[2] | 'as soon as' |
| **kyn**[5] | '[al]though' |
| **kynth** | replaces *kyn*[5] before vowel / h *pre-mutation* |

| | |
|---|---|
| **mar**[4] | 'if' (real or unreal / untrue – if the latter, with [imperfect] subjunctive verb); 'if / whether' (indirect question) *See also* dos *on page 277* |
| **mara** | replaces *mar*[4] before infixed pronoun |
| **mar[a]s** | replaces *mar*[4] before vowel |
| **marnas** | + *nominal sentence structure* 'unless' |
| **na**[2] | 'if not' (unreal / improbable – with [imperfect] subjunctive verb) |
| **pàn**[2] | 'when'; 'while'; 'since' (causal) |
| **[rag] dowt** | + *infinitive construction, na*[2]*-clause (with subjunctive verb)* 'in case' |
| **'tell**[2] | 'that' (further limb of indirect statement – echoing preceding fate·ll[2]) |
| **unweyth a**[4] **/ na**[2] | 'if only' / 'if only not' (unreal – with [imperfect] subjunctive verb) |

## *Question words / phrases*

**a ble**[5] 'where ... from'
**fate·ll**[2] (fatel[2]) 'how'
**fatla**[2] *independent and elsewhere (as* fatl' *before vowel in bos)* 'how'
**[in] pana vaner** 'how'
**pana**[2] (pàn[2]) + *noun* 'what'
**pana bellder** 'how far'; 'how long' (time)
**pana dermyn**[2] (this is a late phrase) 'when'

**pana lies** + *singular noun* 'how many'
**pana lies torn** 'how many times'
**pana re** 'what ones'
**pana sort a**[2] 'what sort of'
**pana vaner** 'what kind of'
**pandra·**[2] *independent and elsewhere (as* pandr' *before vowel in bos)* 'what'

**pandr'orth** 'what about'
**pes** + *singular noun of space / time* 'how many'
**pes termyn** 'how long' (time)
**pesqweyth** 'how often'
**pëth** 'what'
**peur**[5] 'when'
**ple**[5] 'where'
**ple ma / mowns** 'where is / are'
**pleth** otherwise replaces *ple*[5] before vowel in inflected form of bos / mos
**prag** 'why'
**praga** optionally replaces *prag* when independent
**py** + *noun* 'what, which'
**py** + *noun* **pynag** 'whatever, whichever'
**py**[5] 'where ... [to]'
**py lies** 'how many'
**py par** 'what kind of'
**py re** 'which [ones]', 'what ones'

**py seul** *independent* 'how much / many'
**pygebmys** *independent or* + *singular noun* 'how much'; *independent or* + *plural or collective noun* 'how many (much)'
**pygebmys downder** 'how deep'
**pygebmys hës** 'how long' (not time)
**pygebmys les** 'how wide'
**pygebmys uhelder** 'how high / loud'
**pyma / pymowns** 'where is / are' ... [to]
**pyne·yl** 'which' *Only where choice is between two; for wider choice use* py *with* tra *or other noun*
**pyth** replaces *py*[5] before vowel of inflected form of bos / mos
**pyw** 'who'

## *Other words / phrases*

**a'm govys**
'for my sake'
*The phrase is not attested with other possessive pronouns.*

**an**
'the' (for the mutation scheme with this word, consult your textbook – and note some exceptions to the basic rules)

**dhe**[2] (seul[2]) + *comparative* ... **dhe**[2] (seul[2]) + *comparative*
'the more ... the more'

**dhe voy**
'all the more'

**govy** (often introducing subordinate clause or verbal phrase)
'oh dear!'
*Personal forms:* govy, gojy, goe·v, gohy, gony, gowhy, go'y·

**kyn fe** (focusing noun or adjectival / adverbial expression)
'even'

**maga**[5] + *adjective, adverb*
'so'

**mar**[2] + *adjective, adverb*
'so'

**na ve**
introduces infinitive construction to render negative protasis of unreal / impossible conditional sentence
*For possible use of* unweyth *with this phrase, see page 176*

**ot** (awo·t)
replaces *otta* before vowels

**otta** (awotta)
'here / there is / are'
*Personal forms:* otta vy (o·ttama), otta sy, otta va, otta hy, otta ny, otta why, ottensy

# ENGLISH-CORNISH SECTION

The English-Cornish section is an index designed to be used in conjunction with the earlier parts of the book. For every Cornish word you should check the entry in the Cornish-English section or look it up in the separate list of 'grammar words' where it is marked ᴳ. Cross-checking will ensure you choose the right word or phrase for the context, and will help you employ it correctly. Be especially careful to understand entries containing square brackets; and to identify entries that are available in quite limited circumstances (*e.g.* hadre·², in kever), and words / phrases used only with express or implied negatives (*e.g.* den vëth, nameu·r).

## A

**A Level** *n* Level A
**abandon** *v* forsâkya
**abbey** *n* abatty
**abdomen** *n* torr
be **able to** *phr* gallos
**abode** *n* adneth
**abortion** *n* avortans
**about** *prep* a² ᴳ; adro· dhe²; in kever; [ow] tùchya
**above** *adv* wàr vàn
**above** *prep* a-ughᴳ
**above all** *phr* kyns oll
**abrupt** *adj* desempys
**abruptly** *adv* desempys
in the **absence** of *phr* saw
be **absent** *phr* fyllel
**absurd** *adj* absù·rd
**abundant** *adj* pals
**abuse** *v* tebel-dyghtya
**academy** *n* aca·demy
**accelerate** *v* uskys'he·

**accept** *v* degemeres
**accident** *n* gwall; droglam
**Accidents and Emergencies Department (A&E)** *n* [Asran] Droglabmow ha Gorothobmow
**acclaim** *n* gormola
**acclaim** *v* gormel
**accommodation** *n* gwest
**accompanist** *n* keveylyth
**accompany** *v* keveylya
**accomplish** *v* collenwel
**accord** *n* aco·rd
**according to** *phr* herwyth; in herwyth; warle·rghᴳ; orthᴳ
**accordion** *n* acordyon
**account** *n* aco·wnt
**account** *v* acowntya
current **account** *phr* aco·wnt kesres
deposit **account** *phr* aco·wnt arhow

savings **account** *phr* aco·wnt erbysyon
**account for** *phr* styrya
**accountant** *n* acowntyas
**accusation** *n* cùhudhans
**accuse** *v* cùhudha
**ace** *n* âss
**achieve** *v* obery, cowlwil
**achievement** *n* cowlwrians
**acid** *adj* trenk
**acid** *n* trenken
**acknowledge** *v* aswon, alowa, avowa
**acquire** *v* aqwîrya
**Acquired Immune Deficiency Syndrome** (**AIDS**) *phr* Syndrom an Imûndyfyk [Aqwîrys] (SIDA)
**acquisition** *n* cafosyans
**acquit** *v* delyvra
**acre** *n* erow
**across** *prep* dres$^G$
**act** *n* act
**act** *v* obery; gwary
**action** *n* gweythres
**action** *v* gweythresa
**actions** *n* gwrith
**activate** *v* bewhe·
**active** *adj* gweythresek
**activist** *n* gweythresor
**activity** *n* gwrians
**actor** *n* gwarior
**actual** *adj* gwrionedhek
**actually** *adv* in gwrioneth
**acute** *adj* lybm
**acuteness** *n* lymder

**adapt** *v* aswywa
**adapter** *n* aswywor
**add** *v* keworra
**add up** *phr* sùmya
**adder** *n* nader
**addicted to** *phr* in danjer
**addition** *n* keworrans
in **addition to** *phr* kefrë·s ha
**additive** *n* keworransyn
**address** *n* trigva
**adjective** *n* hanow gwadn
**adjust** *v* desedha
**administer** *v* menystra
**administrator** *n* menystror
**admirable** *adj* wordhy
**admiration** *n* estê·m
**admire** *v* estêmya
**admit** *v* alowa, avowa, amyttya
**admittedly** *adv* res yw avowa
**adopt** *v* degemeres, recêva; asvaba
**adore** *v* gordhya [dhe$^2$]; leungara
**adult** *adj/n* tevysak
**advance** *n* avauncyans
**advance** *v* avauncya
**advantage** *n* prow; poynt a brow
**adventure** *n* aventu·r
**adverb** *n* adverb
**adversary** *n* contrary
**advertise** *v* argemydna
**advert[isement]** *n* argebmyn
**advice** *n* cùssul
**advise** *v* cùssulya

**adviser** *n* cùssulyor
**affair** *n* mater, negys
**affection** *n* kerensa
**affectionate** *adj* kerenje'ek
**afflict** *v* grevya dhe[2]
be **afraid** *phr* perthy dowt / own
**after** *prep* wosa; warle·rgh[G]
**after a while** *phr* wosa termyn
**after all** *phr* wosa pùptra·
**afternoon** *n* dohajë·dh
in the **afternoon** *phr* dohajë·dh
**afterwards** *adv* awosa
**again** *adv* arta
**against** *prep* warby·dn[G]
[up] **against** *phr* orth[G]
**age** *n* oos *See also* bloodh
**agency** *n* maino·rieth
**agent** *n* mainor
**aggravate** *v* gwethhe·
**ago** *adv* alebma; nans[G]
in **agony** *phr* in ewn angùs
**agree** *v* acordya, assentya, agria
**agreement** *n* aco·rd, assentyans, agrians
be in **agreement** *phr* bos unverhë·s
**agriculture** *n* amethyans
**aid** *n/v* gweres
**aide** *n* gweresor
**aim** *n* meder
**air** *n* air
**air-sea rescue** *phr* rescous air ha mor

**air traffic controller** *n* rowtor
**aircraft** *n* jyn ebron
**airport** *n* airborth
**aisle** *n* tremenva
**alarm** *n* ala·rm
**alarm clock** *n* dyfunor
**album** *n* albùm
**alcohol** *n* a·lcohol
**algae** *n* alge
**algorithm** *n* awgrym
**ale** *n* coref
brown **ale** *n* coref gorm
pale **ale** *n* coref gell
**alien** *adj* estrednek
**alien** *n* bÿs-estren
**alight** *v* skydnya
**alive** *adj* bew
**all** *adj/pron* oll[G]
above **all** *phr* dres pùptra·
at **all** *phr* màn, cabmen; poynt
**Allah** *n* Allâ·h
**allergic** *adj* allergek
**alley[way]** *n* scochfordh
**alliance** *n* kefrysyans
**allot** *v* kevradna
**allotment** *n* pastel dir
**allow** *v* alowa
**allude to** *phr* campolla andydro
**almond** *n* a·lamand
**almost** *adv* ogas; ogas ha; ogasty·; namna[2] [G]
**alone** *adj* y honen oll
**along** *prep* ahë·s
**alphabet** *n* abecedary
**already** *adv* solabrë·s

**also** *adv* inwe·dh, kefrë·s, maga tâ
**alternate** *v* eylya
**alternative** *adj* ken fordh
**alternative** *n* dêwys; ken fordh
**although** *conj* kyn[5] [G]
**aluminium** *n* alû·mynùm
**always** *adv* pùpprë·s, pùb termyn
**amass** *v* kescruny
**amateur** *adj* amatorek
**amateur** *n* amatou·r
**amateurish** *adj* amatorus
**amaze** *v* gorra marth in
**ambassador** *n* canasor
**ambiguous** *adj* omborthus
**ambition** *n* uhelwhans
**ambitious** *adj* uhelwhansek
**ambivalent** *adj* omborthus
**ambulance** *n* carr clôjy
**ambush** *v* contreweytya
**among** *prep* in mesk; inter[G]
**amplification** *n* whethfyans
**amplify** *v* whethfy
**amuse** *v* dydhana
**amusing** *adj* dydha·n
**anaesthesia** *n* clamder
**anaesthetic** *n* clamderyas
**analogy** *n* ana·lojy
**analysis** *n* dielvednans
**anarchy** *n* dyre·wl
**and** *conj* ha[G]
**anecdote** *n* whedhel
**angel** *n* el
**anger** *n* sorr
**angle** *n* elyn

**Anglican** *adj/n* A·nglycan
**angry** *adj* serrys
**animal** *n* best
**animate** *v* bewhe·
**ankle** *n* ufern
**annex(e)** *n* keworrans
**another** *adj* ken
**another one** *phr* ken onen[G]
**announce** *v* nôtya, declarya
**announcement** *n* derivadow, nôtyans, declaryans
**announcer** *n* derivador
**annoy** *v* ania, serry
**annoyance** *n* anians
**annoyed** *adj* serrys
be **annoyed** *phr* serry
**annual** *adj* bledhednek
**anon** *adv* whare·
**answer** *n* gorthyp
**answer** *v* gortheby
**anti-** *pref* gorth-[2]
**anti-clockwise** *adj* warby·dn an howl
**antibiotic** *n* antybiotek
**antique** *n* hendra
**antler** *n* corn
**antisemitism** *n* gorthyedho·wieth
**ants** *n* mùryon
**anxiety** *n* fienasow
**anxious** *adj* prederus
be **anxious** *phr* perthy awhe·r
**any** *adj* neb[G]; vëth [oll][G]; badna
**any** *pron* neb[G]
**any longer** *phr* na felha

**any more** *phr* namo·y
**any other** *phr* nahe·n
**anyone** *pron* neb[onen][G]; den vëth[G], nagonen[G]
**anything** *pron* nampy·th[G], neptra·[G]; tra vëth[G]
**anyway** *adv* wàr neb cor, in neb câss
**apartment** *n* ranjy
**ape** *n* appa
**apologize** *v* dyharas
**apology** *n* dyharas
**app** *n* gweythres
**appalled** *adj* diegrys
**appalling** *adj* scruthus
**apparatus** *n* darbar
**apparently** *adv* dell hevel
**appear** *v* omdhysqwedhes
**appearance** *n* omdhysqwedhyans; semlant
**appendix** *n* stagell; pedn an colodhyon
**appetite** *n* ewl [boos]
**appetizing** *adj* dâ y vlas
**applaud** *v* plaudya
**apple** *n* aval
**application** *n* govynadow
**apply** *v* gorra; gorra dhe wil; ombrofya
**apply for** *phr* govyn
**appointment** *n* poyntyans
make an **appointment** *phr* settya prës
**appreciate** *v* gwerthveurhe·
**apprentice** *n* prentys
**approach** *v* nes'he·

**appropriate** *adj* desedhus
**appropriately** *adv* ma·nerlych
**approval** *n* comendyans
**approve** *v* comendya
**approximate** *adj* ogas lowr
**approximately** *adv* ogas lowr, aderdro
**apricots** *n* bryketh
**April** *n* mis Ebrel
**apron** *n* apron
**aquarium** *n* pyskva
**Aquarius** *n* An Dowror
**arbitrarily** *adv* herwyth sians
**arbitrary** *adj* herwyth sians
**arch** *n* gwarak
**arch-** *pref* argh-[1]
**architect** *n* penser
**archive** *n* covscrevva
**ardent** *n* gwresak
**ardour** *n* gwres
**argue** *v* argya
**argument** *n* a·rgùment
**Aries** *n* An Hordh
**arithmetic** *n* arsmetryk
**arm** *n* bregh
**arm** *v* arva
**armchair** *n* chair brehek
**arms** *n* devregh
**army** *n* lu
**aroma** *n* sa·woren
**around** *adv* adro·, aderdro
**around** *prep* adro· dhe[2]
all **around** *prep* in kerhyn
**arouse** *v* sordya
**arrange** *v* araya; restry
**arrangement** *n* ara·y; rester

**arrest** *n* dalhen
**arrest** *v* dalhedna
**arrival** *n* devedhyans
**arrive** *v* dos; drehedhes
**arrogance** *n* gooth
**arrogant** *adj* gothys
**arrow** *n* seth
**arse** *n* tin
**art** *n* art
**artery** *n* goth vrâs
**arthritis** *n* fakel mellow
**article** *n* artykyl
**articulated** *adj* kevelsys
**artificial** *adj* creftus
**as** *conj* dell² [G]; ha[G]
**as** *prep* ave·ll[G]; in[G]
[just] **as if** *conj* kepa·r ha pàn² [G]
**ascend** *v* ascendya
be **ashamed** *phr* *meth, kemeres meth
**ash[es]** *n* lusow
**ask** *v* govyn
**ask for** *phr* govyn
**aspect** *n* tremyn
**asphalt** *n* asfalt
**assassinate** *v* moldra
**assault** *n* assaultyans
**assault** *v* assaultya
**assemble** *v* kescorra; omgùntell
**assembly** *n* cùntellva
**assert** *v* declarya
**assertion** *n* declaryans
**assess** *v* arvrusy
**assessment** *n* arvrusyans

**assets** *n* pethow
**assist** *v* gweres
**assistance** *n* gweres
**assistant** *n* darbaror
**association** *n* cowethas
**assume** *v* desevos
**assumption** *n* desef
**assurance** *n* afydhyans
**assure** *v* afydhya
**astride** *prep* gaulak wàr²
**astute** *adj* sley
**astuteness** *n* sleyneth
**at** *prep* in[G]; orth[G]; dhe[G]
**athlete** *n* athlet
**atmosphere** *n* airgelgh
**atom** *n* atom
**atomic** *adj* sprusek
**atrocious** *adj* outrayus
**atrocity** *n* outra·y
**attach** *v* staga
**attachment** *n* stagell
**attack** *n* omsettyans; assaultyans; shôra
**attack** *v* omsettya; assaultya; arveth
**attacker** *n* arvedhyth
**attain** *v* drehedhes
**attempt** *n* assa·y, atte·nt
**attempt** *v* assaya
**attend** *v* bos in, mos dhe²
pay **attention** *phr* attendya
**attic** *n* talyk
**attire** *n* gwysk
**attitude** *n* cowntnans
**attract** *v* tedna, dynya
**attributes** *n* teythy

**auction** *n* strîfwerth
**audacious** *adj* hardh
**audio-video** *adj* cloweles
**August** *n* mis Est
**aunt** *n* modryp
under the **auspices of** *phr* in dadn scoos
**austerity** *n* aspe·ryta
**authentic** *adj* gwir
**authenticate** *v* warrantya
**author** *n* auctour
**authority** *n* aucto·ryta
**autumn** *n* kydnyaf
**available** *adj* dhe gafos

**avalanche** *n* erghslynk
**avenue** *n* rosva
**average** *adj/n* cresek
**avoid** *v* goheles
**awake** *adj* dyfu·n
**award** *n* pewas
**aware** *adj* war
**away** *adv* in kerdh / in kergh; dhe ves
**awful** *adj* dyvla·s, dysawor
**awkward squad** *n* bagas tyckly
**axe** *n* bool
**axis** / **axle** *n* ehel

# B

**babble** *v* clattra
**baby** *n* baby
**babysitter** *n* floghgovior
**back** *adv* tre
**back** *n* tu warle·rgh; kil; keyn
at the **back** *phr* dhele·rgh
**back again** *phr* arta
**background** *n* kilva
**backpack** *n* keynsagh
**backpacker** *n* keynsaghyor
**backslash** *n* lash wàr dhele·rgh
**backwards** *adv* wàr dhele·rgh
**bacon** *n* backen
**bacteria** *n* bacterya
**bad** *adj* drog; poos
**badge** *n* arwedhyk
**badger** *n* brogh
**bag** *n* sagh
**baggage** *n* fardellow

**bagpipes** *n* pibow sagh
**bail** *n* meugh
**bait** *n* trustrùm
**bake** *v* pobas
**balance** *n* omborth
**balance** *v* kesposa; omberthy
**balcony** *n* balcon
**bald** *adj* mol
**bale** *n* pùsorn
**ball** *n* pel; pellen
on the **ball** *phr* lybm y skians
**balloon** *n* balou·n
**ban** *n/v* dyfen
**banana** *n* banâna
**band** *n* menestrouthy
**bandage** *n* lysten
**bandage** *v* lystedna
**bang** *n* bobm, cronk
**bang** *v* cronkya
with a **bang** *phr* sqwat

**bank** *n* arhanty; gladn
**banknote** *n* banknôta
**banner** *n* baner
**banquet** *n* banket
**baptism** *n* besyth
**Baptist** *n* Baptyst
**baptize** *v* besydhya
**bar** *n* barr; predn
**bar** *v* barya; predna
**barbecue** *n* ba·rbecû
**barber** *n* barbour
**bard** *n* bardh
Grand **Bard** *n* Bardh Meur
**bare** *adj* noth; lobm; mol
**bargain** *n* bargen
**bargain** *v* bargednya
a **bargain** *phr* a varhas dhâ
**barista** *n* barryth
**bark** *n* rusk
**bark** *v* hardha
**bark[ing]** *n* hardhva
**barley** *n* barlys
**barman** *n* barryth
**barn** *n* skyber
**barrel** *n* balyer
**barren** *adj* dyfeyth, sëgh
**barrier** *n* baryas
**barrister** *n* dadhlor
**base** *n* sol
**base** *v* grôndya
**basement** *n* selder
**basic** *adj* selvenek
**basin** *n* bason
**basis** *n* selven
**basket** *n* canstel; cowel; costen

**bat** *n* eskelly grehen
**bathe** *v* badhya
**bathroom** *n* golghva
in **batter** *phr* ha kestew in y gerhyn
**battery** *n* batry
**battle** *n* batel
**battle** *v* batalyas
**bay** *n* bay; cabmas; kil
**be** *v* bos
**beach** *n* treth
**beak** *n* gelvyn
**beam** *n* keber; dewyn
**beans** *n* fav
baked **beans** *n* fav pebys
**bear** *n* ors
**beard** *n* barv
**beat** *n* pols
**beat** *v* gweskel; overcùmya
**beautiful** *adj* teg
**beauty** *n* tecter
**because [of]** *phr* dre rêson, drefen; awo·s
**bed** *n* gwely
**bedroom** *n* chambour
**bedsheet** *n* lien gwely
**beef** *n* [kig] bowyn
**beer** *n* coref
**beer mat** *n* straylyk
**beer mug** *n* jorryk
**bees** *n* gwenyn
**beetle** *n* whyl
**beetroot** *n* betys rudh
**befall** *n* codha
**before** *prep* kyns; kyns ès; dhyra·g[G]

**begin** *v* dallath
**beginner** *n* dalathor
**beginning** *n* dallath
on **behalf of** *phr* aba·rth [dhe²]
**behave** *v* omdho·n
**behaviour** *n* omdho·n
**behind** *prep* adrë·v [dhe²]; warle·rgh<sup>G</sup>
**belief** *n* crejyans
**believe** *v* crejy
**bell** *n* clogh
**belly** *n* torr
**belong** *v* longya
**belt** *n* grugys
**bench** *n* scavel, form
**bend** *n* pleg
**bend** *v* plegya; stubma; crobma
**beneath** *prep* in dadn² <sup>G</sup>
**benefit** *n* prow
on **benefits** *phr* ow kemeres pêmons socyal
**bent** *adj* crobm
**berries** *n* greun
**beside** *prep* ryb<sup>G</sup>
**besiege** *v* kerhydna
the **best** *adj* an gwelha
**best regards** *phr* gans gorhemydnow / gor[he]mynadow a'n gwelha
**bet** *n* gwystel
**bet** *v* gwystla
**betray** *v* traita
**better** *adj* gwell
get **better** *v* gwellhe·
**between** *prep* inter<sup>G</sup>

**bewilder** *v* sowthanas
**bewilderment** *n* sowthan
**beyond** *prep* in hans dhe²
**bias** *n* leder
**bib** *n* bronlen
**bicycle** *n* dewros, margh horn
**bid** *n* profyans
**bid** *v* gorhebmyn; profya
**bidding** *n* gorhebmyn
**big** *adj* brâs
The **Big Bang** *phr* An Bobm Brâs
**biker** *n* jyn-dewrosyas
**bikini** *n* bykîny
**bilberries** *n* lus
**bilingual** *adj* dewyethek
**bill** *n* scot
**billionaire** *n* bylyonê·r
**bin** *n* argh
**bind** *v* kelmy
**binoculars** *n* dewweder
**biodegradable** *adj* podradow
**biological** *adj* biologyl
**bird** *n* edhen
**biro** *n* pluven belvleyn
**birth** *n* genesygeth
give **birth to** *phr* denethy
**birthday** *n* pedn bloodh
**biscuit** *n* byskyt; tesen gales
**bisexual** *adj* dewreydhek
**bishop** *n* epscop
**bit** *n* tabm, darn
**bite** *v* dynsel; brathy
**bitter** *adj* wherow
**bitterness** *n* wherowder
**black** *adj* du

**black out** *phr* clamdera
**black pudding** *n* gosogen
**blackberries** *n* mor du
**blackbird** *n* molgh dhu
**blackcurrant** *n* corynt du
**blackmail** *n* godrosladrans
**blackout** *n* clamder
**bladder** *n* gùsygen
**blade** *n* laun
**blame** *n* blam
**blame** *v* blâmya
to **blame** *phr* dhe vlâmya
**blasphemy** *n* bla·sfemy
**blaze** *n* tansys
**bleat** *v* brîvya
**bleed** *v* dyvera goos
**blemish** *n* nàm
**blend** *n* kemysk
**blend** *v* kemysky
**bless** *v* benega
**blessing** *n* bednath
**blind** *adj* dall
**blind** *n* ledn dewl
**blind** *v* dallhe·
**blind people** *n* dellyon
**blister** *n* gùsygen
**blizzard** *n* teweth ergh
**block** *n* stock
**block** *v* lettya
**block [up]** *phr* stoppya
**blog** *n* blòg
**blogger** *n* bloggyor
**blond** *adj* melen y vlew
**blonde** *n* meleganes
**blood** *n* goos
**blossom** *n* flourys gwëdh

**blouse** *n* cris
**blow** *n* bobmen, strocas, sqwat
**blow** *v* whetha; herdhya
**blue** *adj* glas; blou
**blues** *n* hireth
**bluebell** *n* blejen an gùcû
**blueberries** *n* lus
**blunt** *adj* sogh
**blurred** *adj* dyscle·r
**blush** *v* rudhya
wild **boar** *n* torgh coos
**board** *n* astell, bord; kesva
**boast** *n* bost
**boast** *v* bôstya
**boat** *n* scath
**body** *n* corf
**bog** *n* kenegen
**boil** *v* bryjyon
**boiler** *n* caudarn
**bold** *adj* hardh
**boldness** *n* bolder
**bolt** *v* predna
**bomb** *n* tanbellen
**bomb** *v* tanbeledna
**bond** *n* colm
**bone** *n* ascorn
**bonfire** *n* tansys
**book** *n* lyver
**book** *v* ragerhy
**booklet** *n* lyvryk
**boost** *v* kenertha
**boot** *n* trog
**booth** *n* scovva
toll **booth** *n* tollva
**boots** *n* botas

**border** *n* or
**bore** *v* sqwitha
**bored** *adj* sqwith
**boring** *adj* sqwithus
be **born** *phr* bos genys
**borrow** *v* benthygya; kemeres in prest
**both ... and** *conj* ha ... ha$^G$, kefrë·s ... ha$^G$
**bother** *n* trobel
**bother** *v* trobla
**bottle** *n* botel
**bottle bank** *n* bank botel
**bottom** *n* goles; tin
at the **bottom** *phr* awoles
**boundary** *n* cûr
**bouquet** *n* tysk flourys
**bout** *n* torn
**bow** *n* gwarak; colm
**bow tie** *n* colmen bleg
**bowels** *n* colodhyon
**bowl** *n* bolla; scala
**box** *n* box
**box** *v* boxesy
**boy** *n* maw
**boyfriend** *n* caror
**bra** *n* brongolm
**brace** *n* stroth
**bracelet** *n* modrewy
**bracken** *n* reden
**brain(s)** *n* empydnyon
**brake** *n* frodnel
**brake** *v* frodna
**brambles** *n* dreys
**branches** *n* scorr
**brand** *n* merk

**brand new** *adj* nowyth flàm
**brandy** *n* dowr tobm
**brass** *n* brest
**brave** *adj* colodnek
**bravery** *n* colonecter
**breach** *n* torrva
**bread** *n* bara
in **breadcrumbs** *phr* ha browsyon in y gerhyn
**breadth** *n* les
**break** *n* torrva
**break** *v* terry, sqwattya
**breakfast** *n* haunsel
**breast** *n* brodn
**breastfeed** *v* ry brodn dhe$^2$
**breath** *n* anal
**breathe** *v* anella
**breed** *v* maga
**Breton** *n* Bretonek
**Brexit** *n* Brexyt
**brick** *n* bryck
**bridge** *n* pons
**bridle** *n* frodn
**bridle** *v* frodna
**brief** *adj* cot
**briefcase** *n* trog dogvednow
**bright** *adj* spladn
**brightness** *n* splander
**brilliance** *n* splander
**brilliant** *adj* spladn
**brim** *adj* min
**bring** *v* dry; hedhes
**bring near[er]** *phr* nes'he·
**bring up** *phr* maga
**broad** *adj* ledan
**broadband** *n* tres ledan

**broaden** *v* ledanhe·
**brochure** *n* lyvryk
**broccoli** *n* caulvlejen gales
**broken** *adj* trogh
**broker** *n* mainor
**bronze** *n* brons
**brooch** *n* brôcha
**brook** *n* gover
**broom** *n* scubel
**brother** *n* broder
**brow** *n* tâl
**brown** *adj* gell; gorm
**browse** *v* pory
**bruise** *n* brew
**bruise** *v* brewy
**brunette** *adj* tewl hy blew
**brush** *n* scubylen; pyncel
**brush** *v* scubya
**Brussels sprout** *n* caulygen
**bubble** *n* bothel
**bucket** *n* kelorn
**buckle** *n* bockyl
**bud** *n* egyn
**Buddha** *n* Bùdda
**Buddhism** *n* Bù·ddieth
**Buddhist** *n* Bùddyst
**budget** *n* bojet
**buffet** *n* bùffê·
**bug** *n* corbref; defowt
**build** *v* byldya
**builder** *n* bylder
**building** *n* chy
**bulb** *n* bollen
**bulbs** *n* crenwrë·dh

**bulge** *n* bothan
**bull** *n* tarow
**bullet** *n* bùlet
**bulletin** *n* bùltyn
**bully** *n* bùlly
**bully** *v* bùllya
**bump** *n* bonk
**bun** *n* torthen
**bundle** *n* pùsorn
**bungle** *v* camwonys
**burger** *n* borger
**burial** *n* encledhyas
**burn** *v* lesky
**burrow** *v* turya
**burst** *n* tardh
**burst** *v* tardha
**bury** *v* encledhyas
**bus** *n* kyttryn
**bus station** *n* gorsaf bùs
**bus stop** *n* savla bùs
**bush** *n* bùsh
**business** *n* negys
**businesslike** *adj* dyfro·th
**busy** *adj* bysy
**but** *conj* saw[G]; mès[G]
**butter** *n* amanyn
**butterfly** *n* tycky-Duw
**buttock** *n* pedren
**button** *n* boton
**buy** *v* prena
**buyer** *n* prenor
**by** *prep* gans[G]; dre² [G]; warby·dn[G]; er
**by-election** *n* is-dewysyans
**byte** *n* beyt

# C

**cabbage** *n* cavach
**cabin** *n* cabyn
**cabin crew** *n* meyny cabyn
**cabinet** *n* ca·bynet
**cable** *n* capel
**cactus** *n* cactùs
**café** *n* co·ffyva
**cage** *n* bagh; cowel
**cairn** *n* carn
**cake** *n* tesen
**calculate** *v* rekna
**calculation** *n* recken, reknans
**calculator** *n* reknel
**calendar** *n* dedhyador
**call** *n* galow; cry; garm
**call** *v* gelwel
**callus** *n* calesen
**calm** *adj* cosolek
**calm** *n* cosoleth
**calm** *v* coselhe·
**calque** *n* omhevellyans
**camel** *n* cowrvargh
**camera** *n* ca·mera
**camp** *n* camp
**camp** *v* campya
**campaign** *n* caskergh
**camper** *n* havyas campya
**camper van** *n* carven campya
**campsite** *n* campva
**campus** *n* campùs
**can** *n* cafas, cadna
**can** *v* gallos
**canal** *n* dowrgleth
**cancel** *v* dylea

**cancer** *n* canker
**Cancer** *n* An Canker
**candidate** *n* ombrofyor
**candle** *n* cantol
**cannabis** *n* kewarhen
**cap** *n* cappa
**capable** *adj* abyl
**capital** *n* pedn-cyta; kevalaf
**capitalism** *n* kevalavo·rieth
**capricious** *adj* siansus
**Capricorn** *n* An Avar
**capsule** *n* bolhen
**captain** *n* capten
**car** *n* carr [tan]
**car boot sale** *n* basa·r trog
**car park** *n* park kerry
**caramel** *n* ca·ramel
**caravan** *n* ca·ravan
**caravan site** *n* park ca·ravan
**card** *n* carten
**cardboard** *n* pasbord
**cardigan** *n* ca·rdygon
**care** *n* gwith; cur; rach; preder
he doesn't **care** *phr* ny'n deur
**care about** *phr* *bern
**care for** *phr* cherya
take **care** *phr* gorra gwith; kemeres with
**career** *n* resegva
**careful** *adj* war; dour
**carefully** *adv* dour
**care[fulness]** *n* dour
**careless** *adj* lows
**carer** *n* gwethyas

**cares** *n* govyjyon
**caress** *v* chersya
**carnation** *n* jy·lofer
**carnival** *n* ca·rnyval
**carousel** *n* res adro·
**carpenter** *n* ser predn
**carpet** *n* leurlen
**carriage** *n* caryach
**carrots** *n* caretys
**carry** *v* don
**cart** *n* kert
**carve** *v* kervya
**case** *n* trog; câss
in any **case** *phr* in neb câss, wàr neb cor
in **case** *phr* [rag] dowt[G]
in that **case** *phr* dhana, mars yw taclow indelma
**cash** *n* mona parys
**cassette** *n* snod clos
**castle** *n* castel
**cat** *n* cath
**catalogue** *n* ca·talog
**cataract** *n* kednen
**catastrophe** *n* meschau·ns
**catch** *v* cachya
**catch sight of** *phr* aspia
**catch up with** *phr* cachya
**category** *n* class
**caterpillar** *n* prëv del
**cathedral** *n* peneglos
**Catholic** *adj/n* Catholyk
**cattle** *n* gwarthek
**cauliflower** *n* caulvlejen
**cause** *n* ken; skyla
**cause** *v* causya

**caution** *n* rach
**cautious** *adj* war
**cave** *n* cav
**cavity** *n* cow
**CCTV camera** *n* ca·mera clos kelgh
**cease** *v* cessya
**ceasefire** *n* cessyans tedna
**ceiling** *n* nèn
**celebrate** *v* golya; solempnya
**cell** *n* kell; gogell
**cellar** *n* selder
**Celt** *n* Kelt
**Celtic** *adj* Keltek
**cement** *n* cyment
**cemetary** *n* encladhva
**centi-** *pref* centy-[1]
**central heating** *n* gwres cresednek
**centre** *n* cresen
**century** *n* cansvledhen
**cereal** *n* greunvos
**ceremony** *n* sole·mpnyta
**certain** *adj* certan
**certificate** *n* testscrif
**certify** *v* desta
**chain** *n* chain; delk
**chair** *n* chair
**chair** *v* caderya
**chairman** *n* caderyor
**chalk** *n* calhen
**challenge** *v* defia; chalynjya
**chamber** *n* chambour
**champion** *n* campyor
**championship** *n* campyorsys
**chance** *n* chauns

by **chance** *phr* dre hap
**change** *n* chaunj
**change** *v* chaunjya
**channel** *n* canel
**chaos** *n* dera·y
**chap** *n* gwas
**chapel** *n* chapel
**chapter** *n* chaptra
**character** *n* gnas; nas; arweth
**characteristic** *n* nosweth
**charcoal** *n* glow predn
**charge** *n* carg; govyn
**charge** *v* carga; govyn
**charger** *n* cargor
**charitable gift** *n* alusen
**charity** *n* che·ryta
**charm** *n* gorhan
**charm** *v* gorhana
**charming** *adj* gorhanus
**chase** *v* chacya
**chat** *v* clappya
**chatter** *v* clattra
**cheap** *adj* iselbrîs
**cheat** *v* hyga
**check** *n* ardak; checker
**check** *v* checkya
**check in** *phr* omrôlya
**checkmate** *n* cowlardak
**checkout** *n* re·ckenva
**cheek** *n* bogh
**cheeky** *adj* taunt
**cheese** *n* keus
**chef** *n* kegynor
**chemical** *n* chemyk
**cheque** *n* checken
**cherries** *n* keres

**chess** *n* gwëdhboll
**chessboard** *n* checker
**chest** *n* brèst; cofyr
**chestnuts** *n* kesten
**chew** *v* dynsel
**chewing gum** *n* glus knias
**chicken** *n* kig yar
**chief** *adj* chif-[1]
**child** *n* flogh
**chill** *n* yeynder; anwos
**chilli** *n* chylly
**chimney** *n* chymbla
**chin** *n* elgeth
**china** *n* chêny
**china clay** *n* pry gwydn
**chip** *n* scobmyn
**chips** *n* asclas
**chocolate** *n* choclat
**choice** *adj* flour
**choice** *n* dêwys
**choir** *n* cur
**choke** *v* taga
**choking** *adj* tagus
**choose** *v* dêwys
**chop** *v* skethry
**chopstick** *n* gwelen debry
**chord** *n* cord
**chough** *n* palores
**Christian** *adj/n* Cristyon
**Christianity** *n* Cristyoneth
**christen** *v* besydhya
**christening** *n* besyth
**Christmas** *n* Nadelyk
**church** *n* eglos
**churchyard** *n* corflan
**cider** *n* cîder

**cigarette** *n* cygaryk
**cinema** *n* cy·nema
**circle** *n* kelgh; balcon
**circuit** *n* kelgh
**circular** *n* kelghlyther
**circulate** *v* mos adro·
**circumstance** *n* cy·rcùmstans
**circus** *n* cyrcùs
**citizen** *n* dinasyth
**citizenship** *n* dinasy·dhieth
**city** *n* cyta
**civil[ian]** *adj* dinasek
**civilization** *n* wharheans
**civilized** *adj* whar
**claim** *v* pretendya; goledna
**clamp** *n* stroth
**clamp** *v* strotha
**clan** *n* teylu
**clap** *v* tackya dewla
**clarify** *v* clerhe·
**class** *n* class; rencas
**classic** *adj/n* classyk
**classify** *v* classya
**clatter** *v* clattra
**claw** *n* ewyn; paw
**clay** *n* pry
**claypit** *n* poll pry
**clean** *adj* glân
**clean** *v* glanhe·
**clear** *adj* cler; ilyn
**clever** *adj* codnek
**click** *v* clyckya
**client** *n* client
**cliff** *n* âls
**climate** *n* aireth
**climb** *n* crambla

**climber** *n* cramblor
**cling** *v* glena
**clinic** *n* clynyk
**clip** *n* clyp
**cloak** *n* clôk
**cloakroom** *n* clôkva
**clock** *n* clock
**clockwise** *adv* gans an howl
**clog** *v* taga
**close** *adj* ogas
**close** *v* degea
**closed** *adj* degë·s
**cloth** *n* padn; lien; clowt
**clothes** *n* dyllas
**clotted cream** *n* dehen cowlys
**cloud** *n* cloud
**cloudy** *adj* comolek
**clover** *n* mùllyon
**club** *n* clùb
go out **clubbing** *phr* clùbba
**clubs** *n* mùllyon
**clumsy** *adj* cledhek
**coach** *n* caryach; côcha
**coal** *n* glow
**coast** *n* cost
**coaster** *n* straylyk
**coastguard** *n* gwethyas âlsyow
**coat** *n* côta; gwyscas
**coat** *v* kedna
**coat-hanger** *n* gwarak wysk
**coating** *n* kednen
**cock** *n* càl
**cock[erel]** *n* culyak
**cockpit** *n* cabyn lewyador
**cocktail** *n* cocktail

**cocoa** *n* côco
**coconuts** *n* know côco
**cod** *n* barvus
**code** *n* cod
**coffee** *n* coffy
**coffin** *n* geler
**cognate** *adj* unwos
**coin** *n* bath
**cola** *n* côla
**cold** *adj* yêyn
**cold** *n* yeynder; anwos
**coldness** *n* yeynder
**collaborate** *v* kesobery
**collar** *n* bond codna
**collect** *v* cùntell
**collection** *n* cùntellyans
**collective** *adj* cùntellek
**collective** *n* furv gùntellek
**college** *n* coljy
**collide with** *v* omdhehesy warby·dn
**colony** *n* trevesygeth
**colour** *n* colour
**column** *n* coloven
**coma** *n* clavhun
**comb** *n* crib
**comb** *v* cribya
**combination** *n* kesunyans
**combine** *v* kesunya
**come** *v* dos
**come and go** *phr* daromres
**come back** *phr* dewheles
**come near[er]** *phr* nes'he·
**comedian** *n* comedyan
**comedy** *n* co·medy
**comfort** *n* confort

**comfort** *v* confortya
**comfortable** *adj* attê·s
**comic** *adj* comek
**comic** *n* comyk
**command** *n* gorhebmyn
**command** *v* gorhebmyn, comondya
**comment** *n* campoll
**comment on** *v* campolla
**commentary** *n* menegyans resek
**commerce** *n* kenwerth
**commission** *n* comyssyon; ranles
**commissioner** *n* negesyth
**committee** *n* kessedhek; pollgor
**common** *adj* kemyn
**commonwealth** *n* kemeneth
**communicate** *v* kemenessa
**communion** *n* comùn
The **Communist Party** *n* Party an Gemynwer
**community** *n* kemeneth
**compact** *adj* compact
**compact disc** *n* platten gompact
**companion** *n* coweth
**companionship** *n* kescowetha
**company** *n* cowethas; kescowetha
**compare** *v* comparya
**compared with** *phr* adâ·l [dhe²]
**comparison** *n* comparyans

**compartment** *n* sensor
**compass** *n* compas
**compassion** *n* trueth
**compel** *v* constrîna
**compensate** *v* astevery
**compete** *v* kesstrîvya
**competent** *adj* abyl
**competition** *n* kesstrif
**competitor** *n* kesstrîvyor
**complain** *v* croffolas
**complaint** *n* croffal
**complement** *v* collenwel
**complete** *adj* dien; cowl-[2]
**complete** *v* cowlwil
**completely** *adv* glân; cowl-[2]
**complete** *v* collenwel
**complex** *adj* complek
**complicate** *v* completha
**complicated** *adj* completh
**complication** *n* complethter
**compose** *v* composya
**composer** *n* composyth
**compost** *n* teyl
**comprehensive** *adj* compassus
**compromise** *n* kesassoylyans
**compulsory** *adj* constrînus
**computer** *n* amowntyor
**comrade** *n* coweth
**conceal** *v* keles
**conceive** *v* concêvya
**concentrate** *v* kescruny
**concentrate on** *phr* sensy in y breder
**concept** *n* conce·yt
**concern** *n* bern

**concerned** *adj* meur y vern
**concerning** *prep* adro· dhe[2]; in kever; [ow] tùchya
**concert** *n* gool ilow
**concise** *adj* in nebes geryow
**concisely** *adv* in nebes geryow
**conclude** *v* ervira
**conclusion** *n* ervirans
**conclusive** *adj* ervirus
**concrete** *n* concrît
**condemn** *v* dampnya
**condemnation** *n* dampnacyon
**condensation** *n* glûth
**condition** *n* ambos; plit, studh
**conditional** *adj* ambosek
**conditioner** *n* ewnyas
**condom** *n* condom
**conduct** *n* fara
**conductor** *n* gwethyas train
**cone** *n* pykern
**confederation** *n* kefrysyans
**conference** *n* kescùssulyans
**confess** *v* confessya
**confession** *n* confessyon
**confide in** *phr* kyfy dhe[2]
**confidence** *n* omfydhyans
**confidential** *adj* pryva
**confirm** *v* afydhya
**confirmation** *n* afydhyans
**confuse** *v* kemysky; ancombra
**confusing** *adj* ancombrus
**confusion** *n* ancombrynjy
**congratulate** *v* keslowenhe·
**congregation** *n* cùntellva

**congress** *n* cùntelles
**conjunction** *n* kevren
**connect** *v* jùnya
**connected** *adj* kelmys ganso
**conscience** *n* keskians
**consent** *n* assentyans, conse·nt
**consent** *v* assentya
**consequence** *n* sewyans
**conservative** *n* conservegor
The **Conservative Party** *n* Party an Gonservegoryon
**consider** *v* kemeres preder a²
**considerable** *adj* mynsek
**consist of** *phr* consystya a²
**consistent** *adj* kesson
**consolation** *n* confort
**console** *v* confortya
**conspiracy** *n* bras
**constant** *adj* heb hedhy
**constantly** *adv* heb hedhy
**constituency** *n* dêwys-qwartron
**constitution** *n* corflaha
**construct** *v* drehevel
**consult** *v* omgùssulya
**consumer** *n* consûmyor
**contact** *n* kestaf
**contact** *v* omdava gans
**contactless payment** *phr* tylly heb tùchya
**contain** *v* sensy
**container** *n* cafas; sensor
**contaminate** *v* mostya
**contemporary** *adj/n* kevosek
**content** *adj* pës dâ

**contents** *n* contens
**contentious** *adj* cavylek
**continent** *n* brastir
**contingent** *adj* serhak
**continuation** *n* pêsyans
**continue** *v* pêsya
**contraceptive** *n* andenythek
**contract** *n* kevambos
**contrary** *adj* contrary
on the **contrary** *phr* dhe'n contrary, i'n contrary part
**contribute** *v* darbary shara
**contribution** *n* shara
**control** *n* rewl
**control** *v* controllya
**controversial** *adj* dadhlak
**convenient** *adj* vas
**conversation** *n* kescows
have a **conversation** *phr* kescôwsel
**convict** *v* convyctya
**cook** *v* kegy
**cooking** *n* kegy·nieth
**cool** *v* mygla
**co-operate** *v* kesobery
**co-ordinate** *v* kestrevna
**co-ordinated** *adj* kestrevnek
**cope** *v* omweres
**copper** *n* coper
**copy** *n* copy
**copy** *v* copia
**copyright** *n* gwir pryntya
**core** *n* colonen
**cork** *n* corkyn
**corkscrew** *n* alwheth corkyn
**corn** *n* calesen

**corner** *n* cornel
**Cornish** *n* Kernowek
**Cornishman** *n* Kernow
**Cornwall Council** *n* Consel Kernow
**correct** *adj* ewn
**correct** *v* êwna
**correction** *n* ewnans
**correspond** *v* kesscrefa; gortheby
**corridor** *n* tremenva
**corrupt** *adj* pedrys
**corrupt** *v* pedry
**corruption** *n* poder
**cosmetic** *n* afinuster
**cosmos** *n* cosmos
**cost** *n* còst
**cost** *v* costya
**costume** *n* gwysk
**cosy** *adj* cles
**cottage** *n* crowjy
**cotton** *n* coton
**cotton wool** *n* gwlân coton
**couch** *n* gwely dëdh
**cough** *n* pas
**cough** *v* pasa
**council** *n* consel
**count** *v* comptya; nyvera
**counter-** *pref* gorth-[2]
**country** *n* pow; bro; gwlas
**countryside** *n* powdir
**couple** *n* copel
**coupling** *n* kevren
**coupon** *n* colpon
**courgette** *n* pompyonyk gwer
**course** *n* cors; sant

of **course** *phr* heb mar [na martesen]
**court** *n* cort
**courteous** *adj* cortes
**courtesy** *n* cortesy
**courtyard** *n* cort; cauns
**cousin** *n* ke·nderow; keny·therow
**cove** *n* porth
**cover** *n* cudhlen; gorher
**cover** *v* cudha
**covert** *adj* cudh
**cow** *n* buwgh
**coward** *n* coward
**cowardly** *adj* coward
**crab** *n* canker
**crack** *n* crig
**cracked** *adj* trogh
**cradle** *n* lesk
**craft** *n* creft
**craftsman** *n* creftor
**cram** *v* stoffya
**cramp** *n* godra·bm
**cranberries** *n* lus rudh
**crane** *n* garan
**crash** *v* codha in dyfyk
with a **crash** *phr* sqwat
**crash barrier** *n* scoske
**crate** *n* cloos
**crawl** *v* cramyas
**creak** *v* gwîhal
**cream** *n* dehen
**create** *v* formya
**creative** *adj* awenek
**creativity** *n* awen
**crèche** *n* meythrynva

**credit** *n* crejys
**credit card** *n* carten crejys
**creepy-crawly** *n* prëv
**crematorium** *n* corfloskva
**crew** *n* felshyp
**cricket** *n* crycket
**crime** *n* drogober; trespasseth
**criminal** *n* drogoberor
**crinkled** *adj* crigh
**cripple** *v* evredhy
**crisis** *n* terstuth
**crisp** *n* cresyk
**critical** *adj* cablek
**criticism** *n* cabel
**criticize** *v* cably
**croak** *n* ronk
**croak** *v* renky
**crocodile** *n* cro·codyl
**crooked** *adj* cabm
**crop** *n* trevas
**cross** *n* crows
**cross** *adj* crowsek
**cross-bar** *n* trester
**crossed** *adj* crowsek
**crossing** *n* treusva
**crossroads** *n* peswar torn
**crossword** *n* crowseryow
**crouch** *v* plattya
**crow** *n* bran
**crowd** *n* rûth
**crown** *n* cùrun
**crown** *v* cùruna
**crude** *adj* criv
**cruel** *adj* cruel
**cruise** *n* corsyans
**crumbs** *n* browsyon

**crumpets** *n* crampeth tellek
**crumple** *v* crobma
**crumpled** *adj* crobm
**crush** *v* brewy
**crust** *n* cresten
**crutch** *n* croch
**cry** *n* cry; garm
**cry** *v* cria; ola
**cube** *n* cûb
**cubicle** *n* stalla
**cuckoo** *n* cùcû
**cucumber** *n* cû·cùmber
**cue** *n* gwelen
**cuisine** *n* kegy·nieth
**cull** *n* ladhva
**cult** *n* cùlt
**culture** *n* gonysegeth
**cultivate** *v* gonys
**cunning** *adj* sotel
**cunning** *n* sotelneth
**cunt** *n* cons
**cup** *n* hanaf
**cupboard** *n* a·mary
**curb** *v* frodna
**cure** *v* yaghhe·
**curious** *adj* coynt; whensys dhe wodhvos
**curly** *adj* crùllys
**currency** *n* mona
**current** *adj* kesres
**current** *n* fros
**curriculum vitae** *n* resegva bêwnans
**curry** *n* cùrry
**curtain** *n* croglen
**curve** *n* stubm

**curve** *v* stubma
**cushion** *n* pluvak
**custard** *n* cùstard
**custody** *n* gwith
**custom** *n* ûsadow
**customer** *n* cosmer
**customs** *n* tollva
**cut** *n* trogh; torrva

## D

**Dad[dy]** *n* Tasyk
**daffodils** *n* lyly Corawys
**daisy** *n* caja
**damage** *n* damach
**damage** *v* shyndya
**damn** *v* dampnya
**damnation** *n* dampnacyon
be **damned if** *phr* ny + *verb* malbew dàm
**damp** *adj* leyth
**damp** *n* glebor
**dampness** *n* leythter
**dance** *n* dauns; gwary dauns
**dance** *v* dauncya
**dancer** *n* dauncyor
**danger** *n* peryl
**dangerous** *adj* peryllys
**dare** *v* lavasos
**dark** *adj* tewl
**dark** *n* te·wolgow
**darken** *v* tewlhe·
**darkness** *n* tewlder; te·wolgow
**darling** *n* whegen; whegyn
**dart** *n* dart
**dartboard** *n* astell dartys

**cut** *v* trehy
**cutlery** *n* daffar lybm
**cyber-** *pref* cyber-[1]
**cycle** *n* kelghres
**cycle** *v* dewrosa
**cyclist** *n* dewrosyas
**cylinder** *n* cy·lynder
**cynical** *adj* cy·nycus

**dash** *v* stêvya
**date** *n* dedhyans
**daughter** *n* myrgh
**dawn** *n* terry an jëdh
**day** *n* dëdh; jorna; gool
**dazzle** *v* dallhe·
**dead** *adj* marow
**deadline** *n* termyn keas
**deaf** *adj* bodhar
**deafening** *adj* bodharus
**deal with** *phr* dyghtya
**dealer** *n* gwycor
**dear** *adj* ker; wheg
**death** *n* mernans
**debate** *n* dadhel
**debate** *v* dadhla
**debit card** *n* carten debys
**debt** *n* kendon
**decay** *n* podrethes
**decayed** *adj* podrek
**deceit** *n* tùll
**deceive** *v* tùlla
**December** *n* mis Kevardhu
**decent** *adj* onest
**decide [to]** *v* ervira
**deciduous** *adj* del-codha

**decision** *n* ervirans
**decisive** *adj* ervirus
**deck** *n* flûr
**deck chair** *n* chair howl
**declaration** *n* derivadow, declaryans
**declare** *v* declarya
**decline** *n* dyfygyans
**decline** *v* dyfygya
**decorate** *v* afîna
**decoration** *n* afinuster
**dedicate** *v* profya
**deed** *n* ober
**deeds** *n* gwrith
**deep** *adj* down
**deer** *n* carow
roe-**deer** *n* yorgh
**default** *n* defowt
**defeat** *v* fetha
**defect** *n* defowt
**defence** *n* dyffresyans
**defend** *v* dyffres
**defender** *n* dyffresyans
**defibrillator** *n* dyfybrellyor
**deficit** *n* dyfyk
**define** *v* defynya
**definite** *adj* dybla·ns
**definition** *n* defynyans
**definitive** *adj* diambos
**degree** *n* degre·; pryck; gradh
**delay** *n* strech, ardak
**delay** *v* strechya
**delayed** *adj* dylâtys
**delegate** *n* cadnas
**delegate** *v* canasa
**delegation** *n* canaseth

**delete** *v* dylea
**delicacy** *n* bludhecter; tabm dainty
**delicate** *adj* bludh; dainty; tyckly
**delight** *n* delî·t
**delight** *v* delîtya
**delineate** *v* delynya
**delirious** *adj* varies gans fevyr
**deliver** *v* delyvra
**delivery** *n* lyfrêson
**dell** *n* pans
**demand** *n* demo·nd
**demand** *v* demondya
**democracy** *n* democra·tieth
**democratic** *adj* democratek
**demolish** *v* dyswil
**denial** *n* nagh
**dense** *adj* tew
**dentist** *n* densyth
**deny** *v* naha
**deodorant** *n* dyfleryas
**depart** *v* dybe·rth, avoydya
**department** *n* asran
**departure** *n* dyba·rth
**depend on** *phr* cregy / powes wàr[2]
**dependant** *n* serhak
**dependent** *adj* serhak
**deploy** *v* dysplêtya
**deployment** *n* dysplêtyans
**deposit** *v* gorra in arhow
**depraved** *adj* podrek
**depress** *v* dyglodny
**depressed** *adj* dyglon
**depression** *n* cleves dyglon

**depth** *n* downder
**derogatory** *adj* cablek
**descend** *v* skydnya
**desert** *n* dyfeyth
**deserve** *v* dendyl
**design** *n* desî·n
**design** *v* desîna
**desire** *n* whans
**desire** *v* desîrya
**desk** *n* dèsk
**despair** *n* dyspê·r
**despise** *v* despîsya
**despite** *prep* in spit [dhe²] / in despî·t [dhe²]; awo·s
**dessert** *n* sant melys
**destination** *n* pedn an hens
**destine** *v* destna
**destiny** *n* destnans
**destroy** *v* dystrôwy
**detach** *v* dystaga
**details** *n* manylyon
**detain** *v* sensy
**deteriorate** *v* gwetha
be **determined to** *v* bos determys dhe²
**develop** *v* dysplegya
**development** *n* dysplegyans
**device** *n* darbar
**devil** *n* dyowl
**devote oneself** *phr* omry
**dew** *n* glûth
**diabetes** *n* cleves melys
**dialogue** *n* dialog
**diamond** *n* a·damant; dyamont
**diarrhoea** *n* skit

**diary** *n* dedhlyver
**dictate** *v* dythya
**dictionary** *n* gerlyver
**die** *n* dis
**die** *v* merwel *See also* marow
**diet** *n* rewl boos
**differ** *v* dyffra
**difference** *n* dyffrans
**different** *adj* dyhaval; dyffrans
**difficult** *adj* cales
**difficulty** *n* caletter
**dig** *v* palas
**digest** *v* gôy
**digital** *adj* rivednek
**digital versatile disc** (**DVD**) *n* platten [rivednek] liesdefnyth
**diligence** *n* dywysygneth
**diligent** *adj* dywysyk
**dim** *adj* gwadn
**dim** *v* gwanhe·
**dimension** *n* dymensyon
**din** *n* hùbbadùllya
**dining room** *n* rom kydnyow
**dinner** *n* kydnyow
**dinosaur** *n* arghpedrevan
**dip** *n* dyppa
**dip** *v* dyppya
**direct** *adj* dydro·
**direct** *v* kevarwedha; rowtya
**direction** *n* keveryans *See also* qwartron in 'Numerals for Reference'
give **directions** *phr* brednya
**directive** *n* gidlînen
**directly** *adv* dhe blebmyk

**director** *n* kevarwedhor; rowtor
**dirt** *n* most
**dirty** *adj* plos
**disability** *n* dysaby·lyta
**disabled** *adj* dysabyl
**disabled access** *n* entrans rag dysabylyon
**disadvantage** *n* avles
**disagree** *v* dyssentya
**disagreement** *n* dysse·nt
**disappear** *v* mos a wel, vansya
**disappearance** *n* vansyans
**disappoint** *v* tùlla
**disapprove of** *phr* *cas
**disaster** *n* meschau·ns
**disbelief** *n* dyscryjyans
**discern** *v* decernya
**discharge** *v* dyscarga
**disconnect** *v* dygelmy
**discontent** *n* dysconte·nt
**discontented** *adj* drog-pës
**discontinue** *v* astel
**discount** *n* dyscownt
**discourage** *v* dyglodny
**discourteous** *adj* dyscortes
**discourtesy** *n* dysco·rtesy
**discover** *v* dyscudha, dyskevra
**discreet** *adj* doth
**discriminate against** *phr* dysfa·vera
**discrimination** *n* dysfa·verans
**discuss** *v* omgùssulya
**disease** *n* cleves

**disgraceful** *adj* methus
**disguise** *n* tùllwysk
**dish** *n* scudel
**dishonest** *adj* dysle·l
**dishonesty** *n* dyslelder
**disinfectant** *n* dyglevejyas
**dislike** *v* *cas, *drog
**disloyal** *adj* dysle·l
**disloyalty** *n* dyslelder
**dismantle** *v* dysstryppya
**disobedience** *n* dysobeyans
**disobedient** *adj* dywostyth
**disobey** *v* dysobeya
**disorder** *n* dera·y
**dispatch** *v* danvon
**dispel** *v* defendya
**dispenser** *n* spenser
**display** *n* dysplêtyans
**display** *v* dysplêtya
**disposable** *adj* towladow
**dispute** *n* dalva
**dissatisfaction** *n* dysconte·nt
**dissatisfied** *adj* drog-pës
**dissolve** *v* omdedha
**distance** *n* pellder
**distant** *adj* pell
**distinct** *adj* dybla·ns
**distinguish** *v* decernya
**distort** *v* cabma
**distract** *v* trailya adenewen
**distribute** *v* radna in mes
**district** *n* randir *See also* qwartron *in 'Numerals for Reference'*
**ditch** *n* cledh
**dive** *v* dîvya

**diverse** *adj* dyvers
**divide** *v* radna
**diving board** *n* astell dîvya
**divorce** *n* dydhemedhyans
get **divorced** *phr* dydhemedhy
**do** *v* gwil; dyghtya; servya
**do one's best** *phr*
gwil y welha
**do without** *phr* hepcor
**doctor** *n* doctour; medhek
**document** *n* do·cùment
**dodo** *n* dôdô
**dog** *n* ky
**doll** *n* popet
**dollar** *n* dollar
**dolphin** *n* pyffyor
**domino** *n* do·myno
**donkey** *n* asen
**door** *n* daras
**doping** *n* dôpyans
**dot** *n* dyjyn
**doubt** *n* dowt
**doubt** *v* dowtya
without **doubt** *phr* heb mar
[na martesen]
**dough** *n* toos
**doughnuts** *n* know toos
**douse** *v* ladha
**dove** *n* colom
**down** *adv* dhe'n dor, wàr nans
**downhearted** *adj* dyglon
**down[land]** *n* goon
**download** *n* is-carg
**download** *v* is-carga
**downstairs** *adv* awoles; an stairys wàr nans

**drag** *v* draggya; draylya
**dragon** *n* dragon
**drain** *n* dowrgleth
**drain[pipe]** *n* carthpîp
**drama** *n* drâma
**dramatic** *adj* dramatek
**drastically** *adv*
gans meur a gris
**draught** *n* wheth air
**draughts** *n* draghtys
**draw** *n* tedn
**draw** *v* tedna; delynya
**draw lots** *phr* tôwlel predn
**drawer** *n* trog tedna
**drawing** *n* delynyans
**dreadful** *adj* uthyk
**dream** *n* hunros
**dream** *v* hunrosa
**dress** *n* pows
**dress** *v* gwysca
**dressing room** *n* gwyskva
**drill** *n* tardar
**drill** *v* tardra
**drink** *n* dewas
**drink** *v* eva
**drip** *n* dyveren
**drip** *v* dyvera
**drive** *v* drîvya; lewyas
**drive away** *phr* fesya
**driver** *n* lewyor
**driveway** *n* rosva
**driving** *n* lewyans
**driving licence** *n* cubmyas lewyas
**driving test** *n* prov lewyas
**drizzle** *n* glûthglaw

**drones** *n* sùdron
**drop** *n* dyveren
**drop** *v* gasa dhe godha
**drown** *v* budhy
**drug** *n* drogga
**druid** *n* drewyth
**drum** *n* tabour
**drunk** *adj* medhow
**drunkenness** *n* medhowynjy
**dry** *adj* sëgh
**dry** *v* seha
**dry rot** *n* cùsk
**dual carriageway** *n* dewhens
**duchy** *n* dùcheth

# E

**each** *adj* pùb[G]
**each individual** *phr* pùb + *noun* a'y honen
**each [one]** *pron* kenyver[G]
be **eager to** *phr* \*màl
**eagle** *n* er
**ear** *n* scovarn
**early** *adj* ava·rr
**earn** *v* dendyl
**earnest** *adj* dywysyk
**earnestness** *n* dywysygneth
**earphones** *n* scovarnygow
**earthenware** *n* pry
**earthquake** *n* dorgris
**earthworms** *n* bùluk
**east** *adj/n* ÿst
**eastern** *adj* ÿst
**Easter** *n* Pask
**easy** *adj* êsy
**eat** *v* debry

**duck** *n* hos
**dump** *n* poll atal
**dune** *n* towan
**dunk** *v* troghya
**duration** *n* duryans
**during** *prep* dres[G]
**dusk** *n* tewlwolow
**dust** *n* doust
**duty** *n* devar
on / off **duty** *phr* wàr / dhywar dûta
**dwarf** *adj* cor-[2]
**dye** *v* lywa
**dynamic** *adj* dynamek

**echo** *v* dasson
**echo** *v* dasseny
**eclipse** *n* dyfyk
**economical** *adj* erbysus
**economist** *n* eco·nomyst
**economy** *n* eco·nomy
**edge** *n* amal; min
**edit** *v* golegy
**editor** *n* penscrefor
**educate** *v* gorra dhe dhyscans
**education** *n* adhyscans
**educational** *adj* adhyscansek
**eel** *n* sylly
**effect** *n* effeyth
**effective** *adj* effeythus
**effort** *n* strîvyans; ober
make every **effort** *phr* strîvya
**egg** *n* oy
**eisteddfod** *n* esedhvos
**either** *adv* nane·yl

**either ... or** *conj* pò ...pò<sup>G</sup>, bone·yl ... bò<sup>G</sup>
**elastic** *adj/n* elastek
**elbow** *n* elyn
**elect** *n* dêwys
**election** *n* dewysyans
**electric[al]** *adj* tredanek
**electricity** *n* tredan
**electronic** *adj* electronek
**elegance** *n* je·ntylys
**elegant** *adj* jentyl
**element** *n* elven
**elementary** *adj* elvednek
**elephant** *n* olyfans
**eliminate** *v* defendya
**else** *adj/adv* ken
**email** *n* ebost
be **embarrassed** *phr* *meth, kemeres meth
**embarrassment** *n* meth
**embassy** *n* canaseth
**embers** *n* lusow
**embrace** *n* byrlans
**embrace** *v* byrla
**embroider** *v* brosya
**embroidery** *n* brosweyth
**emergency** *n* gorothem
**emergency exit** *n* daras gorothem
**emigrate** *v* dyvroa
**emit** *v* dyllo
**emoji** *n* emôjy
**emotion** *n* muvyans
**emotional** *adj* muvyansek
**emperor** *n* emprour
**emphasis** *n* poslef

**emphasize** *v* posleva
**empire** *n* empîr
**employ** *v* arveth
**employee** *n* arvedhysak
**employer** *n* arvedhor
**employment** *n* arveth
**emptiness** *n* gwacter
**empty** *adj* gwag
**empty** *v* gwakhe·
**enamel** *n* ema·yl
**enchant** *v* gorhana
**enclosed** *adj* clos; gans hebma
**enclosure** *n* clos
**encounter** *v* dierbyna
**encourage** *v* ry colon dhe[2]; kenertha
**end** *n* pedn; dyweth
**end** *v* dewedha
in the **end** *phr* wortyweth
**endanger** *v* peryllya
**enemy** *n* escar; envy
**energetic** *adj* freth
**energy** *n* frethter; nerth
**enforce** *v* constrîna
**engage** *v* omgelmy
**engaged** *adj* bysy
**engine** *n* jyn
**engine house** *n* jynjy
**engineer** *n* injynor
**engineering** *n* injyno·rieth
**English** *n* Sowsnek
**enjoy** *v* enjoya
**enlarge** *v* moghhe·
**enmity** *n* envy
**enormous** *adj* cowrek

**enough** *adj* lowr a[2]
**enough** *adv/n* lowr
**enquire** *v* govyn
**enquiry** *n* govyn[adow]
**ensure** *v* surhe·
**enterprise** *n* aventuryans
**entertain** *v* dydhana
**entertaining** *adj* dydhanus
**entire** *adj* cowal
he is **entitled to** *phr* y'n jeves an gwir dhe[2]
**entrust to** *v* gorra in charj dhe[2]
**envelope** *n* mailyer
**envious** *adj* envies
**environment** *n* kerhydneth
**envy** *n* envy
**envy** *v* perthy envy
**epidemic** *n* cleves epydemek
**epilepsy** *n* drogatty
**epipen** *n* skîtel
**equal** *adj* kehaval
**equilibrium** *n* kespos
**equip** *v* darbary, hernessya
**equipment** *n* daffar, hernes
**era** *n* osweyth
**eradicate** *v* dywredhya
**erase** *v* defendya
**eraser** *n* cravell defendya
**erect** *v* drehevel
**erupt** *v* tardha
**eruption** *n* tardhans
**escape** *v* dia·nk, scappya
**escapism** *n* diankva
**escapist** *adj* diencus
**escort** *v* hùmbronk

**especially** *adv* spessly, kyns oll
**essence** *n* essens
**essential** *adj* dyhepcor
**establish** *v* establyshya
**estate** *n* stât
**estimate** *n* towlcost
**estimate** *v* rekna ogas lowr
**estuary** *n* heyl
**et cetera (etc)** *phr* hag erel
**eternal** *adj* byckenus
**eternity** *n* byckenuster
**ethical** *adj* ewnhensek
**euro** *n* ewro
The **European Union** *n* An Unyans Ewropek
**evangelical** *adj* awaylek
**evasive** *adj* gohelus
**even** *adj* compes; leven
**even** *adv* kefrë·s; kyn fe[G] *See also* unweyth *in 'Numerals for Reference'*
**even though** *phr* [ha] kyn[5] [G]
**evening** *n* gordhuwher
in the **evening** *phr* gordhuwher
this **evening** *phr* haneth
yesterday **evening** *phr* newher
**evenness** *n* levender
**event** *n* wharvos
**ever** *adv* nefra; bythqweth
for **ever [and ever]** *phr* bys vycken [ha bys venary]
**ever again** *phr* nefra namo·y
**evergreen** *adj* bythwer
**every** *adj* pùb[G]

**every one** *pron* pùb huny [oll][G], kettep huny[G]
**every [one]** *pron* kenyver[G]
**everyone** *pron* pùb[onen][G]
**everything** *pron* pùptra·[G]
**everywhere** *adv* in pùb le
**evidence** *n* dùstuny
**evident** *adj* opynwelys
**evil** *adj* tebel-2(1)
**exactly** *adv* pora·n, adhevî·s
**exaggerate** *v* gorlywa
**examination** *n* examnyans; apposyans
**examine** *v* examnya
**example** *n* exampyl
for **example (e.g.)** *phr* rag exampyl
**excavate** *v* palas
**excellent** *adj* brentyn
**execute** *v* execûtya
**execution** *n* execûcyon
**executive** *n* gweythresor
**except** *prep* marnas; saw
**except** *v* exceptya
**except for** *phr* saw
**exception** *n* excepcyon
**exchange** *n* keschaunj
**exchange** *v* keschaunjya
**excite** *v* piga, entanya
get **excited** *phr* frobma
**excitement** *n* frobmans
**exciting** *adj* leun a frobmans, entanus
**exclaim** *n* cria in mes
**excluding** *prep* heb rekna
**excursion to** *phr* tro in

**excuse** *n* ascû·s
**exercise** *n* omassayans
**exhibit** *v* dysqwedhes
**exhibition** *n* dysqwedhyans
**exist** *v* hanvos
**existence** *n* hanvos
**expect** *v* gwetyas
**expectation** *n* gwaityans
**expedition** *n* eskerdh
**expense** *n* còst spênys
**expensive** *adj* ker
**experience** *n* prevyans; experyans
**experiment** *n* arbrof
**experiment** *v* arbrevy
**expert** *n* arbenegor
**explain** *v* clerhe·; styrya
**explode** *v* tardha
**exploration** *n* whythrans
**explore** *v* whythra
**explosion** *n* tardh
**export** *n* esporth
**export** *v* esportha
**expose** *v* dyskevra
**express** *v* gorra in geryow
**expression** *n* tremyn; fygùr a gows
**extend** *v* istydna
**extension** *n* istydnans
**extent** *n* compas
**extinguish** *v* dyfudhy
**extinguisher** *n* dyfudhor
**extra** *adj* addys
**extraordinary** *adj* dres kynda
**extravagance** *n* scùllyans
**extravagant** *adj* scùllyak

extraterrestrial *n* bÿs-estren
extremely *adv* dres ehen
extremist *adj* pendom
eye *n* lagas

eyebrow *n* abrans
eyelash *n* blew an lagas
eyelid *n* crohen an lagas

# F

fabric *n* padn; lien
façade *n* talenep
face *n* fâss; enep
fact *n* feth
in fact *phr* in gwrioneth
factor *n* elven
factory *n* gweythva
fail to *phr* fyllel a[2]
failed *v* ny spêdyas; ny wrug soweny
failure *n* defowt, mothow
faint *n* clamder
faint *v* clamdera
fair *adj* teg
fair *n* fer
fair wear and tear *phr* ûsyans ha swardyans teg
the fairies *phr* an bobel bian
fairness *n* ewnder
fairy cake *n* tesen vian
faith *n* crejyans
faithful *adj* len
faithfulness *n* le·ndùry
fake *adj* fug-[2]
fake *v* conterfeytya
fall *n* coodh
fall *v* codha
false *adj* fâls

fame *n* hanow dâ
family *n* teylu
famous *adj* gerys [dâ], meur y hanow
fancy *n* fancy
fancy dress *n* tùllwysk
fantasy *n* fancy
far *adj* pell
farce *n* gwary fol
farm *n* bargen tir
farm *v* amethy
farmer *n* tiak
farming *n* amethyans
fart *n* brabm
fart *v* brabma
fascist *n* fashyst
fashion *n* fascyon
fashionable *adj* fascyonus
fast *adj* uskys; in rag
fat *adj* tew
fat *n* blonek, berry
fatal *adj* mortal
fate *n* radn, destnans
father *n* tas
fatten *v* tewhe·
favour *n* favour; torn dâ
in favour of *phr* abarth [dhe[2]]
favourable *adj* fa·verus

his **favourite** *adj* an gwelha oll ganso
**fear** *n* own, dowt
**fear** *v* *own, *dowt, perthy dowt / own
**feast** *n* kenwes
**feathers** *n* pluv
**feature** *n* nas
**February** *n* mis Whevrel
**federal** *adj* kefrysek
**federation** *n* kefrysyans
**fee** *n* gober
**feed** *v* maga; meythy; bosa
**feel** *v* clôwes
**feel for** *phr* palvala
**feeling** *n* omglowans
**fellow** *n* gwas, pollat
**female** *adj* benow
**feminine** *adj* benow
**fence** *n* ke
**ferns** *n* reden
**ferry** *n* keybal; treth
**fervent** *adj* gwresak
**fervour** *n* gwres
**festival** *n* gool; golweyth
**fetch** *v* kerhes; hedhes
**fever** *n* fevyr
**few** *adj* bohes[2]
**a few** *phr* nebes[G]
**very few** *phr* very nebes
**fiancé(e)** *n* gour / benyn ambosys
**fiction** *n* fycsyon
**fiddle** *n* crowd
**fidget** *v* fysla
**field** *n* gwel; park

**fight** *n* omlath
**fight** *v* omlath, batalyas
**fight a war** *v* gwerrya
**figs** *n* fyges
**figurative** *adj* fygùrek
**figure** *n* fygùr
**figure of speech** *phr* fygùr a gows
**file** *n* restryn
**fill** *v* lenwel
**filling station** *n* petrolva
**film** *n* kednen
**film** *v* fylmya
**filter** *n* sythel
**filter** *v* sythla
**fin** *n* askel
**final(e)** *n* finweth
**finally** *adv* wàr an dyweth
**finance** *n* arhanso·rieth
**financial** *adj* arhansek
**find** *n* trouvyans
**find** *v* cafos; trouvya
**find out** *phr* desmygy
**fine** *adj* fin; brav
**fine** *n* spal
**finger** *n* bës
**finish** *v* gorfedna
**fire** *n* tan
**fire** *v* gordhyllo
**fire escape** *n* skeul scappya
**firefighter** *n* tangasor
**fireplace** *n* olas
**firework** *n* tan creft
**firm** *adj* ferv
**firm** *n* cowethas
**firmly** *adv* yn fen

**firmly fixed** *phr* fast
at **first** *phr* i'n dallath
**first aid** *n* socour trobm
**first class** *phr* adhevî·s
**fish** *n* pysk
**fish** *v* pyskessa
**fisherman** *n* pùscador
**fishing boat** *n* côk
**fist** *n* dorn
**fit** *adj* in poynt dâ
**fit** *n* shôra
**fit** *v* desedha
**fizzy** *adj* tythus
**fix** *v* staga
**fixed** *adj* stag
**flag** *n* baner
**flakes** *n* scant
**flame** *n* flàm
**flank** *n* tenewen
**flare** *n* fakel
**flash** *v* luhesy
**flashes** *n* luhes
**flask** *n* costrel
**flat** *adj* plat
**flat** *n* ranjy
**flatten** *v* plattya
**flatter** *v* flattra gans
**flavour** *n* sa·woren
**flawless** *adj* heb nàm
**flax** *n* lyn
**fleas** *n* whydn
**flee** *v* fia dhe'n fo
**flesh** *n* kig
**flexible** *adj* heblek
**flick** *n* bobmen scav
**flicker** *v* flyckra

**flies** *n* kelyon
**flight** *n* neyj
**fling** *v* dehesy
**flippers** *n* botas palvek
**flirt** *v* flyrtya
**float** *v* neyja
**flock** *n* gre; hes
**flood** *n* liv
**flooding** *n* budhyans
**floor** *n* leur
**flour** *n* bleus
**flow** *n* fros
**flow** *v* denewy
**flower** *n* flour
**flu** *n* anwosva
**fluent** *adj* frosek
**fluid** *adj* berus
**fluid** *n* berusen
**flush** *v* tedna dowr in
**flute** *n* whybonel
**flutter** *n* treneyja
**fly** *v* neyja [i'n air / ebron]
**foam** *n* ewon
**focus** *v* crespoyntya
**focus [up]on** *phr* dry y fog wàr[2]
**fog** *n* nywl
**foggy** *adj* nywlek
**fold** *n* pleg
**fold** *v* plegya
**folder** *n* plegel
**folk** *n* gweryn
**folktale** *n* drolla
**follow** *v* sewya; holya
**food** *n* boos
**fool** *n* fol

act like a **fool** *phr* dôtya
**foolish** *adj* fol
**foot** *n* troos; tros'hes
**football** *n* pel droos
**footballer** *n* peldrosyas
**footbridge** *n* pons kerdh
**footpath** *n* trûlergh
**footprint** *n* ol
**for** *conj* rag[G]
**for** *prep* rag[G]; dhe[2 G]
**forbid** *v* dyfen, sconya dhe[2]
**force** *n* fors
**forceful** *adj* meur y nell
**forecast** *n* dargan
**forecast** *v* dargana
**forehead** *n* tâl
**foreign** *adj* estrednek
**foreigner** *n* estren
**forge** *v* conterfeytya
**forget** *v* ankevy
**forgive** *v* gava
**forgiveness** *n* gyvyans
**forgo** *v* hepcor
**fork** *n* forgh
**fork** *v* dybe·rth in forgh
**form** *n* form; furvlen
**formal** *adj* furvus
the **former** *pron* y gela[G]
**formula** *n* furvel
**fortunate** *adj* fusyk, gwynvÿs
**fortunately** *adv* i'n gwelha prës
**forum** *n* forùm
**forward slash** *n* lash in rag
**forwards** *adv* in rag

**foul-mouthed** *phr* plos y davas
**found** *v* fùndya
**foundation** *n* selven; fùndyans
**fountain** *n* fenten
**fox** *n* lowarn
**fraction** *n* fracsyon
**fragile** *adj* hedor
**fragrance** *n* sawor
**frame** *n* fram
**frame** *v* frâmya
**framework** *n* cloos
**frantic** *adj* varies
**fraud** *n* fraus
**freckled** *adj* brith
**freckles** *n* brith
**free** *adj* frank
**free** *v* fria
**freedom** *n* franketh
**freemasonry** *n* maso·nieth
**freeze** *v* rewy
**freezer** *n* rewor
**frequency modulation** (**FM**) *n* bludhyans menowghter
**frequent** *adj* menowgh
**fresh** *adj* fresk
**fretting** *n* fienasow
**Friday** *n* De Gwener
**friend** *n* coweth; cothman
**frighten** *v* gorra own in
**fringe** *n* pyllen
**frog** *n* qwylkyn
**from** *prep* a[2 G]; dhywo·rth[G]; dhia[2 G]; rag[G]

**from beneath / under** *phr* ada·dn² G
**front** *n* tu arâ·g; front
in **front** *phr* arâ·g
in **front of** *phr* dhyra·g^G
**frontier** *n* or
**front**[**line**] *n* voward
**frost** *n* rew
**froth** *n* ewon
**frown** *v* plegya tâl
**fruit** *n* frût
dried **fruit** *n* fyges
**frustration** *n* sens a spral
**fry** *v* fria
**frying-pan** *n* lecher
**fuck** *v* kyjya
**fudge** *n* fùj
**fuel** *n* cunys
**fulfil** *v* collenwel, cowlwil
**full** *adj* leun
**fun** *n* sport
make **fun of** *phr* gwil ges a²

**function** *n* gweythres
**function** *v* gweythresa
**fund** *n* arhas
**fund** *v* arhasa
**fundamental** *adj* selvenek
**fundamentalist** *n* selvenegor
**funeral** *n* encledhyas
**fungus** *n* fong
**funnel** *n* corn denewy; chymbla
**funny** *adj* wharthus
**fur** *n* pelour
**furious** *adj* coneryak
**furnish** *v* mebla
**furniture** *n* mebyl
**furthermore** *adv* ha pelha
**fury** *n* conar
**fuss** *v* fysla
**futile** *adj* ufer
**future** *adj/n* devedhek
the **future** *n* an termyn a dheu

# G

**gadget** *n* darbar
**Gaelic** *n* Godhalek
**gain** *n* gwain
**gain** *v* gwainya
**gale** *n* awel
**gallery** *n* soler; oryel
**gallon** *n* gallon
**game** *n* gwary; gam
**gannet** *n* sethor
**gap** *n* ajwy
**gape** *v* dianowy
**garage** *n* carjy

**garden** *n* lowarth
**gardener** *n* lowarthor
**garland** *n* garlont
**garlic** *n* kenyn ewynek
**garret** *n* talyk
**gas** *n* gàs
**gate** *n* yet
**gateway** *n* porth
**gather** *v* cùntell; omgùntell
**gauge** *n* les
**gay** *adj* gay
**gear** *n* maglen

**gel** *n* jèl
**Gemini** *n* An Evellas
**gender** *n* reydh
**gene** *n* genyn
**general** *adj* kemyn
**general** *n* caslewyth
**General Certificate of Secondary Education** (**GCSE**) *phr* Testscrif Ollkemyn [Adhyscans Nessa]
**general practitioner** (**GP**) *n* medhek meyny
**generally** *adv* dre vrâs
**generate** *v* denethy
**generation** *n* ke·nedhel
**generosity** *n* larjes
**generous** *adj* larj
**genetic** *adj* genydnek
**genius** *n* awenyth
**gentle** *adj* clor
**gentleness** *n* clorder
**Gents** *n* Gwer
**genus** *n* kynda
**geographical** *adj* dorydhek
**geography** *n* dory·dhieth
**germ** *n* egyn
**gesture** *n* môcyon
**gesture** *v* gwil môcyon
**get** *v* kerhes; cafos See also he gets
**get away** *phr* scappya
**get off** *phr* skydnya
**get up** *phr* sevel; kemeres in bàn
he **gets** *phr* y'n jeves
**ghost** *n* bùcka, tarosvan

**ghostly** *adj* tarosvanus
**giant** *adj* cowrek
**gift** *n* ro
**gifted** *adj* meur y deythy
**giga-** *pref* gyga-[1]
**gin** *n* jenevra
**ginger** *n* jy·njyber
**girl** *n* mowes, myrgh
**girlfriend** *n* cares
**give** *v* ry
**give back** *phr* dascor
**give up** *phr* omry
**gladly** *adv* dre decter, [oll] a'y vodh
**glance** *n* golok
**glance at** *phr* tôwlel golok wàr[2]
**glass** *n* gweder; gwedren
**glider** *n* gwylanel
**glimpse** *n* golok vian
**glitter** *v* glyttra
**global warming** *phr* tesyans bÿs-efan
**glorious** *adj* gloryùs
**glory** *n* glory
**glove** *n* manek
**glow** *n* golow
**glow** *v* golowy
**glue** *n* glus
**glue** *v* glusa
**gluten-free** *adj* heb glûten
**gnats** *n* gwybes
**go** *v* mos
**go back** *phr* dewheles
**go straight** *phr* mos i'n ewn fordh

**goal** *n* gol
**goat** *n* gavar
**god** *n* duw
**godfather** *n* tasek
he is **going to** *phr* ev a vydn
**gold** *n* owr
**golden** *adj* owrek
**goldfish** *n* owrbysk
**golf** *n* golf
all **gone** *phr* debrys ha deu
**good** *adj* dâ, vas
in **good shape** *phr* in poynt dâ
**good turn** *phr* torn dâ
**goods** *n* gwara
**goodwill** *n* bodh dâ
**goose** *n* goodh
**gorse** *n* eythyn
**gorsedd** *n* gorseth
**gospel** *n* awayl
**govern** *v* governa
**government** *n* governans
**governor** *n* lewyth
**gown** *n* goun
**graceful** *adj* jentyl
**grace[fulness]** *n* je·ntylys
**gracious** *adj* grassyùs
**grade** *n* gradh
**gradually** *adv* tabm ha tabm
**grains** *n* greun
**gram** *n* gram
**grammar** *n* gramer
**grand** *adj* brav
**grandchild** *n* flogh wydn
**grandfather** *n* tas gwydn
**grandmother** *n* dama wydn
**grape** *n* grappa

**grapefruit** *n* aval pa·radhys
**grapple** *v* gwrydnya
**grasp** *n* dalhen
**grasp** *v* dalhedna
**grass** *n* glaswels
**grasshopper** *n* culyak reden
be **grateful to** *phr* bos sensys dhe²
**grave** *adj* sàd
**grave** *n* bedh
**gravel** *n* growyn
**gravity** *n* dyskerheth
**graze** *v* pory
**grease** *n* blonek
**greasy** *adj* blonegek
**great** *adj* meur
**greatly** *adv* brâs
**greatness** *n* meureth
**greed** *n* crefny
**greedy** *adj* crefny
**green** *adj* glas; gwer
**green** *n* glesyn
**greeting** *n* dynargh
send **greetings to** *phr* dynerhy
**gremlin** *n* bùcka
**grey** *adj* loos
**grid** *n* maglen
**grief** *n* grêf
**grieve** *v* kyny
**grill** *n* rastel
**grill** *v* rastella
**grim** *adj* asper
**grimness** *n* aspe·ryta
**grind** *v* mala
**grip** *n* dalhen
**grip** *v* dalhedna

**grit** *n* growyn
**groan** *n* hanajen
**groan** *v* hanaja
**groove** *n* rygol
**grope** *v* palvala
**gross** *adj* cowal
**ground** *n* dor; grônd
**group** *n* bagas
**grow** *v* tevy
**growl** *v* gromyal
**growth** *n* tevyans
bear a **grudge** *phr* perthy grêvons
**grumble** *n* croffal
**grumble** *v* croffolas
**grumbler** *n* grolyak
**grumbling** *adj* grolyak
**grumpy** *adj* crowsek
**guarantee** *n* warrant
**guarantee** *v* warrantya
**guard** *n* gwethyas
**guard** *v* gwardya

**guess** *n* desmyk
**guess** *v* desmygy
**guest** *n* ôstyas
**guesthouse** *n* gwesty
**guide** *n* gedyor
**guide** *v* gedya
**guidebook** *n* gîdlyver
**guideline** *n* gidlînen
**guilty** *adj* cablus
**guitar** *n* gyttern
**gull** *n* gwylan
**gum** *n* glus
**gum(s)** *n* kig an dens
**gun** *n* godn
**gunman** *n* godnor
**gunpowder** *n* polter godn
**gurgle** *n* ronk
**gurgle** *v* renky
**gutter** *n* londer
**guy** *n* gwas
**guy(s)** *addressing sb* sos
**gymnastics** *n* corfassa·y

# H

**hack** *v* terghya in
**haddock** *n* corvarvus
**haggle** *v* bargednya
**hail** *n* keser
**hair** *n* blew
**hairband** *n* snod
**hairdresser** *n* dyghtyor blew
**hairless** *adj* blogh
**hake** *n* denjak
**half an hour** *phr* hanter-our
**hall** *n* hel
**ham** *n* mordhos

**hammer** *n* morthol
**hammer** *v* mortholya
**hamper** *n* spralla
**hand** *n* dorn
on the one **hand** ... **on the other** [hand] *phr* wàr eyl tu ... wàr y gela
on the other **hand** *phr* wàr an tu aral
**hand luggage** *n* scryp
**hand over** *phr* dascor; hedhes
**handbag** *n* sagh dorn

**handful** *n* dornas
**handkerchief** *n* lien dorn
**handle** *n* dorn[la]; scovarn
**handle** *v* handla
**handlebars** *n* dewdhorn
**hands** *n* dewla
**hang** *v* cregy
**happen** *v* wharvos
**happily** *adv* heb awhe·r
**happiness** *n* lowender
**happy** *adj* lowen
**harass** *v* arveth
**harbour** *n* porth
**hard** *adj* cales
**hard shoulder** *n* lin cales
**hardback** *n* aden gales
**hardly** *adv* scant; nameu·r
**hare** *n* scovarnak
**harm** *v* shyndya; grevya dhe[2]
**harmful** *adj* drog
**harmonious** *adj* kesson
**harmony** *n* kessenyans
**harness** *n* hernes
**harness** *v* hernessya
**harp** *n* harp
**harsh** *adj* wherow
**harshness** *n* wherowder
**harvest** *n* trevas
**harvest** *v* don tre
he **has** *phr* y'n jeves
**hashtag** *n* sygen hàsh
**hat** *n* hot
**hate** *v* hâtya
**hatred** *n* cas
**haunt** *v* trobla
**have** *v* cafos See also he has

**hawk** *n* hôk
**hay** *n* gora
**hayfever** *n* cleves strewy
**hazardous** *adj* deantel
**he** *pron* ev[G]
**head** *n* pedn
**headache** *n* drog pedn
**headphones** *n* fônow pedn
**heal** *v* yaghhe·
**health** *n* yêhes
**healthy** *adj* yagh; yahus
**heap** *n* grahell
**heap** *v* grahella
**hear** *v* clôwes
**heart** *n* colon
**heartburn** *n* losk pengasen
**hearth** *n* olas
**heat** *n* gwres
**heat** *v* tobma
great **heat** *n* bros
**heater** *n* tobmor
**heather** *n* grug
**heating** *n* gwres
**heaven** *n* nev
**heavy** *adj* poos
**Hebrew** *n* Ebrow
**hedge** *n* ke
**hedgehog** *n* sort
**heed** *v* gwil vry a[2]
**heel** *n* gwewen
**height** *n* uhelder; bàn
**helicopter** *n* tro-askel
**hell** *n* iffarn
the **hell** *phr* an jowl
**hell of a** *phr* iffarnak
**hello** *interj* halô·

**helmet** *n* basnet
**help** *n* gweres
**help** *v* [ry] gweres
**helper** *n* gweresor
**hen** *n* yar
**her** *adj* hy[3] G
**her** *pron* see 'she'
**herald** *n* herôt
**herb** *n* erba
**herbal tea** *n* tê erba
**herd** *n* gre
**here** *adv* obma
around **here** *phr* i'n côstys-ma
from **here** *phr* alebma, ahanan[G]
**here is / are** *phr* otta[G], ot obma
**herewith** *adv* gans hebma
**hernia** *n* torrva
**hero** *n* gorour
**herrings** *n* hern gwydn
be **hesitant** *phr* perthy danjer
**hesitate** *v* hockya
**hesitation** *n* hockyans
without **hesitation** *phr* heb danjer
**heterosexual** *adj* eylreydhek
**hibernate** *v* gwavgùsca
**hiccup** *n* hyk
**hide** *v* keles
**hideout** *n* covva
**high** *adj* uhel
**high ground** *n* uheldir
**hijack** *v* argibya
**hijack[ing]** *n* argip
**hill** *n* bre

**him** *pron* see 'he'
**hindrance** *n* let
**Hindu** *adj/n* Hyndou
**Hinduism** *n* Hyndou·ieth
**hinge** *n* bagh
**hip** *n* clun
**hire** *v* gobrena
**hire out** *phr* settya wor'gobren
**his** *adj* y[2] G
**history** *n* i·story
**hit** *v* gweskel, sqwattya
**hitch[-hike]** *v* mesya
**hoarse** *adj* hos
**hoax** *n* cast
**hoax** *v* castya
**hobby** *n* hobba
**hold** *v* sensy
**holder** *n* sensor
**hole** *n* toll
make a **hole / holes in** *phr* telly
**holiday** *n* degol
**hollow** *adj/n* cow
**holly** *n* kelyn
**holy** *adj* sans
The **Holy Spirit** *phr* An Spyrys Sans
**home** *adj/adv* tre
**home** *n* olas
at **home** *phr* [in] chy, in tre
**homosexual** *adj* kethreydhek
**homosexuality** *n* kethreydhecter
**honest** *adj* lel
**honesty** *n* lelder
**honey** *n* mel

**honour** *n* enor
**honour** *v* enora; gordhya [dhe²]
**hood** *n* cûgol
**hoodie** *n* garnsy cûgol
**hoof** *n* carn
**hook** *n* bagh
**hook** *v* baha
**hoop** *n* kelgh
**hope** *n* govenek
**hope** *v* *govenek; gwetyas
**hopefully** *adv* dell yw gwaitys
**hopeless** *adj* anteythy
**horizon** *n* gorwel
**horizontal** *adj* leurweth
**hormone** *n* hormôn
**horn** *n* corn
**horoscope** *n* ho·roscôp
**horrible** *adj* casadow, scruthus
**horror** *n* scruth
**horse** *n* margh
**horseman** *n* marhak
**horseradish** *n* marghredyk
**hospital** *n* clôjy
**host** *n* ost; lu
**host** *v* gwesty
**hostage** *n* gwystel
**hostile** *adj* escarus
**hot** *adj* tobm
very **hot** *adj* bros
**hotel** *n* ostel
**hour** *n* our; eur
**house** *n* chy
The **House of Commons** *phr* Chy an Gemyn
The **House of Lords** *phr* Chy an Arlydhy
**household** *n* meyny
**how** *adv* fate·ll² [G], fatla² [G], [in] pana vaner[G]
**how are things?** *phr* fatl'yw genes?
**how are you?** *phr* fate·ll osta?
**how deep** *phr* pygebmys downder[G]
**how far** *phr* pana bellder[G]
**how high** *phr* pygebmys uhelder[G]
**how long** *phr* pygebmys hës[G]; pana bellder[G]; pes termyn[G]
**how loud** *phr* pygebmys uhelder[G]
**how many** *phr* pygebmys[G], pana / py lies[G]; pes[G]; py seul[G]
**how many times** *phr* pana lies torn[G]
**how much** *phr* pygebmys[G]; py seul[G]
**how often** *phr* pesqweyth[G]
**how wide** *phr* pygebmys les[G]
**however** *adv* bytegy·ns
**howl** *n* uj
**howl** *v* uja
**hub** *n* crespoynt
**hug** *n* byrlans
**hug** *v* byrla
**hum** *v* sia
**human being** *n* mab den
**human immune deficiency virus** (**HIV**) *phr* vyrùs an imûndyfyk denyl (VID)

**humane** *adj* whar
**humanitarian** *adj* dengerenje'ek
**humble** *adj* uvel
**humble** *v* uvelhe·
**humid** *adj* leyth
**humidity** *n* leythter
**humiliate** *v* uvelhe·
**humility** *n* uvelder
**humour** *n* hùmor
**hump** *n* bothan
**hunger** *n* nown
**hungry** *adj* nownek; gwag
**hunt** *v* helghya
the local **hunt** *phr* helgh an tyller
**hurdle** *n* cloos
**hurl** *v* dehesy
**hurricane** *n* herdhwyns
**hurriedly** *adv* dre / gans / in / wàr hast
**hurry** *v* fystena
**hurt** *v* hùrtya
**husband** *n* gour
**hut** *n* crow
**hygiene** *n* glanythter
**hygienic** *adj* glanyth
**hymn** *n* hympna
**hypocrisy** *n* fêkyl-jer

# I

**I** *pron* my[G]
**ice** *n* rew
**ice cream** *n* dehen rew
**icing** *n* whegrew
**icon** *n* delow scrin
**icy** *adj* rewys
**idea** *n* tybyans
**ideal** *adj* adhevî·s
**ideal** *n* delvrys
**idealism** *n* delvre·sieth
**idealist** *n* delvresor
**identify** *v* aswon
**identify with** *phr* omunya gans
**identity** *n* honensys
**idiomatic** *adj* teythiak
**idiot** *n* bobba
**idle** *v* sygera
**if** *conj* mar[4] [G]; a[4] [G]
**if necessary** *phr* mars yw res
**if only / if only not** *phr* unweyth a[4] / na[2] [G]
**ignore** *v* sevel orth aswon
**ill** *adj* clâv
**illegal** *adj* ùnlafyl
**illness** *n* cleves
**illusion** *n* tarosvan
**illusory** *adj* tarosvanus
**illustrate** *v* lymna
**illustration** *n* lymnans
**illustrator** *n* lymnor
**imagination** *n* desmygyans
**imaginative** *adj* desmygyansus
**imagine** *v* desmygy
**imitate** *v* gwil warle·rgh
**imitation** *adj* fug-[2]
**immature** *adj* diadhves

**immaturity** *n* diadhvetter
**immediate** *adj* desempys
**immediately** *adv* dysto·wgh, desempys, heb let
**immigrant** *n* envroyas
**immigration** *n* envroans
**immoral** *adj* camhensek
**immune** *adj* diogel
**impatience** *n* fowt perthyans
**impatient** *adj* cot y berthyans
**impede** *n* spralla
**impertinent** *adj* taunt
**implement** *n* toul
**implement** *v* gweythresa
**impolite** *adj* dyscortes
**import** *n* enporth
**import** *v* enportha
**important** *adj* a boos brâs, meur y vern
it is **important** *phr* bysy yw
**impossible** *adj* ùnpo·ssybyl
**imprecise** *adj* andyblans
be **impressed by** *phr* bos kemerys yn frâs gans
**impression** *n* argraf
**imprison** *v* prysonya
**improper** *adj* dysonest
**improve** *v* gwellhe·
**in** *adv* ajy·, aberveth
**in** *prep* in[G]
**in-laws** *phr* tus dâ
**inappropriate** *adj* andesedhus
**incapable** *adj* anabyl
**inch** *n* mesva
**incidentally** *adv* ha ny ow côwsel

**incite** *v* inia
**inclination** *n* stubm; tuedhyans
be **inclined to** *phr* bos whensys dhe[2]
**include** *v* rekna warba·rth; comprehendya
**including** *prep* ha + *noun* intredhans
**income** *n* gwain
**incompetent** *adj* anteythy
**inconvenience** *n* ancombrynjy
**inconvenience** *v* ancombra
**inconvenient** *adj* ancombrus
**increase** *v* moghhe·
**increasingly** *adv* moy ha moy
**indecent** *adj* dysonest
**indeed** *adv* defry·, in gwir
**independent** *adj* dysta·g; anserhak
**index** *n* menegva
**indicate** *v* meneges
**indication** *n* menegyans
**indifferent** *adj* bohes y vern
**indigestion** *n* drog-goans
**indignant** *adj* serrys
be **indignant** *phr* serry
**indignation** *n* sorr
**indispensable** *adj* dyhepcor
**industry** *n* dywysyans
**inexperienced** *adj* heb prevyans
**infect** *v* clevejy
**infection** *n* clevejyans
**infectious** *adj* clevejus
**inflammation** *n* fakel

**inflate** *v* whethfy
**inflation** *n* whethfyans
**influence** *n* awedhyans
**influence** *v* awedhya
**influential** *adj* awedhus
**inform** *v* derivas
**informal** *adj* anfurvus
**information** *n* derivadow, kevarweth
**information point** *n* govynva
**infringement** *n* torrva
**ingredient** *n* defnyth
**inherent** *adj* genesyk
**inherit** *v* e·ryta
**inheritance** *n* ertons
**initiate** *v* sordya
**inject** *v* skîtya
**injection** *n* skîtyans
**injure** *v* pystyga
**injured** *adj* brew
**injury** *n* pystyk
**ink** *n* ink
**innate** *adj* genesyk
**innocence** *n* gwiryonsys
**innocent** *adj* gwiryon, heb drog
**inoculate** *v* breha
**inquest** *n* whythrans
**inquiry** *n* whythrans
**insects** *n* whesker
**inside** *adv* ajy·, aberveth
**inside** *prep* abe·rth in, ajy· dhe[2], aberveth in
**insignificant** *adj* dysty·r
**insincere** *adj* dywiryon
**insincerity** *n* dywiryonsys
**insist** *v* inia
**insistence** *n* iniadow
**inspector** *n* arolegyth
**inspiration** *n* awen
**inspire** *v* aweny
**instal** *v* installya
**instant** *adj* desempys
**instead of** *phr* in le [a[2]]
**instinct(s)** *n* anyen
**institute** *n* fùndyans
**instrumental music** *n* menestrouthy
**instrument(s)** *n* daffar
**insulate** *v* enesegy
**insult** *n* despî·t
**insult** *v* despîtya
**insurance** *n* surynjy
**insure** *v* surhe·
**intact** *adj* dien
**intellect** *n* skians
**intellectual** *adj/n* skiansek
**intelligence** *n* skians
**intelligent** *adj* skentyl
**intend to** *phr* bos porposys dhe[2]
**intense** *adj* crev
**intensify** *v* crefhe·
**intensity** *n* crefter
**intensive care** *n* dourwith
**intent** *n* mydnas
**intention** *n* porpos
**intentionally** *adv* aborpos
**intercept** *v* contreweytya
**interest** *n* les; ôker
be **interested in** *phr* kemeres les in

he is **interested in** *phr* meur yw y les in
**interesting** *adj* a les
**interfere** *v* mellya
**international** *adj* kesgwlasek
The **Internet** *n* An Kesrosweyth
**interpret** *v* interpretya
**interpreter** *n* la·tymer
**interval** *n* spis; powes
**interview** *n* omwel
**intestines** *n* colodhyon
**intimate** *adj* ogas
**into** *prep* in$^G$; abe·rth in, ajy· dhe$^2$, aberveth in
**intolerable** *adj* dywodhaf
**introduce** *v* presentya; comendya
**invalid** *adj* heb bry
**invent** *v* desmygy
**invention** *n* desmyk
**invest** *v* kevarhewy
**investigate** *v* whythra

**investigation** *n* whythrans
**invitation** *n* galow
**invite** *v* gelwel
**invoice** *n* recken
get **involved** *phr* omvagly
**iron** *n* horn; hornel
**iron** *v* levna
**irony** *n* geseth
**irrational** *adj* dyrêson
**irritable** *adj* crowsek
**irritate** *v* serry, ania
**irritated** *adj* serrys
**Islam** *n* Islâ·m
**Islamic** *adj* Islâmek
**island** *n* enys
**isolate** *v* enys'he·
**issue** *n* trogh
**it** *pron* ev$^G$; hy$^G$
**itch** *n* cosva
**itch** *v* cosa
**its** *adj* y$^{2\ G}$, hy$^{3\ G}$
**ivy** *n* idhyow

# J

**jack** *n* knâva
**jackdaw** *n* chôk
**jacket** *n* jerkyn
**jam** *n* jàm
**January** *n* mis Genver
**jar** *n* pot
**jaws** *n* awednow
**jealous** *adj* envies
be **jealous** *v* perthy envy
**jeans** *n* jîns

**Jehovah's Witness** *n* Test Jehova
**jelly** *n* cowles
**jellyfish** *n* blùbber
**Jesus Christ** *n* Jesu Crist
**jet** *n* styf
**Jew** *n* Yêdhow
**jewel** *n* jowal
**jigsaw puzzle** *n* gwary mildam
**job** *n* oberen; soodh
**jog** *v* gobonya

**join** *v* jùnya; omjùnya
**joint** *n* kevals
**joke** *n* ges
**joke** *v* gesya
**joker** *n* jôker
**journalist** *n* jornalyst
**journey** *n* viaj
**joy** *n* lowender, joy
**jubilee** *n* jùbylê
**judge** *n* jùj
**judge** *v* jùjya
**judgement** *n* jùjment; breus
**jug** *n* podyk
**juggle** *v* jùglya
**juice** *n* sùgan
**juicy** *adj* sùgnek
**July** *n* mis Gortheren

**jump** *n* labm
**jump** *v* lebmel
**jump the queue** *phr* dreslebmel an lost
**jumper** *n* gwlanek
**junction** *n* kes'hens
**June** *n* mis Metheven
**jungle** *n* gwylcos
**jurisdiction** *n* danjer
the **jury** *n* dewdhek Cort an Gùrun
**just** *adj* jùst
**just** *adv* knack; nowyth
**just** [**now**] *phr* namnyge·n
**justice** *n* jùstys
**justify** *v* jùstyfia
**jut out** *phr* balegy

# K

**kebab** *n* goleyth Tùrk
**keel** *n* keyn
**keep** *v* sensy, gwetha
**ketchup** *n* sows cogh
**kettle** *n* caltor
**key** *n* alwheth; alwhedhen
**keyboard** *n* alwhedhel
**kick** *v* pôtya
**kidnap** *v* argibya
**kidnap**[**ping**] *n* argip
**kidney** *n* loneth
**kill** *v* ladha
**killer whale** *n* morvil ladha
**kilo-** *pref* kylo-[1]
**kind** *adj* cuv, caradow
**kind** *n* ehen, kynda, sort
of that **kind** *phr* a'n par-na

of this **kind** *phr* a'n par-ma
what **kind of** *phr* pana vaner[G], py par[G]
**kindle** *v* anowy
**king** *n* myte·rn
**kippers** *n* hern opyn
**kiss** *n* abm
**kiss** *v* abma
**kitchen** *n* kegyn
**kitten** *n* cathyk
**knave** *n* knâva
**knead** *v* tosa
**knee** *n* glin
**kneel** [**down**] *v* mos wàr bedn dewlin
**knees** *n* dewlin
**knickers** *n* lavregyn

**knife** *n* collel
**knight** *n* marhak
**knighthood** *n* marhogieth
**knit** *v* gwia
**knock** *v* knoukya
**knot** *n* colm

# L

**label** *n* label; tôkyn
**laboratory** *n* arbrôjy
**labour** *n* lavur
**labour** *v* lavurya
The **Labour Party** *n* Party an Lavur
**lace** *n* lâss
**lack** *n* fowt
**lack** *v* bos heb
be **lacking** *phr* fyllel
**lactose** *n* shùgra leth
**lad** *n* maw, pollat
**ladder** *n* skeul
**Ladies** *n* Benenes
**lady** *n* dama; arlodhes
**ladybird** *n* bùhyk Duw
**lager** *n* coref scav
**lake** *n* lydn
**lamb** *n* ôn; kig ôn
**lame** *adj* cloppek
**lament** *v* kyny
**laminate** *v* plastyfia
**lamp** *n* lugarn
**lamp post** *n* golowbren
**lampshade** *n* skeus lugarn
**land** *n* tir; bro; gwlas
**land** *v* londya; tira
**landing** *n* soler

**know** *v* godhvos; aswon
so far as I **know** *phr* dell gresa'
**know how to** *phr* godhvos
**knowledge** *n* godhvos, skians

**landlord** *n* perhednek; ost
**landslide** *n* dorslynk
**lane** *n* bownder; hens
**language** *n* tavas; yêth
**lap** *n* barlen; troyll
**laptop** *n* amowntyor dewlin
**large** *adj* brâs
**lark** *n* awhesyth
**laser** *n* laser
**lass** *n* maghteth
**last** *adj* dewetha
**last** *v* durya
at **last** *phr* wàr an dyweth
**late** *adj* dewedhes; holergh
**late** *adv* adhewedhes
**latex** *n* glus gwethyn
**Latin** *n* Latyn
**latitude** *n* lesres
the **latter** *pron* an eyl[G]
**lattice** *n* cloos
**laugh** *v* wherthyn
**laugh[ter]** *n* wharth
**launch** *v* launchya
**launder** *v* glanhe·
**law** *n* laha; reth
**lawn** *n* glesyn
**lawn mower** *n* jyn falhas
**layer** *n* gwely, gwyscas

**layout** *n* ara·y
**lazy** *adj* diek
**lead** *n* plobm
**lead** *n* lêsha
**lead** *v* hùmbronk, lêdya
**leader** *n* hùmbrynkyas, lêdyor
**leaf through** *phr* foledna
**leaflet** *n* folednyk
**league** *n* colmeth
**leak** *v* dyscudha
**leak out** *phr* sygera
**lean** *v* posa
**leap** *n* labm
**leap** *v* lebmel
**learn** *v* desky
**learned** *adj* deskys brâs
**learning** *n* dyscas
**leash** *n* lêsha
**least** *adj* lyha
at **least** *phr* dhe'n lyha
**leather** *n* lether, crohen
**leave** *v* dybe·rth
**leave out** *phr* gasa mes
**leaves** *n* del
**lecture** *n* areth
**lecture** *v* arethya
**left** *adj/n* cledh
on the **left** *phr* agle·dh
to the **left of** *phr* agle·dh dhe[2]
**left-handed person** *n* cledhyas
**leg** *n* garr; troos
**legal** *adj* lafyl
**legend** *n* hen-whedhel
**legitimate** *adj* alowadow
**lemon** *n* lymon

**lend** *v* lendya; prestya
**length** *n* hës
**lengthen** *v* hirhe·
**Lent** *n* Corawys
**Leo** *n* An Lew
**less** *adj* le
**lesson** *n* lesson; dyscas
**let** *v* gasa; settya wor'gobren
**let go of** *phr* gasa
**lethal** *adj* mortal
**letter** *n* lyther; lytheren
**lettuce(s)** *n* letys
**level** *adj* gwastas
**level** *n* level
**level** *v* levenhe·
**lever** *n* colpes
**liability** *n* kendon
**liar** *n* gowek
**libel** *n* cabel sclandrus
**liberal** *adj/n* lybral
The **Liberal Democrats** *n* An Democratyon Lybral
**liberty** *n* franketh
**Libra** *n* An Vantol
**library** *n* lyverjy
**licence** *n* cubmyas
**lichen** *n* kewny
**lick** *v* lyckya
**lid** *n* gorher
put the **lid on** *phr* gorhery
**lie** *n* gow
tell a **lie** *phr* gowleverel
**lie down** *phr* growedha
**lieutenant** *n* leftenant
**life** *n* bêwnans
**life jacket** *n* jerkyn sawder

**lifebelt** *n* grugys sawya
**lifeboat** *n* scath sawya
**lifeguard** *n* gwethyas treth
**lifestyle** *n* conversacyon
**lift** *n* iskydnor; gorras
**lift** *v* lyftya
**light** *adj* scav; golow
**light** *n* golow
**light** *v* golowy; gorra tan in; tùchya
**lighten** *v* scafhe·
**lighter** *n* cunor
**lighthouse** *n* golowjy
**lightning** *n* luhes
**like** *adj* haval
**like** *prep* kepa·r ha
he would **like to** *phr* ev a garsa
**like that** *phr* indella
**like this** *phr* indelma
**likeable** *adj* caradow
**lilies** *n* lyly
**limb** *n* esel
**limit** *n* finweth; cûr
**limit** *v* lymytya
over the **limit** *phr* dres an cûr
**limp** *v* cloffy
**limpets** *n* brednyk
**line** *n* lînen
on / off **line** *phr* wàr / dhywar lînen
**linen** *n* lyn
**lining** *n* ispan
**link** *n* kevren
**lion** *n* lion
**lip** *n* gweus

**lipstick** *n* minlyw
**liquid** *n* lydn
**list** *n* rol
**listen** *v* goslowes
**listen to** *phr* cola orth
**literature** *n* lien
**litre** *n* lîter
**litter** *n* stroll
**litter bin** *n* strollargh
**little** *adj* bian; bohes[2]
a **little** *phr* nebes[G], tabm / spot a[2]
very **little** *phr* very nebes
**little by little** *phr* tabm ha tabm
**live** *adj* bew
**live** *v* bewa
**live in** *phr* bos tregys in
**liveliness** *adj* bewder
**lively** *adj* bew[ek], jolyf
**liven up** *phr* bewekhe·
**liver** *n* avy
**lizard** *n* pedrevan
**load** *n* carg
**load** *v* carga
**loaf** *n* torth
**loan** *n* prest
**loathe** *v* abhorrya
**lobby** *n* kenseth
**lobster** *n* legest
**location** *n* tyller
**lock** *n* floren; cudyn
**lock** *v* alwhedha
**locomotive** *n* margh tan
**locust** *n* culyak reden
**lode** *n* goth mûn

**log** *n* etew
**log off** *phr* omdedna
**log on** *phr* omgelmy
**logic** *n* lojyk
**logical** *adj* herwyth lojyk
**logically** *adv* herwyth lojyk
**loneliness** *n* hireth
**lonely** *adj* hirethek; dygoweth
**long** *adj* hir
before **long** *phr* kyns nape·ll
**long ago** *phr* nans yw pell
so **long as** *phr* hadre·2 G
**longing** *n* hireth
**longitude** *n* hesres
**look** *n* golok; tremyn; syght, semlant
**look** *v* meras; yma· syght + *noun / adjective* wàr2
**look for** *phr* whelas
**look out for** *v* aspia orth
be **looking forward to** *phr* *màl
**loop** *n* cabester
**loophole** *n* ajwy
**loose** *adj* lows
**loosen** *v* lowsel
**lord** *n* arlùth
**lorry** *n* kert
**lose** *v* kelly
**loser** *n* collor

# M

**machine** *n* jyn
**mackerel** *n* briel
**mad** *adj* muscok

**loss** *n* coll
get **lost** *phr* mos dhe goll
a whole **lot of** *phr* bùsh brâs a2
**lots of** *phr* lowr / meur a2
**loud** *adj* uhel
**lounge** *n* esedhva
**love** *n* kerensa
**love** *v* cara
make **love** *v* cara warba·rth
**lover** *n* caror
**low** *adj* isel
**lower** *v* iselhe·
**loyal** *adj* lel
**loyalty** *n* lelder
**lubricant** *n* uras
**luck** *n* lùck
**lucky** *adj* fusyk, gwynvÿs
**lucky dip** *n* balyer fortydnys
**luggage** *n* fardellow
**lukewarm** *adj* mygyl
**lull** *v* lùlla
**lullaby** *n* lùll ha lay
**lump** *n* pryl
**lunch** *n* prës ly
**lungs** *n* skevens
**lure** *v* dynya
**lust** *n* lust
**luxurious** *adj* meur attê·s
**luxury** *adj* meur attê·s
be **lying** *phr* bos a'y wroweth

**madam** *addressing sb* madâma
**madness** *n* muscotter
**magazine** *n* lyver termyn

**magic** *n* pystry
**magician** *n* hudor
**magistrate** *n* jùstys
**maid**[**en**] *n* maghteth
**main** *adj* chif-[1]
**maintain** *v* mentêna
**maize** *n* ÿs wheg
**make** *n* merk
**make** *v* gwil; gwil dhe[2]
**make-up** *n* tremlyw
**male** *adj* gourow
**malice** *n* spit
**malicious** *adj* spîtys
**mammal** *n* bronvil
**man** *n* den; gour
**manage** *v* dyghtya, menystra
**management** *n* dyghtyans
**manager** *n* dyghtyor, menystror
**mandate** *n* mandât
**mango** *n* mango
**mania** *n* conar
**manic** *adj* varies
**manifesto** *n* derivadow
**manipulate** *v* handla
**mankind** *n* mab den
**manner** *n* maner, gis
**manufacturing** *n* gwrians
**manure** *n* teyl
**many** *adj* lies; lower [onen][G]
**many** [**a one**] *pron* lies huny
as **many as** *phr* kenyver a[2] [G]
**map** *n* mappa
**march** *n* keskerdh
**March** *n* mis Merth
**march** *v* keskerdhes

**mare** *n* casek
**marijuana** *n* kewarhen
**mark** *n* merk
**market** *n* marhas
stock **market** *n* marhas stockys
**marmalade** *n* kefeth owravallow
**married** *adj* prias
get **married** *v* demedhy
**martyr** *n* merther
**marvellous** *adj* barthusek
**masculine** *adj* gourow
**mash** *v* brewy
**mask** *n* vysour
**mason** *n* mason
**mass** *n* mass; oferen
**massacre** *n* ladhva
**massacre** *v* moldra
**massage** *v* tosa
**mast** *n* gwern
**master** *n* mêster
**mastery** *n* mestrynsys
**mat** *n* strayl
**match** *n* tanbren; fyt
**mate** *n* mâta
**material**(**s**) *n* daffar
**mathematics** *n* calco·rieth
**matter** *n* mater
it doesn't **matter** *phr* ny vern
**mattress** *n* colhes
**mature** *adj* adhves
**mature** *v* adhvejy
**maturity** *n* adhvetter
**maxim** *n* poynt a skians
**maximum** *adj* ughboyntek

**maximum** *n* ughboynt
**May** *n* mis Me
**may** *v* gallos
**maybe** *adv* martesen
**mayonnaise** *n* mayonê·s
**mayor** *n* mer
**me** *pron* see 'I'
**meadow** *n* pras
**meal** *n* prës boos
**mean** *adj* pith
**mean** *v* styrya
**meaning** *n* mênyng; styr
**meanness** *n* pithneth
**means** *n* main; pega·ns
**meanwhile** *adv* i'n mên-termyn
**measure** *n* scantlyn
**measure** *v* musura
**measurement** *n* musurans
**meat** *n* kig
**mechanic** *n* jynweythor
**mechanical** *adj* jynweythek
**mechanism** *n* jynweyth
the **media** *n* an mainys [kemenessa]
**medicine** *n* fysek; medhegieth
**mediocre** *adj* heb teythy specyal
**meditate** *v* ombredery
**medium** *n* main
**meek** *adj* whar
**meet** *v* metya [gans]
**meeting** *n* metyans; cùntellyans
**mega-** *pref* mega-[1]

**melon** *n* pompyon wheg
**melt** *v* tedha
**member** *n* esel
**member of Parliament** (**MP**) *phr* esel seneth
**membership** *n* eseleth
**memory** *n* cov
**mend** *v* êwna, amendya
don't **mention it** *phr* bÿth na lavar a'n dra
**mendacious** *adj* gowek
**mention** *n* mencyon
**mention** *v* gwil mencyon a[2]
**menu** *n* rol vytel; dewysel
**merchant** *n* marchont
**merit** *n* meryt
**merriment** *n* lowender
**merry** *adj* jolyf
**merry-making** *n* jolyfta
**mesh** *n* maglen
**mess** *n* stroll
make a **mess** *phr* strolla
**mess up** *phr* myshevya
**message** *n* messach, cadnas
**messenger** *n* cadnas
**metal** *n* olcan
**metaphor** *n* me·tafor
**method** *n* method
**Methodist** *n* Me·thodyst
**metre** *n* mêter
**miaow** *v* myowal
**mice** *n* logas
**micro-** *pref* mycro-[1]
**microbe** *n* corbref
**microphone** *n* my·crofôn

**microwave [oven]** *n* cordodnor
**midday** *n* hanter-dëdh
**middle** *adj/n* cres
in the **middle of** *phr* in cres
**middle class** *phr* rencas cres
**midges** *n* gwybes
**midnight** *n* hanter-nos
**might** *n* nell; nerth
**migrant** *n* dyvroyas
**migrate** *v* dyvroa
**mild** *adj* clor; whar
**mildew** *n* kewny
**mildness** *n* clorder
**mile** *n* mildi·r
**militant** *adj/n* my·lytant
**military** *adj* a vresel
**milk** *n* leth
**milk** *v* godra
**milkshake** *n* leth shakys
**milli-** *pref* mylly-[1]
**mind** *n* brës
**mindset** *n* keveryans brës
**mine** *n* whel bal
**mineral** *n* mûn
**mineral water** *n* dowr mûn
**mini-** *pref* cor-[2]
**minimal** *adj* ispoyntek
**minimum** *adj* ispoyntek
**minimum** *n* ispoynt
**mining complex** *n* bal
**minister** *n* menyster
**ministry** *n* menystry
**mint** *n* menta
**minus** *prep* marnas
**minute(s)** *n* covnôtyans

**minutes** *n* mynys
**mirror** *n* gweder meras
**miscellany** *n* kemysk
**miserable** *adj* morethek; truan
**misery** *n* duwhan; ponvos
**mislead** *v* camhùmbronk
**Miss** *title* Mêstresyk
**miss** *v* fyllel a weskel; kelly
**mission** *n* myssyon
**mist** *n* nywl
**mistake** *n* fowt
**mistress** *n* mêstres
**misty** *adj* nywl
**misunderstanding** *n* camùnderstondyng
**mix** *n* kemysk
**mix** *v* kemysky
**mixer** *n* jyn kemysky
**mixture** *n* kemysk
**mobile [phone]** *n* kerdhfôn
**mock** *n* mockya
**model** *n* model; ma·nykyn
**moderate** *adj* temprys
**moderate** *v* tempra
**modern** *adj* arnowyth
**modernize** *v* arnowedhy
**modest** *adj* uvel
**modesty** *n* uvelder
**modification** *n* chaunj
**modify** *n* chaunjya
**module** *n* unsys
**mole** *n* go'dho·r
**moment** *n* pryjweyth
at the **moment** *phr* i'n tor'-ma
[for] a **moment** *phr* tùch; udn làm; rag tecken

**momentum** *n* momentùm
**Monday** *n* De Lun
**money** *n* mona
**monk** *n* managh
**monkey** *n* sym
**monster** *n* euthvil
**month** *n* mis
**monument** *n* covep
**mood** *n* cher
**moon** *n* loor
**moor[land]** *n* goon
**mop** *n* scubel wolhy
**moped** *n* whyl tan
**moral** *adj* ewnhensek
**moral** *n* dyscas
**morality** *n* mora·lyta
**morals** *n* conversacyon
**more** *adj/adv* moy
all the **more** *phr* dhe voy[G]
the **more** ... **the more** *phr* dhe² + *comparative* ... dhe² + *comparative*[G]
**more and more** *phr* moy ha moy
**more or less** *phr* moy pò le
**moreover** *adv* ha pelha
**morning** *n* myttyn
in the **morning** *phr* myttyn
**mortal** *adj* mortal
**mortgage** *n* morgaja
**mosque** *n* mòsk
**mosquitos** *n* gwybes
**moss** *n* kewny
**most** *adj* moyha
**mostly** *adv* dre vrâs
**MOT [test]** *n* prov menystry

**moth** *n* gowdhan
**mother** *n* mabm
**mother-in-law** *n* dama dhâ
**mother-tongue** *n* mamyeth
**motion** *n* môcyon; avî·s
**motive** *n* chêson
**motor** *n* jyn
**motorbike** *n* jyn dewros
**motorcyclist** *n* jyn-dewrosyas
**motorway** *n* môtorfordh
**mouldy** *adj* loos
**mound** *n* crug
**mount** *v* iskydna
**mountain** *n* meneth
**mourn** *v* kyny
**moustache** *n* minvlew
**mouth** *n* ganow
**move** *n* gway; remôcyon
**move** *v* gwaya; muvya
**movement** *n* môcyon; muvyans
**mow** *v* falhas
**Mr** *title* Mêster
**Mrs** *title* Mêstres
**Ms** *title* Mêstres
**much** *adv* meur; nameu·r
**mud** *n* lis
**muddle** *n* cabùlva
**muddy** *adj* lisak
**muffle** *v* megy
**mug** *n* cruskyn
**Muhammad** *n* Mùhamad
**multi-storey** *adj* lies-leur
**multiply** *v* lies'he·
**mumbo-jumbo** *n* pystry
**Mum[my]** *n* Mabmyk

murder *v* moldra
murmur *n* hanajen
murmur *v* hanaja
muscle *n* keher
muse *n* awen
museum *n* gwithty
mushroom *n* scavel cronak
mushy peas *n* lobmen pis
music *n* mûsyk
musical *n* gwary ilow
musician *n* mûsycyan

# N

nail *n* ewyn; kenter
nail *v* kentra
naive *adj* anfel
naivety *n* anfelder
naked *adj* noth
name *n* hanow
name *v* henwel
namely *adv* hèn yw dhe styrya
nano- *pref* nano-[1]
have a **nap** *phr* nappya
napkin *n* lien dewla
nappy *n* ledn baby
narrow *adj* cul; idn
narrow *v* culhe·
narrowness *n* culder
nasty *adj* dyvla·s, dysawor, hager-[2]
nation *n* nacyon, ke·nedhel
national *adj* kenedhlek
The **National Health Service** (**NHS**) *phr* An Servys [Kenedhlek] Yêhes

**Muslim** *adj/n* Mùslym
he [really] **must** *phr* res [porre·s] yw dhodho
he **must** [**have**] *phr* res yw
mustard *n* kedhow
mute *adj* avlavar
mutual *adj* kesparthek
muzzle *n* minfron
my *adj* ow[3] [G]
mysterious *adj* kevrinek
mystery *n* kevrin

**National Insurance number** *phr* nyver Surynjy Kenedhlek
The **National Lottery** *n* An Lo·ttery [Kenedhlek]The **National Trust** *n* An Fydhyans Kenedhlek
native *adj* genesyk
natural *adj* naturek
nature *n* natur; gnas; nas
nausea *n* whejuster
navel *n* begel
navy *n* morlu
near *adj* ogas
near *prep* in ogas; [in] ogas dhe[2]
nearby *adv* in ogas; rybon[G]
nearer *adj* nes
nearest *adj* nessa
neat *adj* glanyth
neatness *n* glanythter
necessary *adj* a res
neck *n* codna; gwarr
need *n* othem

**need** *v* *othem
**needle** *n* najeth
**negative** *adj* negedhek
**neglect** *v* gasa dhe goll
**neighbour** *n* kentrevak
**neighbourhood** *n* kentrevogeth
**neighbouring** *adj* kentrevak
**neither** *adv* nane·yl
**neither ... nor** *conj* na ... na[G], nane·yl ... na[G]
**nephew** *n* noy
**nerve** *n* nerv
**nervous** *adj* nervus
**nest** *n* neyth
**nest** *v* neythy
**net** *n* roos
**net[t]** *adj* ilyn
**nettles** *n* lynas
**network** *n* rosweyth
**never** *adv* nefra; bythqweth
**never again** *phr* nefra namo·y
**nevertheless** *adv* byttele·
**new** *adj* nowyth
**news** *n* nowodhow
**newsletter** *n* kelghlyther
**newspaper** *n* paper nowodhow
**next** *adj* nessa; an + *noun* a dheu
**nice** *adj* wheg; dainty
**niceness** *adj* whecter
**niece** *n* nith
**night** *n* nos
last **night** *phr* newher
**nightie** *n* pows nos

**nightingale** *n* eosyk
**nightmare** *n* hunlef
**nipple** *n* tethen
**nits** *n* nedh
**no** *adj* vëth [oll][G]; badna
**no longer** *phr* na felha
**no matter** *phr* na fors
**no more** *phr* namo·y
**no one** *pron* den vëth[G], nagonen[G]
**no other** *phr* nahe·n
in **no other way** *phr* nahe·n
he has **no time for** *phr* ny syns ev oy a²
**noble** *adj* brentyn
**nod** *v* inclynya pedn
**noise** *n* tros
**noisy** *adj* meur y dros
**nomination** *n* hanwans
**nonetheless** *adv* byttele·
**nonsense** *n* flows
**noodle** *n* noudel
**noose** *n* cabester
**nor** *conj* na[G]
**normal** *adj* normal
**Norman** *adj/n* Norman
**north** *adj/n* north
**northern** *adj* north
**nose** *n* dewfrik
**nostalgia** *n* hireth
**nostalgic** *adj* hirethek
**not** *adv* ada·r[G] *Not a general purpose word! The negative is most frequently expressed by a particle.*

**not a squeak** *phr* na gyk na myk
**not at all** *phr* màn, cabmen
**not counting** *phr* heb[G]
**not often** *phr* nameu·r
**not to mention** *phr* heb côwsel a²
**notable** *adj* a vry
**note** *n* nôten, nôtyans
**note** *v* nôtya
**nothing** *pron* tra vëth[G]
**notice** *n* avî·s; gwarnyans
**notice** *v* merkya
**notoriety** *n* drog-hanow
**notorious** *adj* drog-gerys
**noun** *n* hanow crev
**nourish** *v* maga
**novel** *n* novel
**November** *n* mis Du
**now** *adv* lebmyn, i'n eur-ma
**now** *interj* now
by **now** *phr* nans[G]

**now and then** *phr* lebmyn hag arta
**now that** *conj* abà·n² [G]
**nozzle** *n* tron
**nuance** *n* arlyw
**nuance** *v* arlywa
**nuclear** *adj* sprusek
**nude** *adj* noth
**nudity** *n* notha
**numb with cold** *phr* crobm
go **numb with cold** *phr* crobma
**number** *n* nùmber; nyver
**number** *v* nùmbra
**numeral** *n* nyveren
**numerous** *adj* lies
**nurse** *n* clôjior
**nursery** *n* meythrynva
**nursery school** *n* scol veythryn
**nuts** *n* know
**nylon** *n* nylon

# O

**oar** *n* rev
**oats** *n* kergh
**obedience** *n* obeyans
**obedient** *adj* gostyth
**obese** *adj* gorbeskys
**obey** *v* obeya
**object** *n* tra; objeta
**objective** *n* medras
**obligation** *n* kendon
**obligatory** *adj* constrînus
**oblige** *v* constrîna
**oblong** *adj/n* hirbedrak

**obscene** *adj* vil
**obscure** *v* tewlhe·
**observe** *v* aspia orth
**obsessed** *adj* obsessys
**obstacle** *n* let
**obtain** *v* gwainya
**obvious** *adj* ape·rt
**occasion** *n* ocasyon
**occasionally** *adv* lebmyn hag arta
**occupy** *v* ocûpya
**occur** *v* wharvos

**occurrence** *n* wharvos
**October** *n* mis Hedra
**odd** *adj* dybarow; coynt
**oddness** *n* co·yntùry
**of** *prep* a² G *But not a universal substitute for the genitive construction!*
**off** *adv* dhe ves
**off** *prep* dhywar² G
**offence** *n* offe·ns
**offend** *v* offendya
**offender** *n* trespassor
**offer** *n* profyans
**offer** *v* profya, offra
**office** *n* soodh; sodhva
**officer** *n* sodhak
**official** *adj* sodhogyl
**official** *n* sodhak
**official status** *n* gre sodhogyl
**often** *adv* yn fenowgh; nameu·r
**oh** *interj* ogh
**oh dear** *phr* govy^G
**oil** *n* oyl
**oil** *v* oylya
**okay** *adj/interj* dâ lowr
**old** *adj* coth
grow **old** *phr* cothhe·
**olive oil** *n* olew
**olives** *n* greun olew
The **Olympics** *n* An Gwariow Olympek
**ombudsman** *n* negesyth golyas
**omit** *v* gasa mes
**omit to** *phr* fyllel dhe²

**on** *prep* wàr² G
**on to** *phr* wàr² G
**once again** *phr* unweyth arta
**one** *pron* onen^G; den
[the] **one** *adj* an eyl^G
the **one** ... **the other** *pron* an eyl ... y gela^G
the **ones** *pron* an re^G
**onions** *n* onyon
**onlooker** *n* meror
**only** *adv* ma's; only, yn udnyk
**ooze** *v* sygera
**opaque** *adj* dyscle·r
**ope[way]** *n* ôp
**open** *adj* egerys, opyn
**open** *v* egery
The **Open University** *n* An Benscol Egor
**opener** *n* egerel
**opening** *n* egor
**opera** *n* gwary kenys
**operate** *v* gweytha
**operation** *n* oberyans medhek
**opinion** *n* tybyans, breus, opynyon
in his **opinion** *phr* dh'y vrës / vreus ev, orth y vrës / vreus
**opinion poll** *n* sowndyans
**opponent** *n* contrary
**opportune** *adj* in prës dâ
**opportunely** *adv* in prës dâ
**opportunist** *n* oportûnyst
**opportunity** *n* chauns, spâss
**oppose** *v* gortheneby
**opposite** *adj* contrary
**opposite** *prep* adâ·l [dhe²]

The **Opposition** *n* An Enebyans
**oppress** *v* compressa
**optionally** *adv* adhewys
**or** *conj* pò[G]
**or** [**otherwise**] *phr* poke·n[G]
**orange** *adj* rudhvelen
**orange** *n* owraval
**orchestra** *n* o·rchestra
**order** *n* ordyr; arhadow
**order** *v* erhy
in **order not to** *phr* rag na[2] [G]
in **order to** *phr* rag [may[5]] [G]
**ordinary** *adj* kemyn
**organ** *n* organ
**organic** *adj* organek
**organization** *n* cowethyans
**organize** *v* trevna
**orientation** *n* keveryans
**origin** *n* devedhyans
**original** *adj* gwredhek
**original** *n* mamscrif
**originate** *v* sordya
**origin**(**s**) *n* dalathfos
**ornament** *n* tegen
**ornamental** *adj* tegednek
**orphan** *adj/n* omdhevas
**orthodontist** *n* orthodontyth
**orthopaedic** *adj* orthopedek
**ostrich** *n* strus
**other** *adj* aral

the **other** [**one**] *phr* an aral[G]
the **others** / **other ones** *phr* an re erel[G]
**otherwise** *adv* ken; poke·n[G]
he **ought to** [**have**] *phr* y coodh / codhvia dhodho
**our** *adj* agan[G]
**out** *adj* marow
**out** *adv* avês; [in] mes
**out** *v* dyskevra
**out of** *phr* [in] mes a[2]
**outline** *v* linedna
**outlook** *n* gologva
**outrage** *n* outra·y
**outrageous** *adj* outrayus
**outside** *adv* avê·s; [in] mes
**outside** *prep* avê·s dhe[2]
**oval** *adj* hirgren
**oven** *n* forn
**over** *prep* a-ugh[G]; dres[G]
**overcome** *v* overcùmya
**overdraft** *n* gordenva
**overflow** *v* fedna
**overtake** *v* passya
**overturn** *v* omwheles
**owe** *v* bos in kendon rag
**owl** *n* ûla
**own** *adj* honen[G]
**own** *v* perhedna
**owner** *n* perhen

# P

**pack** *v* trùssa
**package** *n* fardel

**packet** *n* fardellyk
**pact** *n* kevambos

**paddle** *n* rev
**paddle** *v* revya; kerdhes i'n dowr
**padlock** *n* hesp cregys
**page** *n* folen
**pain** *n* pain
a real **pain** *phr* meur a bonvos
**pain in the arse** *phr* torment tin
**paint** *n* paint
**paint** *v* paintya; lymna
**painter** *n* lymnor
**painting** *n* lymnans
**pair** *n* copel
**pal** *n* mâta
**palace** *n* palys
**pale** *adj* gwydnyk
**paleness** *n* gwynder
**palm** *n* palv; palm
The **Palmer Award** *n* An 'Pewas Perghyryn'
**pan** *n* padel
**pancakes** *n* crampeth
**pane** *n* qwarel
**panel** *n* panel
**panties** *n* lavregyn
**pantomime** *n* a·nterlyk Nadelyk
**pants** *n* lavrak bian
**paper** *n* paper
**paperback** *n* aden vedhel
**parachute** *n* lamlen
**paradise** *n* pa·radhys
**paradox** *n* gow gwir
**parallel** *adj* keslînek
**paralyse** *v* paljia

**paranoid** *adj* pa·ranoyd
**parents** *n* kerens
**parish** *n* plu
**park** *v* parkya
**parliament** *n* seneth
**parrot** *n* po·pynjay
**parsnips** *n* panes
**part** *n* radn; part
take **part in** *phr* kemeres radn in
in these **parts** *phr* i'n côstys-ma
**participant** *n* kevradnak
**participate** *v* kevradna, kemeres radn
**particularly** *adv* spessly
**partner** *n* kespar
**partnership** *n* kescowethyans
**party** *n* kyffewy; party
**party** *v* kyffewya
**pass** *v* tremena, passya; istydna
**pass away** *phr* tremena
**passage** *n* tremenva
**passenger** *n* tremenyas
**passion** *n* passyon
**passport** *n* tremengubmyas
**password** *n* ger tremena
**past** *prep* dres$^G$
the **past** *n* an termyn eus passys
**pasta** *n* pasta
**paste** *n* toos
**pastry** *n* fûgen
**pasty** *n* pasty
**patch** *n* clowt

**patch** *v* clowtya
**path** *n* trûlergh
**patience** *n* perthyans
**patient** *adj* meur y berthyans
**patient** *n* clâv
**patron** *n* tasek
**pattern** *n* patron
**pause** *n* powes
**pause** *v* hedhy, powes
**pavement** *n* cauns
**paw** *n* paw
**pawn** *n* gwerynor
**pay** *v* tylly
**pay [out]** *phr* pê
**payment** *n* pêmont
**peace** *n* cres
**peace and quiet** *phr* cosoleth
**peach** *n* aval gwlanek
**peacock** *n* payon
**peak** *n* bleyn
**peanuts** *n* know dor
**pearl** *n* perl
**pears** *n* per
**peas** *n* pis
**peasant** *n* gwerynor
**pebbles** *n* bùly bian
**peculiar** *adj* dybarow
**peculiarity** *n* coyntys
**pedal** *n* trosel
**pedal** *v* trosella
**pedestal** *n* troos
**peel** *v* dyrusca
**peeler** *n* dyruskel
**peg** *n* ebyl
**pen** *n* pluven
**pencil** *n* pluven blobm; pyncel

**pendulum** *n* polsor
**penetrate** *v* dewana
**penis** *n* càl
**penny** *n* dynar
**pension** *n* pensyon
**Pentecost** *n* Pencast
**people** *n* pobel
**pepper** *n* puber
bell **pepper** *n* pubryn
**per cent** *phr* an cans
**perceive** *v* [godhvos] convedhes
**percentage** *n* cansran
**perfect** *adj* perfeth
**perfection** *n* perfethter
**perfectionist** *n* perfethyth
**performance** *n* gwrith
**perfume** *n* scent
**perhaps** *adv* martesen, par hap
**period** *n* amseryow
**perish** *v* mos dhe goll
**permanent** *adj* fast
**permission** *n* cubmyas
**permit** *v* ry cubmyas rag
**persecute** *v* persecûtya
**persist** *v* durya
**person** *n* den, person
**personal identification number (PIN)** *phr* nyver aswonvos [personek]
**personnel** *n* felshyp
**perspiration** *n* whës
**perspire** *v* whesa
**persuade** *v* perswâdya
**perverted** *adj* podrek

**pet** *n* mil dov
**pet** *v* chersya
**petition** *n* petycyon
**petrol** *n* petrol
**pharmacist** *n* apo·tecary
**phenomenon** *n* feno·menon
**phenomenal** *adj* barthusek
**photo**[**graph**] *n* skeusen
**photograph** *v* fotografya
**photographer** *n* skeusednor
**photography** *n* skeuse·dnieth
**phrase** *n* lavaren
**physical** *adj* fy·sycal
**piano** *n* pyâno
**pick**[**-axe**] *n* pyck
**pickle** *n* pyckel
**pickle** *v* pyckla
**picnic** *n* croust
**picture** *n* pyctour
**pie** *n* pasty
**piece** *n* darn
**pier** *n* cay
**pierce** *v* gwana; telly
**piercing** *n* tegen telly
**pig** *n* porhel
**pigeon** *n* colom
**pile** *n* grahell
**pile** *v* grahella
**pilchards** *n* hern
**pill** *n* pelednyk
**pillow** *n* pluvak
**pilot** *n* lewyador
**pimple** *n* cùriak
**pin** *n* pyn
**pin** *v* pydna
**pinch** *n* pynch

**pinch** *v* pynchya
**pineapple** *n* pînaval
**pink** *adj* gwynru·dh
**pint** *n* pynt
**pioneer** *n* ragresor
**pipe** *n* pib; pibel
**Pisces** *n* An Pùscas
**piss** *n* pysas
**piss** *v* pysa
**pit** *n* pyt; poll
**pitch** *n* gwel, park
**pity** *n* trueth; dieth
**pity** *v* kemeres trueth a[2]
**pizza** *n* pîtsa
**place** *n* tyller, plâss
**place** *v* gorra
**place mat** *n* straylyk
**plagiarism** *n* lien-ladrans
**plague** *n* pla
**plaice** *n* lith
**plain** *n* plain
**plainly** *adv* dhe blebmyk
**plait** *n* pleth
**plait** *v* plethy
**plan** *n* cùssul, towl; towlen
**plan** *v* cùssulya, tôwlel; towledna
**planet** *n* planet
**plant** *n* plans; gweythva
**plant** *v* plansa
**plants** *n* losow
**plaster** *n* plaster; plestryn
**plastic** *n* plastek
**plate** *n* plât
**platform** *n* cay
**plausible** *adj* gwirhaval

**play** *n/v* gwary
**player** *n* gwarior
**playground** *n* garth gwary
**plaything** *n* gwariel
**pleasant** *adj* wheg, plesont
**pleasantness** *n* whecter
**please** *v* plegya dhe² / gans
**please** *interj* mar pleg,
my a'th / a'gas pës,
dre gortesy
**pleased** *adj* pës dâ
**pleasure** *n* plesour
**plenty of** *phr* cals a²; pals
**plot** *n* bras; plot; splat
**plough** *n* a·radar
**plough** *v* aras
**plug** *n* ebyl; ebylyor
**plug in** *phr* ebylya
**plum** *n* plùmen
**plumber** *n* plobmor
**plural** *n* furv liesek
**pocket** *n* pocket
**podiatrist** *n* trosvedhek
**podium** *n* arethva
**poem** *n* bardhonek
**poet** *n* prydyth
**poetry** *n* prydy·dhieth
**point** *n* poynt
**pointed** *adj* pigvon
**pointer** *n* poyntyor
**pointless** *adj* cog
**poison** *n* poyson
**poison** *v* posnya
**poke** *n* pock
**poke** *v* pockya
**police** *n* creslu

**police officer** *n* gwethyas cres
**policy** *n* po·lycy
**polish** *n* cor lenter
**polish** *v* polsya
**polite** *adj* cortes
**politeness** *n* cortesy
**political** *adj* gwlasek;
poly·tycal
**politician** *n* gwlasegor
**politics** *n* gwlasegeth; po·lytek
**pollute** *v* defolya
**pompous** *adj* bobansus
**pond** *n* lagen
**pony** *n* merhyk
**pool** *n* poll; bylyard tavern
**poor** *adj* bohosek; truan
**popcorn** *n* ÿs crack
**pope** *n* pab
**popular** *adj* meurgerys
**popularity** *n* kerensa
gans an bobel
**population** *n* poblans
**porch** *n* portal
**pork** *n* kig porhel
**pork scratchings** *n* cravyon
mogh
**pornographic** *adj* pornografek
**porpoise** *n* morhogh
**porridge** *n* yos kergh
**port** *n* porth; portwîn
**portable** *adj* hedhon
**portal** *n* portal
**portfolio** *n* omgemeryans
**portion** *n* shara
**portray** *v* portraya

**position** *n* tyller; savla; stauns, stubm; soodh
**position** *v* desedha
**positive** *adj* po·sytyf
**possess** *v* perhedna
**possessions** *n* pethow
**possible** *adj* po·ssybyl
**post** *n* peul; post; pôsten; soodh
**post office** *n* sodhva bost
**postage** *n* lytherdoll
**postcode** *n* pôstcôd
**poster** *n* poster
**postpone** *v* dylâtya
**pot** *n* pot
**potato** *n* patâta
**pouch** *n* pors
**pound** *n* poos; puns
**pour** *v* dyvera, denewy
**poverty** *n* bohosogneth
**powder** *n* polter
**power** *n* gallos; nell; nerth; vertû
**powerful** *adj* gallosek
**practical** *adj* pra·ctycal
**practice** *n* practys; omassayans
**practise** *v* practycya; omassaya
**praise** *n* gormola
**praise** *v* gormel
**pram** *n* caryach baby
**prawn** *n* legestyk
**pray** *v* pejy
**prayer** *n* pejadow

The **Prayer Book Rebellion** *phr* Rebellyans Lyver Pejadow
**preach** *v* progeth
**precarious** *adj* deantel
**precedent** *n* exampyl kyns
**precipice** *n* clegar
**precise** *adj* kewar
**precisely right** *phr* kewar
**precision** *n* kewerder
**predict** *v* dargana
**prediction** *n* dargan
**predominance** *n* gwarthevyans
**prefer** *v* \*gwell
**pregnant** *adj* behek
**prejudice** *n* ragvreus
**pre-menstrual tension** (**PMT**) *phr* tenva kyns mislif
The **Premier League** *n* An Colmeth Adhevî·s
**prepare** *v* darbary; parusy
**preposition** *n* ragêr
**prescription** *n* gorhebmyn medhek
**present** *adj* present
**present** *n* present; ro
**present** *v* presentya
**presentation** *n* presentyans
**presently** *adv* whare·
**preserve** *v* gwetha
**preside** *v* caderya
**president** *n* pre·sydent
**press** *n* gwask
**press** *v* gwasca; levna
**pressure** *n* gwascas
**prestige** *n* roweth

**pretend** *adj* fug-
**pretty** *adj* teg
**prevent** *v* lettya
**previously** *adv* kyns
**price** *n* pris
**prick** *v* piga
**prickle** *n* dren
**pride** *n* gooth
take **pride in** *phr* bos balgh a[2]
**priest** *n* pronter
**primary school** *n* scol elvednek
**prince** *n* pensevyk
**princess** *n* pensevyges
**principal** *adj* chif-[1]
**principally** *adv* kyns oll
**principle** *n* penrewl
**print** *n* prynt
**print** *v* pryntya
**prison** *n* pryson; bagh
**prisoner** *n* prysner
**privacy** *n* pryvetter
**private** *adj* pryva
**prize** *n* pris, pewas
**probable** *adj* gwirhaval
**probably** *adv* dre [bùb] lycklod
**problem** *n* caletter; cudyn; problem
**proceed** *v* mos in rag
**process** *n* argerdh
**procession** *n* keskerdh
move in **procession** *v* keskerdhes
**prod** *n* pock
**prod** *v* pockya
**produce** *v* ascor

**product** *n* ascoras
**profession** *n* galwans
**professional** *adj* galwansek
**professor** *n* professour
**profit** *n* gwain, profyt
**profound** *adj* down
**progress** *n* avauncyans
**program** *n* towlen
**program** *v* towledna
**programme** *n* raglen; program
**progress** *v* avauncya
**prohibit** *v* dyfen
**prohibition** *n* dyfen
**project** *n* keweyth
**promise** *n* promys
**promise** *v* dedhewy
**promising** *adj* leun a dhedhewadow
**promote** *v* avauncya
**promotion** *n* remôcyon
**promotional code** *n* cod marhasa
**pronoun** *n* raghanow
**pronunciation** *n* leveryans
**proof** *n* prov
**proper** *adj* onest
**prophet** *n* profet
**proportion** *n* kemusur
**proportional /**
**proportionate** *adj* kemusur
**proposal** *n* profyans
**propose** *v* profya
**proprietor** *n* perhednek
**prose** *n* pros
**prosecute** *v* darsewya
**prosper** *v* soweny

**prosperity** *n* sowena
**prostitute** *n* hôra
**protect** *v* gwetha; dyffres
**protection** *n* dyffresyans
child **protection** *n* diogelyans flogh
**protector** *n* dyffresyas
**protest** *n* protestyans
**protest** *v* protestya
**Protestant** *adj/n* Pro·testant
**proud** *adj* gothys
**prove** *v* prevy
**proverb** *n* lavar coth
**provide** *v* provia
**provision** *n* provians
**provoke** *v* provôkya
**proxy** *n* cadnas vôtya
**prudence** *n* furneth
**prudent** *adj* fur
**prune** *v* dyvarra
**psychological** *adj* enevek
**psychology** *n* ene·vieth
**pub** *n* tavern
**public** *adj* poblek
the **public** *n* an bobel
**publicize** *v* poblegy
**publish** *v* dyllo
**publisher** *n* dyllor
**pudding** *n* pùdyn
**puddle** *n* lagen
**pull** *n* tedn
**pull** *v* tedna
**pull back** *phr* kildedna

**pullover** *n* gwlanek
**pulpit** *n* gogell
**pulse** *n* pols
**pump** *n* pùmp
**pump** *v* pùmpya
**pumpkin** *n* pompyon
**pun** *n* gwary ger
**punctually** *adv* abo·ynt
**punish** *v* pùnsya
**punishment** *n* pù·nyshment
**pupil** *n* scolor; descor
**puppet** *n* popet
**puppy** *n* colyn
**purchase** *n* prenas
**purchase** *v* prena
**purchaser** *n* prenor
**pure** *adj* pur
**purple** *adj* glasru·dh
**purpose** *n* porpos
on **purpose** *phr* aborpos
**purr** *v* pùrrya
**purse** *n* pors
**pus** *n* podrethes
**push** *n* pock
**push** *v* pockya
**pushchair** *n* cadar herdhya
**put** *v* gorra
**put on** *phr* gwysca
**put up with** *phr* perthy
**puzzle** *n* desmyk *See also* gwary mildam
**pyjamas** *n* pyjamas

# Q

**quality** *n* qwa·lyta; gnas

**quarrel** *n* dalva

**quarrel** *v* omdhal
**quarry** *n* mengleth
**quay** *n* cay
**queen** *n* myternes
**question** *n* qwestyon
**questionnaire** *n* govynador
**queue** *n* lost
**quick** *adj* uskys
as **quick as I could / you can** *phr* scaffa gyllyn / gylta

# R

**rabbit** *n* conyn
**race** *n* hil; resegva
**racism** *n* hile·gieth
**rack** *n* cloos, rastel
**racket** *n* hùbbadùllya
**radiator** *n* tobmor
**radical** *adj* ra·dycal
**radio** *n* radyo
**radish** *n* redyk
**raffle** *n* gwary dall
**rag** *n* pyllen
**rail** *n* lînen
**railings / rails** *n* clether
**railway** *n* hens horn
**rain** *n* glaw
**rain** *v* gwil glaw
**rainbow** *n* gwarak an glaw
**raise** *v* derevel
**ramble** *v* gwandra
**ramp** *n* iskynva
**rank** *n* renk
**rape** *v* defolya
**rare** *adj* tanow

pretty damn **quick** *phr* toth men
**quiet** *adj* cosel
**quirk** *n* coyntys
**quite** *adv* lowr; teg
**quite a few** *phr* lower
**quiz** *n* qwyz
**quorum** *n* qwôrùm
**quotation** *n* devyn
**quote** *v* devydnes

**rarely** *adv* bohes venowgh, namenowgh
**rascal** *n* gal
**rasp** *n* ronk
**rasp** *v* renky
**raspberries** *n* avan
**rasping** *adj* ronk
**rate** *n* kevrath
**rates** *n* toll adneth
**rather** *adv* kyns
**rating** *n* scor
**ration** *n* ewnran
**rational** *adj* resonek
**rats** *n* logas brâs
**rattle** *v* rugla
**raucous** *adj* ronk
**raw** *adj* criv
**ray** *n* dewyn
**razor** *n* alsen
**reach** *v* hedhes; drehedhes
**react** *v* gortheby
**reaction** *n* gorthyp
**reactor** *n* dasoberor
**read** *v* redya

**readiness** *n* paruster
**ready** *adj* parys
get **ready** *v* parusy
**ready meal** *n* prës parys
**readily** *adv* iredy
**real** *adj* gwir
**reality** *n* gwrioneth, realeth
virtual **reality** *n* realeth furvwir
**reality TV** *n* pellwolok realeth
**realize** *v* [godhvos] convedhes
**really** *adv* dhe wir
**rear** *v* maga
**reason** *n* rêson; chêson; skyla
for some **reason** *phr* neb ken
**reasonable** *adj* resonus
**rebel** *v* rebellya
**receipt** *n* aqwîtyans
**receive** *v* degemeres, recêva
**recently** *adv* agensow
**reception** *n* recepcyon
**recess** *n* kil
**recession** *n* kildro
**recipe** *n* rece·yt
**recipient** *n* degemeror
**reciprocal** *adj* kesparthek
**recognize** *v* aswon
**recommend** *v* comendya
**recommendation** *n* comendyans
**reconnaissance** *n* aspians
**record** *n* covath; record
**record** *v* recordya
**recover** *v* sawya
**rectangle** *n* hirbedrak
**rectangular** *adj* hirbedrak
**recyclable** *adj* dassteusadow

**recycle** *v* dassteusya
**red** *adj* rudh
**reduce** *v* lehe·
**reel** *n* rôlbren
**refer to** *phr* campolla
**referee** *n* breusor
**reference** *n* campoll; dùstuny
**referendum** *n* referendùm
**refill** *v* daslenwel
**reflect** *v* dastewynya; ombredery
**reform** *v* dasformya
**refrain** *n* pedn pùsorn
**refrain from** *phr* sevel orth
**refresh** *v* dyseha
**refreshing** *adj* ow tyseha [yn] teg
**refrigerator** *n* yeynor
**refuge** *n* harber
**refugee** *n* foesyk
**refusal** *n* nagh
**refuse** *v* naha
**regard** *n* bry
have a high **regard for** *phr* acowtya
**regime** *n* mestrynsys
**regiment** *n* re·jyment
**region** *n* randir
**regional** *adj* randirek
**register** *n* covrol
**register** *v* covscrefa
**regret** *n* edrek
**regret** *v* *edrek
**regulate** *v* rêwlya
**regulation** *n* rewlyans
**rehearsal** *n* assa·y

**rehearse** *v* assaya
**reindeer** *n* carow Loghlyn
**reinforce** *v* crefhe·
**reject** *v* sconya
**rejoice** *v* lowenhe·
**relate to** *phr* perthyn dhe²
**related** *adj* kelmys ganso; unwos
**relating to** *phr* adro· dhe², [ow] tùchya
in **relation to** *phr* in kever
**relationship** *n* perthynas; kescowethyans; caro·rieth
**relative** *adj* perthynek
**relatively** *adv* yn keverek
**relatives** *n* kerens
**relativity** *n* perthynecter
**relax** *v* dysqwitha
**relaxing** *adj*
teg y dhysqwithans
**relevant** *adj* longus
**reliable** *adj* diogel
**reliance** *n* fydhyans
**religion** *n* crejyans
**religious** *adj* cryjyk
**reluctant** *adj* [oll] a'y anvoth
be **reluctant** *phr* *poos
**reluctantly** *adv* [oll] a'y anvoth
**rely on** *phr* scodhya wàr²
**remain** *v* remainya
the **remainder** *n* an remnant
**remake** *v* dasqwil
**remark** *n* lavar
**remark** *v* nôtya
**remember** *v* perthy cov, remembra

**remind** *v* dry dhe gov
**remote control** *n* sethor
**remove** *v* remuvya
**remunerate** *v* gobra
**rendezvous** *v* omvetya
**renew** *v* nowedhy
**renewable [energy]** *n* nerth nowedhadow
**renovate** *v* nowethhe·
**rent** *n* rent
**rent** *v* gobrena
**rent out** *phr* settya wor'gobren
**repair** *n* ewnans
**repair** *v* êwna
**repay** *v* attylly
**repayment** *n* atta·l
**repeat** *v* dasleverel
**repent** *v* repentya
**repentance** *n* repentons
**reply** *n* gorthyp
**reply** *v* gortheby
**report** *n/v* derivas
**reporter** *n* derivador
**represent** *v* representya
**representative** *n* cadnas
**reproach** *n* kereth
**reproach** *v* keredhy
**reptile** *n* cramvil
**republic** *n* poblegeth
**repulsive** *adj* casadow
**reputation** *n* hanow
**request** *n* govyn[adow]
**request** *v* govyn
**require** *v* reqwîrya
**requirement / requisition** *n* gorholeth

**rescue** *v* sawya
**rescuer** *n* den rescous
**research** *n* whythrans
**research** *v* whythra
**reservation** *n* ardak
**reserve** *v* ragerhy
**reserves** *n* creunyon
**reservoir** *n* pollgreun
**resign** *v* omdhysodha
**resist** *v* sevel orth
**resistance** *n* gorthsaf
**resources** *n* asnodhow
**respect** *n* bry, revrons
**respect** *v* gwil revrons dhe², gwil vry a²
**respectable** *adj* wordhy
**respond** *v* gortheby
**response** *n* gorthyp
**responsibility** *n* charj, omgemeryans
take **responsibility for** *phr* omgemeres rag
**rest** *n/v* powes
have a **rest** *phr* gwil powes
the **rest** *n* an gwedhyl
**restaurant** *n* bosty
**restore** *v* dasqwil
**restrict** *v* strotha; culhe·
**result** *n* sewyans
**result** *v* omsewya
as a **result** *phr* dre hedna
**retaliate** *v* attylly
**retaliation** *n* attal
**retain** *v* sensy
**retire** *v* omdedna
**retirement** *n* omden

**retreat** *v* kildedna
**retrieve** *v* dascafos
**return** *v* dewheles; dascor
**reveal** *v* dyscudha
**revenge** *n* venjyans
**revenue** *n* rent
**review** *n* dasqwel
**review** *v* dasqweles
**revise** *v* amendya; dastesky
**revive** *v* dasvewa
**revolution** *n* omdrailyans; wheldro
**reward** *n* we·ryson
**reward** *v* rewardya
**rhetorical** *adj* arethek
**rheumatism** *n* cleves esyly
**rhyme** *n* rim
**rhythm** *n* rythym
**ribbon** *n* rybyn
**ribs** *n* asow
**rice** *n* ris
**rich** *adj* rych
**riches** *n* rychys
**riddle** *n* desmyk
**ride** *n* viaj; jaunt
**ride** *v* marhogeth
**rider** *n* marhak
**ridge** *n* crib, keyn
**ridiculous** *adj* wharthus
**right** *adj* ewn; compes; dyhow
**right** *adv* knack
**right** *n* an dâ; gwir; dyhow
he is **right** *phr* y'n jeves an gwir
on the **right** *phr* adhyhow
put **right** *phr* amendya

to the **right of** *phr* adhyhow dhe²
**right angle** *n* elyn pedrak
**rigid** *adj* dywethyn
**rigour** *n* dour
**rind** *n* rusk
**ring** *n* kelgh; besow
**ring** *v* seny
**ringtone** *n* ton seny
**riot** *n* gùstel
**rip** *v* sqwardya
**ripe** *adj* adhves
**ripen** *v* adhvejy
**ripeness** *n* adhvetter
**rise** *v* derevel
**risk** *n* peryl
**risk** *v* chauncya
**river** *n* ryver
**road** *n* fordh
**roar** *n* uj
**roar** *v* uja
**roast** *v* rôstya
**roast meat** *n* goleyth
**rob** *v* rafna
**robber** *n* rafnor
**robbery** *n* rafnans
**robe** *n* pows
**robin** *n* rudhak
**robot** *n* robot
**rock** *n* carrek
**rock** *v* lesca
**rocket** *n* fusen
**rocky** *adj* caregek; carnak
**rod** *n* gwelen
**roll** *n* rol
**roll** *v* rollya

**roller** *n* rôlbren
**Roman** *adj/n* Roman
**romantic** *adj* romantek
**roof** *n* to
**room** *n* spâss, tyller; rom
**roots** *n* gwrëdh
**rope** *n* lovan
**roses** *n* ros
**rot** *n* poder, podrethes
**rot** *v* pedry
**rota** *n* kelghrester
**rotten** *adj* poder
**rough** *adj* garow
**round** *adj* rônd
**round** *n* tro
**roundabout** *n* fordh adro·
**route** *v* rowtya
**router** *n* rowtor
**row** *n* res; kedry·dn
**row** *v* revya
**royal** *adj* rial
**royalty** *n* mûndalas
**rub** *v* rùttya
**rubber** *n* rùber
**rubbish** *n* atal
**rucksack** *n* gwarsagh
**rude** *adj* dyscortes
**rudeness** *n* dysco·rtesy
**rugby** *n* rùgby
**ruin** *n* magor
**ruin** *v* myshevya
**rule** *n* rewl
**rule** *v* rêwlya
**rule lines** *phr* linedna
**rule the roost** *phr* rowtya
**ruler** *n* linednor

**rum** *n* dowr tobm molâ·ss
**rummage** *v* turya
**rumour** *n* whedhel
the **rumour mill** *phr* scavel an gow
**rumpled** *adj* crigh
**run** *v* ponya; resek; brednya; governa

## S

**sack** *n* sagh
**sack** *v* gordhyllo
**sacred** *adj* sacrys
**sacrifice** *v* offrydna
**sad** *adj* trist
**sad state of affairs** *phr* trueth
**saddle** *n* dyber
**safe** *adj* saw
**safeguard** *n* scoos
**safety** *n* sawder
**safety belt** *n* grugys sawder
**Sagittarius** *n* An Sethor
**sail** *n* gool
**sail** *v* golya
**sailboard** *n* astell gool
go **sailboarding** *phr* astell-wolya
**sailor** *n* marner
**St Meriadoc** *n* Meriasek
**St Michael** *n* Myhal Sans
**St Piran** *n* Peran
for my **sake** *phr* a'm govys[G]
for the **sake of** *phr* rag kerensa
**salad** *n* salad
**salary** *n* gober

**run out** *phr* dyfygya
**runway** *n* hens tira
**rush** *v* stêvya
**rustle** *v* rùstla
**rusty** *adj* gossenek
**rut** *n* rygol
**ruthless** *adj* dybyta
**rye** *n* sugal

**sale** *n* gwerth
**salesman** *n* gwerthor
**salmon** *n* sowman
**salt** *n* holan
**salty** *adj* holanek
at the **same time** *phr* i'n kettermyn
the **same** *adj* an keth[G]
the **same thing** *phr* an keth hedna[G]
**sanction(s)** *n* kessydhyans
**sanctuary** *n* sentry
**sand** *n* tewas; treth
**sandwich** *n* breghtan
**sarcastic** *adj* sarcastek
be **sat** *phr* bos a'y eseth
**satellite** *n* loren
**satire** *n* geseth
**satirize** *v* scornya
**satisfaction** *n* contentyans
**satisfied** *adj* pës dâ
**satisfy** *v* contentya
**satnav** *n* hensador [lorednek]
**Saturday** *n* De Sadorn
**sauce** *n* sows
**saucepan** *n* padel dhorn

**saucer** *n* padellyk
**sausage** *n* selsygen
**save** *n* sylwans
**save** *v* sylwel; sawya; erbysy
**savings** *n* erbysyon
**saviour** *n* savyour
**saw** *n* hesken
**saw** *v* heskedna
**Saxon** *adj/n* Saxon
**say** *v* leverel
**scaffolding** *n* scaffôtys
**scale** *n* gradhva; skeul
**scales** *n* scant; mantol
**scampi** *n* legestyk Bay Dûlyn
**scan** *v* scanya
**scandal** *n* sclander; bysmê·r
**scandalous** *adj* sclandrus
**scanner** *n* scanyor
**scar** *n* crithen
**scarce** *adj* scant, tanow
**scarcely** *adv* scant; nameu·r
**scarecrow** *n* bùcka
**scarf** *n* lien codna
**scene** *n* gwel
**scent** *n* scent
**sceptical** *adj* skeptycal
**schedule** *n* towlen
**schedule** *v* towledna
**scheme** *n* rester
**school** *n* scol
**science** *n* sciens
**scientific** *adj* sciensek
**scientist** *n* sciensyth
**scissors** *n* gweljow bian
**scold** *v* tavasa
**scones** *n* scons

**scoop** *n* loas
**score** *n* scor
**scorn** *v* scornya
**Scorpio** *n* An Scorpyon
**scramble** *v* crambla; scrambla
**scrape** *v* cravas
**scraper** *n* cravell
**scratch** *v* cravas
**scratch card** *n* carten cravas
**scream** *n* uj
**scream** *v* uja
**screen** *n* skew; scrin
**screw** *n* screw
**screwdriver** *n* trogentrel
**script** *n* scriven; scrypt
**scruple(s)** *n* danjer
**sculpture** *n* gravyans
**scum** *n* kellyn
**sea** *n* mor
**seagull** *n* gwylan
**seal** *n* reun
**seal** *v* staunchya
**sealed** *adj* staunch
**search** *n* whythrans
**search** *v* whythra
**search engine** *n* jyn whelas
**seashore** *n* morrep
**season** *n* sêson
**seasonal** *adj* a'n sêson
**seat** *n* eseth
**seaweed** *n* goubman
**second** *adj* nessa *Only when the focus is a sequence! See also* secùnd *in 'Numerals for Reference'*
**second** *n* secùnd

**second-hand** *phr* dasleuvus
**secondary school** *n* scol nessa
**secret** *adj* kevrinek, in dadn gel
**secret** *n* kevrin
**secretary** *n* scrivynyas
**secretly** *adv* in dadn gel
**section** *n* trogh
**sector** *n* dyberthva
**secure** *adj* saw, diogel
**security** *n* sawder
**security [check]** *n* checkva
**security guard** *n* gwethyas sawder
**see** *v* gweles
**see-saw** *n* astell omborth
**see-through** *adj* boll
**seed** *n* has
**seek** *v* whelas
**seem** *v* hevelly
**seep** *v* sygera
**seize** *v* dalhedna
**seldom** *adv* bohes venowgh, namenowgh
**select** *v* dêwys
**selection** *n* dêwys
**self** *n* honen[G]
**self-** *pref* honen-[2 G]
**self-sacrifice** *n* omoffrydnans
**selfish** *adj* honenus
**selfishness** *n* honenuster
**sell** *v* gwertha
**seller** *n* gwerthor
**senate** *n* seneth
**send** *v* danvon

**sense** *n* sens; styr
make **sense** *phr* bos rêson
**sense of humour** *phr* sens a dhydhan
**sensible** *adj* fur
**sensitive** *adj* se·nsytyf
**sensitivity** *n* sensyty·vyta
**sentence** *n* lavar
**sentimental** *adj* amuvyansek
**separate** *adj* dybarow
**separate** *v* dybe·rth
**separation** *n* dyba·rth
**September** *n* mis Gwyngala
**sequence** *n* res
**serial** *adj* kevresek
**series** *n* kevres; steus
**serious** *adj* sevur; sàd
**seriousness** *n* sevureth
**sermon** *n* progeth
**serpent** *n* serpont
**serpentine** *n* sarfven
**servant** *n* servont
**serve** *v* servya
**server** *n* servyas
**service** *n* servys
**services** *n* othomva
**serviette** *n* lien dewla
**session** *n* esedhvos
**set** *v* settya; desedha; sedhy; dosbartha
**set in order** *phr* ordna
**set up** *phr* fastya
**setback** *n* let
**settee** *n* gwely dëdh
**setting** *n* desedhans
**settlement** *n* trevesygeth

**severe** *adj* wherow
**severity** *n* wherowder
**sew** *v* gwrias
**sex** *n* reydh; carnal joy
**sexism** *n* sexy·stieth
**sexual orientation** *n* keveryans reydhek
**shade** *n* goskes; arlyw
**shade** *v* goskesy
**shadow** *n* skeus
**shady** *adj* skeusek
**shaft** *n* shafta
**shake** *v* shakya; crena
**shale** *n* shal
**shallow** *adj* bas
**shallowness** *n* baster
**sham** *adj* fug-[2]
**shame** *n* meth, sham
**shame** *v* shâmya
**shameful** *adj* methus
**shameless** *adj* dyve·th
**shamelessness** *n* dyvethter
**shampoo** *n* shampou·
**shape** *n* shâp
**shape** *v* shâpya
**share** *n* kevran; shara
**share** *v* kevradna
**shareholder** *n* kevradnor
**shark** *n* morvleyth
**sharp** *adj* lybm; sherp
**sharpen** *v* lebma
**sharpness** *n* lymder
**shatter** *v* brewy
**shave** *v* dyvarva; dyvlewa
**shaver** *n* dyvarvor; dyvlewor
**shawl** *n* whytel

**she** *pron* hy[G]
**shed** *v* dyvera
**sheep** *n* davas
**sheet** *n* ledn
**shell** *n* crogen; tanbellen
**shell** *v* tanbeledna
**shellfish** *n* pùscas crogednek
**shelter** *n* goskes; scovva
**shelter** *v* goskesy
**shelving** *n* estyll
**sherry** *n* sherys
**Shia** *adj* Shiek
**Shia** *n* Shiyas
**shield** *n* scoos
**shine** *n* càn
**shine** *v* spladna
**ship** *n* gorhal
**shipwreck** *n* torrva
**shirt** *n* cris
**shit** *n* caugh
**shit** *v* cauha
**shoal** *n* hes
**shock** *n* scruth
**shocked** *adj* diegrys
**shocking** *adj* scruthus
**shoe** *n* eskys
**shoot** *v* tedna
**shop** *n* shoppa
**shop** *v* prenassa
**short** *adj* cot
**short-sighted** *adj* cot y wolok
**shortage** *n* dyfyk
**shortcut** *n* cot'hens, scochfordh
**shorten** *v* cot'he·
**shorts** *n* lavrak cot

**shot** *n* tedn
he **should** [**have**] *phr* y coodh / codhvia dhodho
**shoulder** *n* scoodh
**shoulders** *n* gwarr
**shout** *n* cry
**shout** *v* cria
**shove** *v* herdhya
**shovel** *n* rev
**shovel** *v* revya
**show** *n* dysqwedhyans; show
**show** *v* dysqwedhes
**shower** *n* cowas; cowasva
take a **shower** *phr* cafos cowas
**shred** *v* frega
**shrewd** *adj* fel
**shrewdness** *n* felder
**shriek** *n* scrij
**shriek** *v* scrija
**shrimp** *n* bîbyn-bûbyn
**shrine** *n* scrin
**shrink** *v* omdedna
**shut** *adj* degë·s
**shut** *v* degea
**shutter** *n* keas fe·nester
**shuttle**[**cock**] *n* gwenol
be **shy** *phr* *meth
**shyness** *n* meth
**sick** *adj* clâv; whejus
be **sick** *phr* wheja
**side** *n* tu; tenewen; parth
on this **side of** *phr* a'n barth / tu-ma dhe[2]
**siege** *n* esedhva

**sieve** *n* crôder
**sigh** *n* hanajen
**sigh** *v* hanaja
**sight** *n* gwel, syght
**sign** *n* sin, arweth
**sign** *v* sîna
**signal** *n* sin, arweth
**signal** *v* sîna, arwedha
**signature** *n* sînans
**significant** *adj* a bris
**Sikh** *adj/n* Sik
**Sikhism** *n* Sî·kieth
**silence** *n* taw
**silence** *v* destewel
**silent** *adj* tawesek
fall **silent** *phr* tewel
**silk** *n* owrlyn
**silly** *adj* cog
**silver** *n* arhans
**similar** *adj* haval
**similarity** *n* hevelepter
**simile** *n* comparyans
**simple** *adj* sempel
**simplify** *v* sempelhe·
**simulate** *v* omhevelly
**simulation** *n* omhevellyans
**sin** *n* pehadow
**sin** *v* peha
**since** *conj* abà·n[2 G]; pàn[2 G]
**since** *prep* dhia[2 G]
**sincere** *adj* gwiryon
**sincerity** *n* gwiryonsys
**sing** *v* cana
**singer** *n* canor
**single** *adj* heb kespar
**singular** *n* furv unplek

**sink** *n* new
**sink** *v* budhy; sedhy
**sinner** *n* pehador
**sip** *n* lemygya
**sir** *addressing sb* sera
**sister** *n* whor
**sit** [**down**] *phr* esedha
be **sitting** *phr* bos a'y eseth
**sitting room** *n* rom esedha
be **situated** *phr* bos desedhys
**situation** *n* plit
**size** *n* brâster, myns
**sizeable** *adj* mynsek
**skeleton** *n* corf eskern
**sketch** *n* tedn; skech
**ski** *n* sky
**ski** *v* skia
**skid** *v* slyppya
**skilful** *adj* sley
**skilfulness** *n* sleyneth
**skill** *n* creft
**skill**(**s**) *n* gallos
**skin** *n* crohen
**skip** *n* kybell atal
**skirt** *n* losten
**skull** *n* crogen pedn
**sky** *n* ebron
**skylark** *n* awhesyth
**slab** *n* legh
**slack** *adj* lows
**slander** *n* cabel sclandrus
**slant** *n* leder
**slant** *v* ledry
**slap** *n* sqwat
**slap** *v* sqwattya
**slate** *n* lehen

**slaughter** *n* ladhva
**slaughter** *v* ladha
**slavery** *n* kethneth
**sleaze** *n* podrethes
**sledge** *n* carr slynkya
**sleep** *n* cùsk
**sleep** *v* cùsca; nappya
**sleeper** *n* trester
**sleeping bag** *n* sagh cùsca
**sleet** *n* dowrergh
**sleeve** *n* brehal
**sleigh** *n* carr slynkya
**slender** *adj* moon
**slice** *n* tregh
**slide** *n* slynkva
**slide** *v* slynkya
**slim** *adj* moon
**slim** *v* monhe·
**slip** *v* slynkya; slyppya
**slip road** *n* slynkfordh
**slipper** *n* pawgen
**slogan** *n* garm
**slope** *n* leder
**slope** *v* ledry
**slot** *n* bùlgh
**slot machine** *n* bathador
**slow** *adj* lent; ow kelly
**slugs** *n* glûthvelwes
**slush** *n* lûbergh
**small** *adj* bian
**small change** *n* mona munys
**smallholding** *n* pastel dir
**smart** *adj* fur
**smart casual** *phr* dyllas compes-powes
**smash** *v* brewy

**smear** *n* bysmê·r
**smear** *v* drogura
**smell** *n* smellyng; odour; sawor
**smell** *v* clôwes, sawory; yma· odour + *noun / adjective* wàr²
**smelly** *adj* mousak
**smile** *n* minwharth
**smile** *v* minwherthyn
The **Smith** *n* An Gov
**smoke** *n* mog
**smoke** *v* megy
**smooth** *adj* leven
**smooth** *v* levna
**smoothness** *n* levender
**smother** *v* megy
**smoulder** *v* sygera
**smuggler** *n* franklondyor
**snack** *n* croust
**snag** *n* cudyn
**snails** *n* melwhes
**snake** *n* serpont
**snatch** *n* kibya
**sneeze** *n* strew
**sneeze** *v* strewy
**sniff** *v* frony
**snooker** *n* snouker
**snore / snort** *n* ronk
**snore / snort** *v* renky
**snout** *n* tron
**snow** *n* ergh
**snow** *v* gwil ergh
**snowstorm** *n* teweth ergh
**snug** *adj* cles

**so** *adv* mar² [G], maga⁵ [G]
[and] **so** *phr* ytho·[G]
**so many / much** *phr* kebmys[G]
**soak** *v* glehy
**soap** *n* seban
**sober** *adj* sàd; dyvedhowon
**social media** *phr* wàr vainys cowethasek
**socialist** *n* socyalyth
**society** *n* cowethas; an gowethas
**sock** *n* lodryk
**socket** *n* crow
**sofa** *n* gwely dëdh
**soft** *adj* medhel
**soften** *v* medhelhe·
**softness** *n* medhelder
**software** *n* medhelweyth
**soil** *n* gweras
**soldier** *n* soudor
**sole** *n* gothen
**solemn** *adj* solempna
**solicitor** *n* atorny
**solid** *adj/n* solyd
**solidarity** *n* solyda·ryta
**solitary** *adj* dygoweth
**solution** *n* assoylyans
**solve** *v* assoylya
**some** *adj* neb[G]; nebes[G]
**some** *pron* re[G]; nebes[G]
**somehow** *adv* [in] / wàr neb fordh, [in] neb maner
**someone** *pron* neb[onen][G]
**something** *pron* nampy·th[G], neptra·[G]
**sometime** *adv* nepprë·s

**sometimes** *adv* traweythyow
**somewhere** *adv* neb le
**son** *n* mab
**song** *n* cân
**soon** *adv* [yn] scon
as **soon as** *phr* kettel[2] [G]
as **soon as** [ever] peskytter may[5] [G]
**soot** *n* hylgeth
**sore** *n* brew
**sorrow** *n* duwhan
**sort** *n* ehen, kynda, sort
some **sort of** *phr* neb sort a[2]
what **sort of** *phr* pana sort a[2] [G]
**sort out** *phr* restry
**soul** *n* enef
**sound** *n* son
**sound** *v* seny, sowndya
**soup** *n* cowl
**sour** *adj* trenk
**source** *n* penfenten
**south** *adj/n* soth
**southern** *adj* soth
**sow** *v* gonys has
**spa** *n* fentenva
**space** *n* efander; spâss
**spade** *n* pal
**spaghetti** *n* spagetty
**spar** *n* predn
**sparkling** *adj* tythus
**sparks** *n* gwrîhon
**sparrow** *n* golvan
**speak** *v* côwsel
**special** *adj* specyal
**specialist** *n* arbenegor

**specialize** *v* arbenegy
**species** *n* ehen
**specific** *adj* specyfyk
**specimen** *n* spe·cymen
**speckled** *adj* brith
**speckles** *n* brith
**spectacle** *n* gwary mir
**spectator** *n* meror
**speech** *n* cows; areth
**speed** *n* toth
at full **speed** *phr* toth men
**speed bump** *n* godolhyn lent'he·
**speed camera** *n* ca·mera toth
**speed up** *phr* uskys'he·
**speedily** *adv* snèl
**speedy** *adj* snèl
**spell** *v* spellya
**spend** *v* spêna
**sperm** *n* has
**spicy** *adj* spîsek
**spiders** *n* kefnys
**spike** *n* kenter
**spill** *n* scùllyans
**spill** *v* scùllya
**spin** *n* troyll
**spin** *v* troyllya
**spinach** *n* spynach
**spiral** *n* troyll
**spirit** *n* spyrys
**spit** *v* trewa
**spite** *n* spit
in **spite of** *phr* in spit [dhe[2]] / in despî·t [dhe[2]]; awo·s
**spiteful** *adj* spîtys
**splash** *v* lagya

**splendid** *adj* spladn, rial
**splendour** *n* splander
**splinter** *n* skethryk
**splinter group** *n* bagas dybe·rth
**split** *n* fâls
**split** *v* falja
**spoil** *v* dyswil; chersya re
**spokesman** *n* leveryas
**sponge** *n* sponj
**sponsored by** *phr* in dadn veugh
**sponsorship** *n* meugh
**spoon** *n* lo
**spoonful** *n* loas
**sport** *n* sport
**sportsman** *n* sportyas
**spot** *n* spot
**spots** *n* brith
**spotted** *adj* brith
**spouse** *n* prias
**spray** *v* styfa
**spread** *n* spredyas
**spread** *v* lêsa; spredya; omlêsa
**spreadsheet** *n* leslen
**spring** *n* fenten; gwaynten
**sprinkles** *n* whegyjyon
**spy** *n/v* aspias
**squander** *v* scùllya
**square** *adj* pedrak
**square** *n* pedrak; plain
**squash** *n* sqwash
**squash** *v* gwrydnya
**squeak / squeal** *v* gwîhal
**squeeze** *v* strotha, gwrydnya

**squirm** *v* omwenel
**squirrel** *n* gwywer
**squirt** *n* skit
**squirt** *v* skîtya
**stable** *adj* fast
**stable** *n* stâbel
**stadium** *n* stadyùm
**staff** *n* lorgh; felshyp
**stage** *n* stap; gwaryva
**stain** *n* nàm
**stain** *v* nabma
**stained glass** *n* gweder lyw
**stairs** *n* stairys
**stake** *n* gaja
**stale** *adj* coth
**stalk** *n* garren
**stall** *n* stalla
**stall** *v* dyfygya
**stallion** *n* stallyon
**stammer** *v* hockya in y gows
**stamp** *n* stampen
**stamp** *v* stampya; stankya
**stamp duty** *n* stampdoll
**stance** *n* stauns
**stand** *n* sensor
**stand out** *phr* balegy
**stand [up]** *phr* sevel
**standard** *n* sqwir
The **Standard Written Form** (**SWF**) *n* An 'Furv Scrifys Savonek' (FSS)
on **standby** *phr* ow cortos yn parys; sqwychys dhe barys
**standing** *n* roweth
be **standing / stood** *phr* bos a'y sav

258

**staple** *n* cromgenter
**staple** *v* cromgentra
**stars** *n* ster
**start** *n* dallath
**start** *v* dallath; sordya; tanya
**state** *n* stât; plit, studh
**state** *v* meneges
**statement** *n* derivadow, menegyans
**station** *n* gorsaf
**station** *v* settya
**statue** *n* delow
**stay** *n* godrik
**stay** *v* godrega; remainya
**steady** *adj* ferv
**steak** *n* stêk
**steal** *v* ladra
**steam** *n* ethen
**steam** *v* ethedna
**steam engine** *n* jyn ethen
**steel** *n* dur
[very] **steep** *adj* dyserth
**steeple** *n* tour
**steer** *v* lewyas
**steering** *n* lewyans
**stem** *n* garren
**step** *n* stap
**step by step** *phr* stap ha stap
**stepladder** *n* steppyow
**stew** *n* bros
**stick** *n* gwelen; lorgh
**stick** *v* glena
**stiff** *adj* serth
**stile** *n* camva
**still** *adj* heb gàs
**still** *adv* whath

**sting** *n* bros
**sting** *v* brosa
**stinginess** *n* pithneth
**stingy** *adj* pith
**stink** *v* flerya
**stir** *v* cabùly
**stirrup** *n* gwarthowl
**stock** *n* stock
**stock** *v* stoffya
**stocking** *n* loder
**stockpile** *v* stoffya
**stomach** *n* pengasen
**stone** *n* men
**stool** *n* scavel
**stop** *v* lettya; hedhy; sevel
**stopper** *n* corkyn
**store** *n* gwithva
**storey** *n* leur
**storm** *n* teweth
**story** *n* whedhel
**stove** *n* forn
**straight** *adj* compes; strait; serth
**straighten** *v* composa
**straighten [out]** *phr* dygabma
**strain** *v* sythla
**strainer** *n* sythel
**strange** *adj* stranj
**strangeness** *n* stranjnes
**stranger** *n* estren
**strangle** *v* taga
**strap** *n* cron; cabester
**straw** *n* cala; gwelen eva
**strawberries** *n* syvy
**stream** *n* fros; gover
**stream** *v* frosa

**street** *n* strêt
**strength** *n* crefter
**strengthen** *v* crefhe·
**stress** *n* tenva; poslef
**stress** *v* posleva
**stressful** *adj* tydn
**stretch** *v* tedna
**stretcher** *n* grava
**strict** *adj* stroth, sevur
**strike** *n* astel ober
**strike** *v* frappya; astel ober
go on **strike** *phr* astel ober
**striker** *n* astelor
**strimmer** *n* falgh raf
**string** *n* corden
**strip** *n* sketh
**strip** *v* stryppya
**strip down** *phr* dysstryppya
**stripe** *v* lînen
**stripper** *n* omdhiscores
**strive** *v* strîvya
**stroke** *n* strocas
**stroke** *v* palva
**stroll** *n* tro kerdhes
**stroll** *v* rôsya
**strong** *adj* crev
**structural** *adj* starnedhek
**structure** *n* starneth
**stubborn** *adj* pedn cales
**stubborn person** *n*
pedn cales
**student** *n* studhyor; descor
**study** *n* rom studhya; studhva
**study** *v* studhya
**stuff** *n* stoff
**stuff** *v* stoffya

**stuffing** *n* stoffyas
**stuffy** *adj* clos
**stumble** *v* trebuchya
**stump** *n* kef; stock
**stunt** *n* prat
**stupid** *adj* gocky
**stupidity** *n* gockyneth
**sturdy** *adj* stordy
**stutter** *v* hockya in y gows
**style** *n* gis; gis screfa
**sub-** *pref* is-[1]
**subject** *n* sojeta
**subject[-matter]** *n* defnyth
**submarine** *n* lester sedhy
**submerge** *v* sedhy
**subscribe** *v* ragprena
**subscribe to** *phr* ragprena eseleth in
**subscription** *n* ragpren
**subsidy** *n* gweres mona
**substance** *n* sùbstans; stoff
**subtle** *adj* fel; sotel
**subtlety** *n* felder; sotelneth
**subtract from** *phr* kemeres dhywo·rth
**succeed** *v* soweny; spêdya
**success** *n* spêda
**such** *adj* a'n par-na
**suck** *v* sùgna
**sudden** *adj* desempys
**suddenly** *adv* desempys
**suffer** *v* godhaf
**sufficient** *adj* lowr
**suffocate** *v* taga
**suffocating** *adj* tagus
**sugar** *n* shùgra

**suggest** *v* cùssulya, profya
**suggestion** *n* cùssul, profyans
commit **suicide** *phr* omladha
**suit** *n* sewt
**suitability** *n* gwywder
**suitable** *adj* gwyw
**suitcase** *n* trog dyllas
**sulk** *v* mûtya
**sultry** *adj* tesak
**sum** *n* sùm
**summary** *n* derivas cot
**summer** *n* hâv
**summit** *n* barr
**summon** *v* cria
**sun** *n* howl
**sunblock** *n* dehen spral
**sunburnt** *adj* howl-leskys
**Sunday** *n* De Sul
**sunlight** *n* howl
**Sunni** *adj* Sùnek
**Sunni** *n* Sùnyas
**sunny** *adj* howlek
**sunset** *n* howlsedhas
**suntan** *n* lyw howl
**supermarket** *n* gorvarhas
**supervision** *n* gwith
**supper** *n* boos soper
**supple** *adj* gwethyn
**supplement** *n* keworrans
**supplement** *v* gorra moy dhe[2]
**supplier** *n* provior
**supply** *n* provians
**supply** *v* provia
**support** *n* scodhyans
**support** *v* scodhya
**supporter** *n* scodhyor

**suppose** *v* soposya
**supposedly** *adv*
dell yw prederys
**supremacy** *n* gwarthevyans
**sure** *adj* sur
make **sure** *phr* diogelhe·
**surely** *adv* iredy
**surf** *n* mordardh
**surf** *v* mordardha; rôsya
**surface** *n* arenep
**surfboard** *n* astell mordardha
**surgeon** *n* chyrùrjyen
**surgery** *n* chyrù·rjery;
medhegva
**surprise** *n* sowthan
**surprise** *v* sowthanas
be **surprised** *phr* \*marth
**surprisingly** *adv* er y varth
**surreal** *adj* sùrreal
**surround** *v* kerhydna
**surveillance** *n* aspians
**survey** *n* arwhythrans
**suspect** *v* drogdyby
**suspend** *v* astel
**suspense** *n* fienasow
**suspension bridge** *n* pons cregys
**suspicion** *n* gorgis; skeus
**suspicious** *adj* skeusek
**swallow** *n* gwenol
**swallow** *v* lenky
**swan** *n* swàn
**swap** *n* keschaunj
**swap** *v* keschaunjya
**swarm** *n* hes
**swat** *v* sqwattya

**swear** *v* lia; cùssya
**sweat** *n* whës
**sweat** *v* whesa
**sweater** *n* gwlanek
**sweatshirt** *n* cris whës
**sweep** *v* scubya
**sweet** *adj* wheg
**sweet** *n* whegyn
**sweet and sour** *phr* melys ha wherow
**sweetcorn** *n* ÿs wheg
**sweetener** *n* melysor
**sweetness** *n* whecter
**swell** *v* whedhy
**swelling** *n* whedh
**swift** *adj* scav
**swim** *v* neyja [i'n dowr]
**swimming pool** *n* poll neyja

**swimshorts** *n* lavrak neyja
**swimsuit** *n* dyllas neyja
**swing** *n* lesk; lesk lovan
**swing** *v* lesca
**switch** *n* sqwychel
**switch off / on** *phr* sqwychya mes / rag
**swoop** *v* stêvya
**sword** *n* cledha
**symbol** *n* arweth
**symbolic** *adj* arwedhek
**sympathy** *n* tregereth
**synod** *n* seneth
**syringe** *n* skîtel
**syrup** *n* syrop
**system** *n* kevreth
**systematic** *adj* kevrethek

# T

**T-shirt** *n* cris T
**table** *n* bord; tâbel
**tablecloth** *n* lien bord
**tablet** *n* lehen
**tact** *n* tact
**tag** *n* sygen
**tail** *n* lost
**tail-end** *n* tin
**tailor** *n* trehor
**take** *v* kemeres
**take off** *phr* disky; dallath
**take-off** *n* dallath
**tale** *n* whedhel
**talent** *n* talent
**talk** *n* cows; areth
**talk** *v* côwsel; arethya

**talks** *n* kescows
**tame** *adj* dov
**tame** *v* dova
**tan** *n* lyw howl
**tangled** *adj* camnedhys
**tank** *n* tank; argh
**tap** *n* tap
**tape** *n* tâpa; snod
**target** *n* costen
**tart** *n* tart
**task** *n* oberen
**taste** *v* sawory; yma· sa·woren + *noun / adjective* wàr[2]
**tasty** *adj* blesys dâ
**tattoo** *n* corflywans
**Taurus** *n* An Tarow

**taut** *adj* tydn
**tax** *n* toll
**tax** *v* tolly
**taxi** *n* taxy
**taxi** *v* rollya
**tea** *n* tê
**tea towel** *n* lien seha lestry
**teacake** *n* torthen tê
**teach** *v* desky dhe²
**teacher** *n* descador
**team** *n* para
**teapot** *n* pot tê
**tear** *n* sqward
**tear** *v* sqwardya
**tear** *n* dager
**tear up** *phr* frega
**technical** *adj* technegyl
**technician** *n* technegor
**technique** *n* technyk
**technology** *n* technolo·gieth
**telephone** *n* pellgowsor
**telephone** *v* pellgôwsel
**telescope** *n* gweder aspia
**television** *n* pellwolok
**tell** *v* derivas
**temperature** *n* gwres
**temple** *n* templa
**temporarily** *adv* rag tro
**temporary** *adj* rag tro
**tempt** *v* temptya
**temptation** *n* temptacyon
**tendency** *n* tuedhyans
**tender** *n* medhel; tydn
**tenderness** *n* medhelder
**tendon** *n* giewen
**tennis** *n* tenys

**tension** *n* tenva
**tent** *n* tent
**tera-** *pref* tera-¹
**term** *n* termyn
**terms and conditions** *phr* ambosow aco·rd
**terrace** *n* terras
**terrain** *n* tireth
**terrible** *adj* uthyk
**terrify** *v* brawehy
**terror** *n* euth
**terrorism** *n* euthweyth
**terrorist** *n* euthwas
**test** *n* prov
**test** *v* prevy
**testimony** *n* dùstuny
**tether** *n* stagell
**tether** *v* staga
**text** *n* text
**text** *v* textya
**textile** *n* gwia
**than** *conj* ès dell² ᴳ, agè·s dell² ᴳ
**than** *prep* èsᴳ, agè·sᴳ
**thank** *v* aswon grâss dhe²
**thank you** *phr* meur ras / gromercy [dhis / dhywgh why]
**thanks** *n* grâss
**that** *adj* -naᴳ
**that** *conj* fate·ll² ᴳ, 'tell² ᴳ, dell² ᴳ
**that is (i.e.)** *phr* hèn yw
**that is to say** *phr* hèn yw dhe leverel
**that [one]** *pron* hednaᴳ, hodnaᴳ

**thaw** *v* tedha
**the** *definite article* an[G]
**theatre** *n* gwaryjy; plain an gwary
**theft** *n* ladrans
**their** *adj* aga[3] [G]
**them** *pron* see 'they'
**theme** *n* them
**then** *adv* ena, i'n eur-na; dhana, ytho·[G]
by **then** *phr* nans[G]
**theory** *n* damcanep
in **theory** *phr* warle·rgh an abecedary
**there** *adv* ena; dy
from **there** *phr* alena
**there is / are** *phr* otta[G]
**thereby** *adv* dredhy[G]
**therefore** *adv* rag hedna
**thermometer** *n* gwresel
**thermostat** *n* sqwychel gwres
**these [ones]** *pron* an re-ma[G]
**they** *pron* y[G]
**thick** *adj* tew
**thicken** *v* tewhe·
**thief** *n* lader
**thin** *adj* tanow
**thin [out]** *phr* tanowhe·
**thing** *n* tra
**think** *v* predery; tyby; sensy
**thirst** *n* sehes
be **thirsty** *phr* *sehes
**this** *adj* -ma[G]
**this [one]** *pron* hebma[G], hobma[G]
**thong** *n* cron

**thorn** *n* dren
**those [ones]** *pron* an re-na[G]
**though** *conj* kyn[5] [G]
**thought** *n* preder; tybyans
**thrash** *v* cronkya
**threads** *n* neus
**threat** *n* godros
**threaten** *v* godros
**threatening** *adj* godrosek
**threshold** *n* treuthow
**thrifty** *adj* erbysus
**throat** *n* briansen
**through** *prep* dre[2] [G]
**throw** *n* towl
**throw** *v* tôwlel
**thrust** *v* herdhya
**thunder[bolt]** *n* taran
**Thursday** *n* De Yow
**ticket** *n* tôkyn
return **ticket** *n* tôkyn mos ha dewheles
single **ticket** *n* tôkyn mos only
**ticket machine** *n* tokynador
**tickle** *n* cosva
**tide** *n* mortid
high **tide** *n* morlanow
low **tide** *n* mordrik
**tidiness** *n* kempensys
**tidy** *adj* kempen
**tidy** *v* kempedna
**tie** *n* colm, lâss; colm codna
**tie** *v* kelmy
**tiger** *n* tîger
**tight** *adj* tydn; stroth
**tighten** *v* strotha
**tights** *n* tydnyow

**tile** *n* [pry]lehen
**time** *n* termyn; prës; eur; treveth
**time** *v* rekna termyn
all the **time** *phr* prèst
for the **time being** *phr* rag an present termyn
in **time** *phr* i'n kettermyn
it is **time to** *phr* prës yw
on **time** *phr* adermyn
**timer** *n* euryor
**timetable** *n* euryador
**tin** *n* sten; cadna; cafas
**tingle** *n* cosva
**tingle** *v* cosa
**tinner** *n* stenor
**tint** *n* arlyw
**tint** *v* arlywa
**tiny** *adj* munys
**tip** *n* bleyn; grastal
**tire** *v* sqwitha
**tired** *adj* sqwith
**tiring** *adj* sqwithus
**title** *n* tytel
**to** *prep* dhe² G; bys in; bys dhe²
**toad** *n* cronak
**toadstool** *n* scavel cronak
**toast** *n* bara cras
**toast** *v* eva yêhes
**tobacco** *n* backa
**today** *adv* hedhyw
**toe** *n* bës troos
**toffee** *n* clyjjy
**together** *adv* warba·rth
**toil** *n* lavur

**toil** *v* lavurya
**toilet(s)** *n* pryvedhyow
**token** *n* tôkyn
**tolerance** *n* godhevyans
**tolerate** *v* godhaf, perthy
**toll** *n* toll
**tomato** *n* aval kerensa
**tomb** *n* bedh
**tomorrow** *adv* avorow
**ton** *n* tona
**tone** *n* ton
**tongue** *n* tavas
**tonight** *adv* haneth
**too** *adv* inwe·dh, kefrë·s, maga tâ
**too many** *phr* re aga nùmber
**too [much]** *phr* re²
**tool** *n* toul
**tooth** *n* dans
**toothache** *n* drog dens
**toothbrush** *n* scubylen dens
**toothpaste** *n* toos dens
**top** *n* gwartha; pedn; top
at the **top** *phr* awartha
**topic** *n* testen
**topless** *adj* brodn-noth
**topping** *n* cappa
**tor** *n* carn
**torch** *n* torchen
**torment** *n* torment
**torment** *v* tormentya
**tortoise** *n* cronak ervys
**torture** *n* torment
**torture** *v* tormentya
**total** *n* cowlsùm

**total [up]** *phr* rekna cowlsùm
**touch** *n* tùch
**touch** *v* tava; handla
**touch [on]** *phr* tùchya
**tough** *adj* gwethyn
**tourism** *n* toury·stieth
**tourist** *n* touryst
**tournament** *n* tournay
**towards** *prep* tro / wor'tu ha
**towel** *n* towal
**tower** *n* tour
**town** *n* tre
**toy** *n* gwariel
**trace** *n* ol
**track** *n* hens
**tracksuit** *n* reswysk
**tractor** *n* jyn tedna
**trade** *n* kenwerth
**trade** *v* kenwertha
**trader** *n* gwycor
**tradition** *n* tradycyon
**traditional** *adj* trady·cyonal
**traffic** *n* daromres
**traffic jam** *n* daromdak
**traffic light** *n* golow trafyk
**tragedy** *n* tra·jedy
**trailer** *n* kert adrë·v
**train** *n* train
**trainer** *v* descador; eskys sport
**traitor** *n* traitour
**tram** *n* tràm
**trample** *v* stankya
**trampoline** *n* lamwely
**tranquil** *adj* cosolek

**tranquility** *n* cosoleth
**transfer** *v* treusperthy
**transformer** *n* treusfurvyor
**transgender** *adj* treusreydhek
**translate** *v* trailya
**translation** *n* trailyans
**transmit** *v* treuscorra
**transport** *v* carya
**transport[ation]** *n* caryans
**trap** *n* maglen
**trauma** *n* trauma
**travel** *v* viajya
**tray** *n* servyour
**tread** *n* gothen
**treasure** *n* tresour
**treasurer** *n* alwhedhor
**treat** *n* favour
**treat** *v* dyghtya
**treatment** *n* dyghtyans
**treaty** *n* kevambos kesgwlasek
**trees** *n* gwëdh
**tremble** *v* crena
**trench** *n* cledh
**trespasser** *n* camdremenyas
**trial** *n* trial
**trial and error** *phr* experyans
**triangle** *n* trielyn
**tribunal** *n* sedhek brusy
**trick** *n* cast, prat; tryck
**trick** *v* castya
**tricky** *adj* tyckly
**trifle** *n* trufyl
**trifling** *adj* trufyl
**trigger** *n* trygger
**trigger** *v* sordya

**trinket** *n* tegen
**trip** *v* trebuchya
**troll** *n* troll
**trolley** *n* kertyk
**troop** *n* bagas
**trouble** *n* ponvos, trobel
**trouble** *v* trobla
**trousers** *n* lavrak
**trout** *n* truth
**truck** *n* kert
**true** *adj* gwir
**trump** *n* trùmp
**trumpet** *n* hirgorn
**trunk** *n* cofyr; tron
[tree] **trunk** *n* gwedhen-ven
**trust** *n* trèst; fydhyans
**trust** *v* *trèst; trestya dhe²
**trustee** *n* fydhyador
**truth** *n* gwrioneth
**try to** *phr* whelas
**tub** *n* kybell
**tube** *n* piben
**Tuesday** *n* De Merth
**tuft** *n* tos
**tug** *n* tedn

**tug** *v* tedna
**tulip** *n* blejen tù·lyfant
**tumour** *n* tevyans
**tumultuous** *adj* tervus
**tuna** *n* tûna
**tune** *n* ton
**tune** *v* tônya
**tunnel** *n* keyfordh
**turban** *n* tù·lyfant
**turkey** *n* yar gyny
**turmoil** *n* tervans
**turn** *n* tro; torn
**turn** *v* trailya
[each] in **turn** *phr* pùb wàr y dorn
**turn aside** *phr* trailya adenewen
**twilight** *n* tewlwolow
**twin** *n* gevell
**twirl / twist** *n* troen
**twirl / twist** *v* troyllya
**type** *n* tîp
**typical** *adj* tîpek
**tyrant** *n* turont
**tyre** *n* bonden

# U

**ugliness** *n* hacter
**ugly** *adj* hager
**ultrasound** *n* ughson
**umbrella** *n* glawlen; to sun **umbrella** *n* howllen
**unbearable** *adj* dywodhaf
**uncertain** *adj* ancertan
**uncle** *n* êwnter

**uncomfortable** *adj* anê·s; heb confort
**unconditional** *adj* diambos
**unconscious** *adj* dyswa·r
**uncover** *v* dyscudha
**under** *prep* in dadn² G
**underline** *v* islînya
**underpants** *n* lavrak bian

**understand** *v* [godhvos] convedhes, ùnderstondya
**understanding** *n* ùnderstondyng
**undertake** *v* omgemeres
**undertaking** *n* omgemeryans; ambos
**undress** *v* disky
get **undressed** *adj* omdhisky
**unemployed** *adj* dywe·yth
**unethical** *adj* camhensek
**uneven** *adj* dygompes
**unfair** *adj* ane·wn
**unfaithful** *adj* dysle·n
**unfortunate** *adj* anfusyk
**unfortunately** *adv* i'n gwetha prës, soweth
**unfurl** *v* dysplêtya
**unhappy** *adj* morethek
**unhealthy** *adj* anyagh; anyahus
**uniform** *n* unwysk
**unify** *v* unya
**unimportant** *adj* dyboo·s, bohes y vern
[trade] **union** *n* kesunyans lavur
**unique** *adj* udnyk
**unit** *n* unsys
**unite** *v* unya
The **United Nations** *n* An Kenedhlow Unyes
**unity** *n* unsys
**universe** *n* keynvÿs
**university** *n* penscol
**unjust** *adj* anjù·st

**unkind** *adj* dygu·v
**unless** *conj* marnas[G]
**unlike** *adj* dyhaval
**unload** *v* dyscarga
**unlock** *v* dialwhedha
**unlucky** *adj* anfusyk
**unmarried** *adj* dybrias
**unnecessarily** *adv* heb othem
**unnecessary** *adj* heb othem
**unpack** *v* dydrùssa
**unparalleled** *adj* dybarow
**unpleasant** *adj* anwhek
**unplug** *v* dysebylya
**unreasonable** *adj* avresonus
**unripe** *adj* criv
**unroll** *v* dyrollya
**unruly** *adj* dyre·wl
**unscrew** *v* dyscrewya
**unsuitable** *adj* anwyw
**unsure** *adj* ansur
**untie** *v* dygelmy
**until** *conj* erna[2 G], bys may[5 G], bys pàn[2 G]
**until** *prep* bys in; bys dhe[2]; bys
**unveil** *v* dyscudha
**unwilling** *adj* anvodhek
**unwrap** *v* dysmailya
**up** *adv* in bàn
**up to** *phr* bys in; bys dhe[2]
**up to date** *phr* kesres
**up to now** *phr* bys i'n eur-ma
**update** *v* kesres'he·
**uphold** *v* mentêna
**upload** *n* ugh-carg
**upload** *v* ugh-carga

**upon** *prep* wàr² G
**upright** *adj* serth
**upset** *v* omwheles; dystempra
**upstairs** *adv* wàr vàn; in bàn
**urge** *v* inia
be **urgent** *phr* bos res porre·s
**urinate** *v* pysa
**urine** *n* pysas
**us** *pron* see 'we'
**use** *v* ûsya

make **use of** *phr* gwil defnyth a²
**use up** *phr* spêna
he **used to** *phr* ev a wrug ûsya
**useful** *adj* vas, a brow, dhe les
**useless** *adj* dyle·s
**user-friendly** *adj* hegar dhe ûsya
as **usual** *phr* dell yw ûsys, i'n fordh ûsys
**utilize** *v* gwil defnyth a²

## V

**vacant** *adj* gwag
**vacuum** *n* gwacter
**vacuum cleaner** *n* scubel sùgna
**vagina** *n* cons
**vague** *adj* dyscle·r
in **vain** *phr* in vain
**valid** *adj* crev
**validity** *n* crefter
**valley** *n* valy
**valuable** *adj* talvesek
**value** *n* valew
**value** *v* talveja
**value added tax** (**VAT**) *n* toll daswerth
**valve** *n* clapes
**van** *n* carven
**vanilla** *n* vanylla
**vanish** *v* vansya
**vape** *v* ethedna
**variable** *adj* chaunjus
**variety** *n* sort
**various** *adj* dyvers

**varnish** *n* vernysh
**varnish** *v* vernsya
**vary** *v* varia
**vase** *n* lester
**veal** *n* kig leugh
**vegetable** *adj* losowek
**vegetables** *n* losow debry
**vegetarian** *n* kigsconyor
**vegetation** *n* losow
**vehement** *adj* ter
**vehicle** *n* degador
**veil** *n* veyl
**veil** *v* cudha
**vein** *n* gwythien
**velvet** *n* paly
**veneer** *n* argen
**venture** *n* aventuryans
**venture** *v* aventurya; lavasos
**verb** *n* verb
**verify** *v* composa
**verruca** *n* gwenogen troos
**verse** *n* gwers
**vertical** *adj* serth

**very** *adv* pòr, fèst
**vessel** *n* lester
**vestige** *n* ol
**vet** *n* milvedhek
**vexation** *n* ponvos
**vice-** *pref* is-[1]
**victim** *n* vyctym
**victory** *n* vy·ctory
**view** *n* vu
**vigorous** *adj* freth
**vigour** *n* frethter
**village** *n* treveglos
**vinegar** *n* aysel
**vintage** *n* trevas
**vinyl** [**record**] *n* platten vînyl
**violence** *n* garowder
**violent** *adj* garow
**violet** *adj* glasru·dh
**violin** *n* crowd
**VIP** *n* onen a'n vrâsyon
**viper** *n* nader
**viral** *adj* vyral

**virginity** *n* gwerghsys
**Virgo** *n* An Werhes
**virtual** *adj* furvwir
**virtue** *n* vertû
**visit** *n* vysyt
**visit** *v* vysytya
summer **visitor** *n* havyas
**vocabulary** *n* gerva
**vodka** *n* dowr bian
**voice** *n* lev
**void** *n* gwacter
**volcano** *n* loskveneth
**volume** *n* kevrol; uhelder
**voluntary** *adj* bodhek
**volunteers** *n* bodhogyon
**vomit** *v* wheja
**vote** *n* vôta
**vote** *v* vôtya
**voucher** *n* colpon
**voyage** *n* viaj
**vulnerable** *adj* dyscoo·s
**vulture** *n* hôk caryn

# W

**wager** *n* gaja
**wage**(**s**) *n* gober
**waist** *n* wast
**waistcoat** *n* crispows
**wait** *v* gortos
**waiter** *n* servyas
**wake** [**up**] *v* dyfuna
**walk** *n* kerdh
**walk** *v* kerdhes; lavurya
**walker** *n* kerdhor
**wall** *n* fos
**wallet** *n* tygen mona

**wallop** *n* whaf
**wallpaper** *n* paper gwal
old **walls** *n* magor
**wander** *v* gwandra
**want** *v* *whans; whansa
**want to** *phr* bos whensys dhe[2]
**war** *n* bresel
**ward** *n* dyberthva
**wardrobe** *n* dyllasva
**warfare** *n* gwerryans
**warm** *adj* tobm

**warn** *v* gwarnya
**warning** *n* gwarnyans
**warrant** *n* warrant
**warrant** *v* warrantya
**warranty** *n* warrant
**wart** *n* gwenogen
**wash** *v* golhy; omwolhy
**wasps** *n* gùhy
**waste** *n* scùllyans
**waste** *v* scùllya
**wasteful** *adj* scùllyak
**watch** *n* euryor
**water** *n* dowr
hot **water** *n* dowr pooth
**waterfall** *n* dowrlam
**watering can** *n* cafas dowrhe·
**wave** *n* todn
**wax** *n* cor
**wax** *v* cora
**way** *n* fordh
by the **way** *phr*
ha ny ow côwsel
a good [long] **way** *phr* pols dâ
a little **way** *phr* pols bian
in any other **way** *phr* nahe·n
some **way** *phr* pols
**we** *pron* ny[G]
**weak** *adj* gwadn
**weaken** *v* gwanhe·
**wealth** *n* rychys
**weapon** *n* arv
**weather** *n* awel; ebron
**weave** *v* gwia
**web** *n* gwias
**webcam** *n* ca·mera gwias
**website** *n* gwiasva

**wedding** *n* demedhyans
**Wednesday** *n* De Merher
**week** *n* seythen
**weekend** *n* penseythen
**weep** *v* ola
**weigh** *v* mantolly; posa
**weird** *adj* ùncoth
**welcome** *n* wolcùm
**welcome** *v* wolcùbma
**welfare** *n* les
**well** *interj* wèl
**well** *n* pith
as **well** *phr* inwe·dh, kefrë·s, maga tâ
as **well as** *phr* kefrë·s ha
**Welsh** *n* Kembrek
**west** *adj/n* wèst
**western** *adj* wèst
**wet** *adj* glëb
**wet** *n* glebor
**wet** *v* glebya
**wetsuit** *n* sewt staunch
**whack** *n* whaf
**whale** *n* morvil
**what** *adj* pana[2] [G], py[G]
**what** *pron* pandra·[2] [G], pëth[G]; an pëth a[2] [G]
**what about** *phr* pandr'orth[G]
**what ones** *phr* pana / py re[G]
**what's-her-name** *phr* myrgh hy dama
**what's-his-name** *phr* mab y dhama
**what's more** *phr* ha pelha
**what's the time?** *phr* py eur yw?

**what's the use?** *phr* pana brow?
**what's your name?** *phr* pëth yw dha / agas hanow?
**whatever** *pron* [pùp]pyna·g [oll] a² ᴳ
**wheat** *n* gwaneth
**wheel** *n* ros
**wheelbarrow** *n* grava ros
**wheelchair** *n* cadar rosow
**wheelie bin** *n* argh atal
**wheeze** *v* whybana
**when** *adv* peur⁵ ᴳ, pana dermyn² ᴳ; may⁵ ᴳ
**when** *conj* pàn² ᴳ
**whenever** *conj* pesqweyth [oll] [ma]y⁵ ᴳ, bÿth pàn² ᴳ
**where** *adv* ple⁵ ᴳ; [le] may⁵ ᴳ
**where ... from** *phr* a ble⁵ ᴳ
**where ... [to]** *phr* py⁵ ᴳ
**where is / are** *phr* ple ma / mowns ᴳ
**where is / are ... [to]** *phr* pyma / pymowns ᴳ
**wherever** *conj* ple pyna·g [ma]y⁵ ᴳ
**which** *adj* py ᴳ
**which** *pron* pyne·yl ᴳ; pëth a² ᴳ
**which [ones]** *pron* py re ᴳ
**[for] a good [long] while** *phr* pols dâ
**[for] a little while** *phr* pols bian
**[for] some while** *phr* pols
**while** *conj* pàn² ᴳ
**whim** *n* sians
**whirl** *n* troyll

**whirl** *v* troyllya
**whiskers** *n* minvlew
**whiskey** *n* dowr tobm Wordhen
**whisky** *n* dowr tobm Alban
**whisper** *n* whystrans
**whisper** *v* whystra
**whistle** *n* whyban; whythell
**whistle** *v* whybana
**whistle-blower** *n* cùhudhor a'n tu aberveth
**whistling** *n* whyban
**white** *adj* gwydn
**whiteness** *n* gwynder
**Whitsun** *n* Pencast
**who** *pron* pyw ᴳ; [neb] a² ᴳ
**all who** *phr* myns / seul a² ᴳ
**whoever** *pron* [pùp]pyna·g [oll] a² ᴳ
**whole** *adj* cowal
**on the whole** *phr* dre vrâs
**the whole** *adj* an holl² ᴳ
**to whom** *phr* [neb] may⁵ ᴳ
**why** *adv* prag ᴳ
**wicked** *adj* camhensek, tebel-²⁽¹⁾
**wide** *adj* efan; ledan
**widen** *v* efanhe·; ledanhe·
**widowed** *adj* gwedhow
**wife** *n* gwreg
**WiFi** *n* dywyver
**wild** *adj* gwyls
**wilderness** *n* gwylfos
**will** *n* mydnas; lyther kebmyn
**he will** *phr* ev a wra
**willing** *adj* bolùnje'ek

**willingly** *adv* heb awhe·r
**willpower** *n* nerth y vydnas
**win** *n* gwain
**win** *v* gwainya
**wind** *n* gwyns
**wind** *v* gwia
**wind turbine** *n* melyn wyns
**windmill** *n* melyn wyns
**window** *n* fe·nester
**window sill** *n* legh fe·nester
**windscreen** *n* skewwyns
go **windsurfing** *phr* astell-wolya
**windy** *adj* gwynsak
**wine** *n* gwin
**wing** *n* askel
**wink** *v* gwynkya
**winner** *n* gwainyor
**winter** *n* gwâv
**wipe** *v* glanhe·
**wipe [up]** *phr* deseha
**wiper** *n* desehor
**wire** *n* gwyver
**wireless** *adj* dywyver
**wisdom** *n* furneth
**wise** *adj* fur
**wish** *n* whans
**wish** *v* whansa
**wish to** *phr* bos whensys dhe²
**witch** *n* gwragh
**with** *prep* gans[G]; ha[G]
**wither** *v* gwedhra
**within** *prep* abe·rth in, ajy·dhe², aberveth in; kyns pedn
**without** *prep* heb[G]
**witness** *v* desta

**witty** *adj* dydha·n
**wizard** *n* pystrior
**wobbly** *adj* omborthus
**wolf** *n* bleydh
**woman** *n* benyn
**womb** *n* bris
**wonder** *n* marth
**wonder** *v* gwil marthùjyon; govyn orth y honen
**wonderful** *adj* marthys
**wonderfully** *adv* marthys
**wood** *n* predn; coos
**woodlouse** *n* gwragh
**woodpecker** *n* casek coos
**wool** *n* gwlân
**woolly** *adj* gwlanek
**word** *n* ger
**work** *n* gweyth; lavur; whel; ober; scrif
**work** *v* lavurya
**work at** *phr* gonys; gweytha orth
**worker** *n* gweythor; gwerynor
**working class** *phr* rencas lavur
**working party** *n* bagas lavur
**workman** *n* oberwas
**works** *n* gweythva
**world** *n* bÿs
in the **world** *phr* in oll an bÿs
The **World Cup** *n* Hanaf an Bÿs
**worn out** *phr* gwyskys ha deu
**worried** *adj* prederus
**worry** *n* preder; trobel
**worry** *v* predery; trobla

**worse** *adj* lacka
**worship** *n* golohy
**worshipper** *n* gologhyas
the **worst** *adj* an + *noun* lacka oll
it would be / have been **worth** *phr* y tal / talvia [dhodho]
**worthy** *adj* wordhy
**wound** *n* goly; brew
**wound** *v* golia
**wrap** *n* mailyans; whytel
**wrap** *v* mailya
**wrapper** *n* mailyans

**wreath** *n* garlont
**wreck** *n* gwreck
**wrestle** *v* omdôwlel
**wrestling** *n* omdowl
**wrinkle** *n* crigh
**wrinkled** *adj* crigh
**wrist** *n* codna bregh
**write** *v* screfa
**writer** *n* screfor
**writing** *n* scrif
**wrong** *adj* cabm; camhensek
**wrong** *n* an drog

# X

**X-ray** *n* golowyn X

# Y

**yard** *n* lath
**yawn** *v* dianowy
**year** *n* bledhen; bloodh
last **year** *phr* warleny
this **year** *phr* hevleny
**year group** *n* bagas kevos
**yearn for** *phr* yêwny
**yeast extract** *n* godroth burm
**yell** *n* uj

**yell** *v* uja
**yellow** *adj* melen
**yesterday** *adv* de
**yet** *adv* whath
**yield** *v* dascor
**yoghurt** *n* yogùrt
**you** *pron* ty[G]; why[G]
**young** *adj* yonk
**your** *adj* dha[2] [G]; agas [G]
**youth** *n* yowynkes

# Z

**zigzag** *adv* igam-ogam
**zip** *n* zyp

**zone** *n* grugys
**zoo** *n* milva

# KEY VERB TABLES FOR REFERENCE

Forms are given for careful but unpedantic speech. Alone or combined with a verb-noun, present participle or past participle, they are sufficient to express every verbal idea in ordinary conversation.

## BOS

*Imperative*
**bëdh, bedhowgh**

| *Present copula* | *Present local / auxiliary* | *Present habitual / Future* |
|---|---|---|
| **oma** | **e·soma** | **be·dhama** |
| *or* **o'vy** | *or* **eso'vy** | *or* **bedha'vy** |
| **osta** | **esta** | **bedhys jy** |
| **yw va** *or* **ywa** | **yma·** / **usy va** | **bëdh ev** |
| **yw hy** | **yma·** / **usy hy** | **bëdh hy** |
| **yw** | **yma·** / **usy** / **eus** | **bëdh** |
| **on ny** | **eson ny** | **bedhyn ny** |
| **o'why** | **eso'why** | **bedho'why** |
| **yns y** | **ymo·wns** / **usons y** | **bedhons y** |

*Note:* **usy** *also* **ujy**

| *Imperfect copula* | *Imperfect local / auxiliary* | *Imperfect habitual / Future in the past* |
|---|---|---|
| **en vy** | **esen vy** | **bedhen vy** |
| **es jy** | **eses jy** | **bedhes jy** |
| **o va** | **esa va** | **bedha va** |
| **o hy** | **esa hy** | **bedha hy** |
| **o** | **esa** | **bedha** |
| **en ny** | **esen ny** | **bedhen ny** |
| **e'why** | **ese'why** | **bedhe'why** |
| **êns y** | **esens y** | **bedhens y** |

*Note:* **usy** / **eus** / **esa** *are not used in nominal sentence structure*

| Preterite | Conditional | Present subjunctive | Imperfect subjunctive |
|---|---|---|---|
| **beuma** or **beu'vy** | **bien vy** | **byma** or **bi'vy** | **ben vy** |
| **beusta** or **beus jy** | **bies jy** | **bosta** | **besta** or **bes jy** |
| **beu va** | **bia va** | **bo va** | **be va** |
| **beu hy** | **bia hy** | **bo hy** | **be hy** |
| **beu** | **bia** | **bo** | **be** |
| **beun ny** | **bien ny** | **bon ny** | **ben ny** |
| **be'why** | **bie'why** | **bo'why** | **be'why** |
| **bowns y** | **biens y** | **bowns y** | **bêns y** |

## BOS IN SENSE OF 'HAVE / GET'

| Present | Future | Imperfect | Imperfect habitual / Future in the past |
|---|---|---|---|
| **y'm beus** | **y'm bëdh** | **y'm bo** | **y'm bedha** |
| **y'th eus** | **y'fëdh** | **y'th o** | **y'fedha** |
| **y'n jeves** | **y'n jevyth** | **y'n jeva** | **y'n jevedha** |
| **y's teves** | **y's tevyth** | **y's teva** | **y's tevedha** |
| **y'gan beus** | **y'gan bëdh** | **y'gan bo** | **y'gan bedha** |
| **y'gas beus** | **y'gas bëdh** | **y'gas bo** | **y'gas bedha** |
| **y's teves** | **y's tevyth** | **y's teva** | **y's jevedha** |

| Preterite | Conditional |
|---|---|
| **y'm beu** | **y'm bia** |
| **y'feu** | **y'fia** |
| **y'n jeva** | **y'n jevia** |
| **y's teva** | **y's tevia** |
| **y'gan beu** | **y'gan bia** |
| **y'gas beu** | **y'gas bia** |
| **y's teva** | **y's tevia** |

Where mixed mutation occurs in you-singular (familiar) forms, this is caused by dropped 'th[5], not by the particle y[5]. Mixed mutation is therefore retained if the particle is changed to a[2] or re[2].

## MYDNAS *as auxiliary followed by verb-noun*

| Present auxiliary (making future tense) | Imperfect auxiliary (making future in the past) | Conditional auxiliary (making conditional tense) | Subjunctive auxiliary (making future subjunctive) |
|---|---|---|---|
| **mana'vy** *or* **mydna'vy** | **mydnen vy** | **mynsen vy** | **mednen vy** |
| **mynta** *or* **mydnys jy** | **mydnes jy** | **mynses jy** | **mednes jy** |
| **mydn ev** | **mydna va** | **mynsa va** | **mydna va** |
| **mydn hy** | **mydna hy** | **mynsa hy** | **mydna hy** |
| **mydn** | **mydna** | **mynsa** | **mydna** |
| **mydnyn ny** | **mydnen ny** | **mynsen ny** | **mednyn ny** |
| **mydno'why** | **mydne'why** | **mynse'why** | **medno'why** |
| **mydnons y** | **mydnens y** | **mynsens y** | **mednons y** |

Throughout, first syllable y may become e *except* in the subjunctive. And s may become j in the conditional. All but present may also be used with earlier meaning 'wish to', in which sense there is also a preterite.

## DOS

| Past participle | Imperative |
|---|---|
| **devedhys** | **deus**, **dewgh** |

*Subjunctive phrase followed by verb-noun, forming verb in protasis of unreal conditional sentence. Note that the conjunction is always* mar[4].

**mar teffen vy ha**
**mar teffes jy ha**
**mar teffa va ha**
**mar teffa hy ha**
**mar teffa ha**
**mar teffen ny ha**
**mar teffo'why ha**
**mar teffons y ha**

# GWIL

*Past participle*
**gwrës**

*Imperative*
**gwra**, **gwrewgh**

*Present habitual / Future*

gwrama
or **gwra'vy**
gwrêta
or **gwres jy**
gwra va
gwra hy
gwra
gwren ny
gwre'why
gwrowns y

*Imperfect / Future in the past*

gwren vy

gwres jy

gwre va
gwre hy
gwre
gwren ny
gwre'why
gwrêns y

*Preterite*

gwrug [a]vy

gwrusta
or **gwrussys jy**
gwrug ev
gwrug hy
gwrug
gwrussyn ny
gwrusso'why
gwrussons y

*Conditional*

gwrussen vy
gwrusses jy
gwrussa va
gwrussa hy
gwrussa
gwrussen ny
gwrusse'why
gwrussens y

*Subjunctive*

gwrellen vy
gwrelles jy
gwrella va
gwrella hy
gwrella
gwrellen ny
gwrello'why
gwrellons y

All forms of gwil except the verb-noun and the past participle may be used as an auxiliary + verb-noun.

In conversation it will be useful to recognize some common *inflected preterites* of other verbs. You might hear the regular 'you' forms: -sys jy and -so'why in questions addressed to you. The 'he/she' form, frequent in statements, usually ends in -as or -ys, depending on the verb. The former reverses any affection seen in the verb-noun: *e.g.* sonas though seny. Note irregular deuth 'came', dros 'brought', dug 'carried', êth 'went', ros 'gave'. And you may hear an occasional bare ty-imperative: generally just the *root* of the verb, without affection – final y is dropped.

## GALLOS

| Present | Imperfect | Conditional | Subjunctive |
|---|---|---|---|
| gallama *or* galla'vy | gyllyn vy | galsen vy | gallen vy |
| gylta *or* gyllyth jy | gyllys jy | galses jy | galles jy |
| gyll ev | gylly va | galsa va | galla va |
| gyll hy | gylly hy | galsa hy | galla hy |
| gyll | gylly | galsa | galla |
| gyllyn ny | gyllyn ny | galsen ny | gallon ny |
| gyllo'why | gylle'why | galse'why | gallo'why |
| gyllons y | gyllens y | galsens y | gallons y |

## GODHVOS

| Present | Future | Imperfect |
|---|---|---|
| gorama *or* gòn vy | godhvedha'vy | godhyen vy |
| gosta *or* godhes jy | godhvedhys jy | godhyes jy |
| gor ev | godhvyth ev | godhya va |
| gor hy | godhvyth hy | godhya hy |
| gor | godhvyth | godhya |
| godhyn ny | godhvedhyn ny | godhyen ny |
| godho'why | godhvedho'why | godhye'why |
| godhons y | godhvedhons y | godhyens y |

| Conditional | Subjunctive |
|---|---|
| gothvien vy | gothfen vy |
| gothvies jy | gothfes jy |
| gothvia va | gothfa va |
| gothvia hy | gothfa hy |
| gothvia | gothfa |
| gothvien ny | gothfen ny |
| gothvie'why | gothfo'why |
| gothviens y | gothfens y |

## RY & DRY

*Imperative*

**ro** (roy)
**rewgh**

**dro** (doroy)
**drewgh**

## KEMERES

*Imperative*

**kebmer**
**kemerowgh**

## GASA

*Imperative*

**gas**
**gesowgh**

## MOS

*Past participle*

**gyllys**

*Imperative*

**kê**
**ewgh** (kewgh)

## CARA

*Conditional followed by verb-noun*
*Sense is 'would like to' / 'want to'*

**carsen vy**
**carses jy**
**carsa va**
**carsa hy**
**carsa**
**carsen ny**
**carse'why**
**carsens y**

## Imperative / subjunctive endings

Optionally, o may be replaced by e in imperative and subjunctive endings, except in the present subjunctive of bos.

## Past participle

The normal ending is -ys (triggering affection in *some* verbs). But note exceptions unyes and ûsyes. Ûsys is generally reserved for 'usual'.

# NUMERALS FOR REFERENCE

If you are in doubt about the grammar of numerals, consult *Desky Kernowek* or another good textbook.

0     **màn**

*Cardinals (one, two etc)*

| | | | |
|---|---|---|---|
| 1 | **onen** *(also pronoun)* **udn*** + *noun* | 21 | **onen warn ugans** **udn*** + *noun* **warn ugans** |
| 2 | **dew**$^2$ (**dyw**$^2$ *feminine*) | 39 | **nawnjek warn ugans** |
| 3 | **try**$^3$ (**teyr**$^3$ *feminine*) | 40 | **dewgans** (dew ugans) |
| 4 | **peswar** (**peder** *feminine*) | 41 | **onen ha dewgans** **udn*** + *noun* **ha dewgans** |
| 5 | **pymp** | | |
| 6 | **whegh** | | |
| 7 | **seyth** | 50 | **deg ha dewgans** *or* **hanter-cans** |
| 8 | **eth** | | |
| 9 | **naw** | 59 | **nawnjek ha dewgans** |
| 10 | **deg** | 60 | **try ugans** |
| 11 | **udnek** | 61 | **onen ha try ugans** **udn*** + *noun* **ha try ugans** |
| 12 | **dewdhek** | | |
| 13 | **tredhek** | | |
| 14 | **peswardhek** | 79 | **nawnjek ha try ugans** |
| 15 | **pymthek** | 80 | **peswar ugans** |
| 16 | **whêtek** | 81 | **onen ha peswar ugans** **udn*** + *noun* **ha peswar ugans** |
| 17 | **seytek** | | |
| 18 | **êtek** | | |
| 19 | **nawnjek** | | |
| 20 | **ugans** | 99 | **nawnjek ha peswar ugans** |

\*     Contact mutation as for **an**

**dew** vs **dyw** is just a spelling convention

| | | | |
|---|---|---|---|
| 100 | **cans** (*pl* cansow) | 1,000 | **mil**[2] (*pl* milyow) |
| 200 | **dew cans** | 2,000 | **dyw vil**[2] |
| 300 | **try cans** (try hans) | 3,000 | **teyr mil**[2] (tremil[2]) |
| 400 | **peswar cans** | 4,000 | **peder mil**[2] |

1,000,000 is **mil vil** or **udn mylyon**

1,000,000,000 is **udn bylyon**

*Ordinals (first, second etc)*

| | | | |
|---|---|---|---|
| 1 | **kensa** | 24 | **pe·swora warn ugans** |
| 2 | **secùnd** | 25 | **pympes warn ugans** |
| 3 | **tressa** (tryja) | 26 | **wheffes warn ugans** |
| 4 | **pe·swora** (pe·swara) | 27 | **seythves warn ugans** |
| 5 | **pympes** | 28 | **êthves warn ugans** |
| 6 | **wheffes** (whegves) | 29 | **nawves warn ugans** |
| 7 | **seythves** | 30 | **degves warn ugans** |
| 8 | **êthves** | 31 | **unegves warn ugans** |
| 9 | **nawves** (nawes) | 40 | **dewgansves** |
| 10 | **degves** | 50 | **hanter-cansves** |
| 11 | **unegves** | 60 | **tryugansves** |
| 12 | **dewdhegves** | 80 | **peswar ugansves** |
| 13 | **tredhegves** | 100 | **cansves** |
| 14 | **peswardhegves** | 1000 | **milves** |
| 15 | **pymthegves** | | |
| 16 | **whêtegves** | | |
| 17 | **seytegves** | | |
| 18 | **êtegves** | | |
| 19 | **nawnjegves** | | |
| 20 | **ugansves** | | |
| 21 | **kensa warn ugans** | | |
| 22 | **secùnd warn ugans** | | |
| 23 | **tressa warn ugans** | | |

*Example phrases*

**an dhew** both, **aga dew** / **pùbonen a'n dhew** both of them, **aga thry** / **pùbonen a'n try** the three of them

*Times (once, twice etc)*

| | | | |
|---|---|---|---|
| 1 | **unweyth** | 5 | **pymp gweyth** |
| | *with express negative* | 6 | **whegh gweyth** |
| | *also* 'even' | 7 | **seythqweyth** |
| 2 | **dewweyth** (dywweyth) | 8 | **êthweyth** |
| 3 | **tergweyth** | 9 | **naw gweyth** |
| 4 | **pedergweyth** | 10 | **degweyth** |
| 100 | **canqweyth** | 1000 | **milweyth** |

*Fractions*

**hanter** half, **hantera** *verb* halve, **tressa radn** third, **qwartron** quarter (**qwartron** *m qwartronys* also 'direction; district')
**udn radn in teyr** one third, **dyw radn in teyr** two thirds
**udn qwartron** one quarter, **try qwartron** (try whartron) three quarters

*Multiples*

**unplek** single, **dewblek / dobyl** double, **dobla** *verb* double, **tryflek** treble, **tryflegy** *verb* treble

*Simple calculations*

**A ha B yw / a wra C**
A plus B is C *or*
A and B make C

**A marnas B yw / a wra C**
A minus B is / makes C

**A [lies'hës] B gweyth yw C**
A multiplied by / times B is C

*See above for special forms*

**A rydnys inter B yw C**
A divided by B is C

*Example dates*

an êthves mis Est êtek [cans], eth ha dewgans
(8 August 1848: birth of Henry Jenner)
an seythves warn ugans mis Me nawnjek [cans], nawnjek ha dewgans
(27 May 1959: passing of R. Morton Nance)
an tredhegves mis Metheven dyw vil ha seytek
(13 June 2017: '30 years on')

# CONTACT MUTATIONS FOR REFERENCE

In conversation do not worry overmuch if some mutations are missed. In fact the rules for leniting g are really more like guidelines. And spirantization of a verb-noun after ow 'my' ('me' with verb-noun) may be 'hyper-correct'.

## *Second state* (lenition)

**b > v**

**c > g**  No change after s, th

**ch > j**

**d > dh**  No change before û = yoo
Occasionally no change after s (*e.g.* after nos, tus)

**g > zero**  **gl**, **gr** often unchanged; growedha / groweth / grugys > wrowedha / wroweth / wrugys
Monosyllables usually unchanged
And many loan-words also resist this change

**go > wo**

**goo > wo**

**gou > wo**

**gù > wo**

**gû > wo**

**gu > wu**

**gw > w**

**k > g**  No change after s, th

**m > v**

**p > b**  No change after s, th

**qw > g**  No change after s, th

**t > d**  No change after s, th

In loan-words **go** sometimes > **o**: *e.g.* arolegyth, an orseth

## Second state in speech but not in writing
f > v  fl, fr unchanged

Some also argue for **s** > **z**. But the evidence for such a regular mutation is not strong. The pronunciation of s as [z] is better regarded as a matter determined by phonetic environment.

## Third state *(spirantization)*
c > h  cl, cr unchanged
k > h  kn unchanged
qw > wh
p > f
t > th

## Fourth state *(provection)*
b > p
d > t
g > c / k
gw > qw

## Fifth state *(mixed)*

| | | | |
|---|---|---|---|
| b > f | > v after th | gou > who | > wo after th |
| d > t | | gù > who | > wo after th |
| g > h | gl, gr unchanged | gû > who | > wo after th |
| | | gu > whu | > wu after th |
| go > who | > wo after th | gw > wh | > w after th |
| goo > who | > wo after th | m > f | > v after th |

But 're'th fo' in wishes. Note also unique *nasal* mutation dor > an nor (in special sense 'earth as opposed to heaven').

# 'OUTBURSTS'

The main part of the dictionary contains a few short interjections (*e.g.* now, ogh), as well as basic expressions for 'please' and 'thank you'. But here is an array of words and phrases that will make conversation more lively, and which seem to invite an exclamation mark.

Singular you-forms (familiar) are given throughout, except where only a polite form would be used. Plural / polite forms can often be substituted: *e.g.* by changing dhis to dhywgh [why] or dhewy.

## *Hello and goodbye*

| | |
|---|---|
| **Bednath Duw genes!** | Hello! Goodbye! |
| **Bys avorow!** | Till tomorrow! |
| **Bys-bys!** | Bye-bye! Cheerio! |
| **Bys whare·!** | I'll be back! |
| **Da weles!** | So long! See you! |
| **Deus ajy·!** | Come in! |
| **Dohajë·dh dâ!** | Good afternoon! |
| **Dùrda dhewy!** | How do you do? |
| **Dùrnosta dhis!** | Good night! |
| **Duw genes!** | Goodbye! |
| **Farwè·l!** | All the best! |
| **Gordhuwher dâ!** | Good evening! |
| **Hayl dhis!** | Hello! Hi [there]! |
| **Lowena dhis!** | Hi [there]! |
| **Myttyn dâ!** | Good morning! |
| **Nos dâ!** | Good night! |
| **Remai·n in dadn dava [gene']!** | Keep in touch! |
| **Wèl, campoll an jowl!** | Well, talk of the devil! |
| **Wolcùm!** | Welcome! |

*Good wishes*

**Bledhen Nowyth dâ!** — Happy New Year!
**Fortyn dâ!** — Good luck!
**God-spêda dhis!** — All the best!
**Nadelyk lowen!** — Merry Christmas!
**Pedn bloodh lowen [ha meur anodhans]!** — Happy birthday! Many happy returns [of the day]!
**Sowena!** — All the best!

*Being courteous*

**Dùrdala dhis!** — Thank you!
**Gav dhybm!** — Excuse me! (interrupting, going past)
**Me a'm beus oll an blam!** — [It's] my fault entirely!
**Ny vedhaf mynysen!** — I shan't (won't) be a moment!
**Praydha!** *or* **Y praya!** — Excuse me? (preface to question / request)

*Getting attention*

**Ay!** — Hey! Ahoy!
**Cou-î!** — Coo-ee!
**Den i'n mor!** — Man overboard!
**Harow!** — Help!
**Hay!** — Hey! Phew!
**How** *or* **Ow!** — Hello! (surprise)
**Maydes!** — Help!

*In good company*

**Arta!** — Encore!
**Brav!** — Bravo!
**Clow clow!** — Hear hear!
**Kernow bys vycken!** — Cornwall for ever!
**Ober dâ!** — Proper job!
**Oyeth!** — Hear hear!

| | |
|---|---|
| **Tergweyth hurâ· rag** ...! | Three cheers for ...! |
| **Yêhes dâ dhis!** | Cheers! (toast) |

## With the young (and not so young)

| | |
|---|---|
| **Bo-gik!** | Peek-a-boo! |
| **Bou!** | Boo! |
| **Chùg chùg!** | Come along now! |
| **Cùsk cosel!** | Sleep tight! Sweet dreams! |
| **Myam myam!** | Yum yum! Yummy! |
| **Sa' sa'!** | There there! |
| **Taw tavas!** | Hush now! |
| **Thùck!** | Yuck! |

## I'm the boss

| | |
|---|---|
| **Avau·nd!** | Get lost! |
| **Bëdh war!** | Careful! Look out! |
| **Darwar!** | Watch out! |
| **Deus!** | Come on! |
| **Dewla in bàn!** | Hands up! |
| **Dhe'n dor gans** ...! | Down with ...! |
| **Dhe'n jowl an dermynogyon**! | Every man for himself! |
| **Gas cres!** | Cut it out! |
| **Gas dha son!** | Stop your noise! |
| **Gas ev in y wres y honen!** | Let him stew! |
| **Gwella dha jer!** | Cheer up! |
| **Gwra derivas dhybm!** | Let me know! |
| **Gwra kestedna dha honen!** | Pull yourself together! |
| **Han-na!** | Fetch! (to dog) |
| **Ho!** | Whoa [there]! |
| **In mes genes!** | Get out! |
| **In sol!** | Up you get! |
| **Kê wàr dha gàm!** | Steady on! Don't overdo it! |
| **Kebmer with!** | Take care! |
| **Kebmer with a'n step!** | Mind the step! |
| **Mir!** | Look! |

| | |
|---|---|
| **Na wra vry orto!** | Take no notice [of him]! |
| **Otta dha shara!** | That's your lot! |
| **Sav in nes!** | Stay where you are! |
| **Syns dha glap!** | Shut up! Stow it! |
| **Tàn hebma!** | Take this! Hold this! |
| **Taw dha vin!** | Shut up! Stow it! |
| **Voyd alebma / a'm syght!** | Out of my sight! |

## Making a point

| | |
|---|---|
| **Col orthy'!** | Mark my words! |
| **Jevody·!** | I'm telling you! |
| **Re Dhuw a'm ros!** | Honestly! |
| **Re Synt Defry·!** | I'm not joking! |

## Reacting to people and events

The social conventions that originally governed what Cornish expressions were appropriate in what contexts can no longer be reconstructed. Anyway, they would not accord with modern values. The Revival may eventually establish conventions of its own. For those with a contemporary appetite for crudity, a few **** entries are included; they can be translated easily enough. But traditional Cornish 'strong language' drew rather upon shared Catholic beliefs, universal horror of the plague, and fascination with the hangman's noose.

| | |
|---|---|
| **A!** | Ah! |
| **Aba·rth an pla!** | Damn! Blast! |
| **Â gans dha whedhlow!** | Get away [with you]! |
| **Adhevî·s!** | Excellent! Super! |
| **Agh!** | Ugh! |
| **Ahâ·!** | Aha! |
| **An den truan!** | Poor devil! |
| **An milyk truan!** | Poor thing! The poor darling! |
| **Anhegol!** | Incredible! Unbelievable! |

| | |
|---|---|
| **Ass osta dâ!** | That's good of you! How kind of you! |
| **Ass yw dieth!** | What a pity! What a shame! |
| **Ass yw dyvla·s** (dyfla·s)! | [That's] disgusting! |
| **Ass yw mothow!** | What a disaster! |
| **Ass yw omgyjyor!** | **** |
| **Ass yw scogyn!** | What an idiot! |
| **Besias saym!** | Butter-fingers! |
| **Bohes chauns!** | Fat chance [of that]! |
| **Brabm an gath!** | Cobblers! |
| **Brentyn!** | Wonderful! Splendid! |
| **Bÿth ny vedna'!** | No way! (refusal) |
| **Cabmen vëth!** | Not in the least! Not in the slightest! |
| **Cales lùck!** | Hard luck! |
| **Camdybys osta!** | You're wrong! |
| **Cudyn vëth!** | No problem! |
| **Dâ aqwîtys osta!** | [It] serves you right! |
| **Dâ lowr!** | OK! Okay! |
| **Dàr!** | What! (surprise) *Often followed immediately by negative question (without interrogative particle): e.g. Dàr, ny wosta?* What! Don't you know? |
| **Dhe'th cregy**! | Damn you! |
| **Do way!** | Now now! |
| **Drocka los** (loos)! | What a pain! |
| **Drog yw gene'!** | Sorry! |
| **Duwhanhë·s oma!** | I am sooo sorry! |
| **Dyowlyk bian ywa!** | The little devil! The rascal! |
| **Ea / Nâ!** | Yes! / No! |
| **Ea mar pleg! / Na vana', gromercy dhis!** | Yes please! / No thank you! |
| **Ea, mar teffen ha cafos an chauns!** | Chance would be a fine thing! |

| | |
|---|---|
| **Ellas!** | Alas! Oh dear! |
| **Er y wuw!** | Worse luck! |
| **Fate·ll esta ow lavasos!** | How dare you! |
| **Faven gog!** | Not a dicky-bird! |
| **Flows ha whedhlow!** | Stuff and nonsense! |
| **Forsô·th!** | True! |
| **Fy!** | Rot! |
| **Gas dha flows!** | Don't talk rubbish! |
| **Ges a wres!** | You're joking! |
| **Gool ha gwary!** | Fun and games! |
| **Gwir pora·n!** | Quite right! |
| **Gwir yn tien!** | Spot on! |
| **Gwrës dâ!** | Well done! |
| **Gwynvÿs!** | That was lucky! |
| **Heb mar na ma's!** | No buts! |
| **Hebma a gòst dhis!** | You'll pay for this! |
| **Hèn yw onen dâ!** | That's rich! |
| **Horsen plos!** | Son of a bitch! |
| **In lagas dha din!** | **** |
| **Keslowena!** | Congratulations! |
| **Kewar yn tien!** | Exactly! Precisely! |
| **Kyj an air!** | **** |
| **Lowena re'th fo ganso!** | Good luck with it! |
| **Lowr yw dhe brevy perthyans Job!** | It's enough to try the patience of a saint! |
| **Mal!** | Damn! |
| **Malbew dàm ny'n gwrêta!** | Like hell you will! |
| **Malbew onen!** | Not [a single] one! |
| **Malbew vadna!** | Not a drop! |
| **Mewl yw hedna dhe'm breus avy·!** | I call that a disgrace! |
| **Na fors!** | Never mind! |
| **Na le!** | No less! |
| **Ny amo·wnt màn!** | It's no use! |
| **Ny'n jeves chauns canary!** | He hasn't a bat's chance in hell! |
| **Ny rov oy!** | I couldn't care less! |

| | |
|---|---|
| Ny wòn malbew dàm! | Blowed if I know! |
| Nyns yw marth! | No wonder! |
| Owt warnas! | Blast you! Confound you! |
| Pandra· vern? | So what? |
| Pandr'yw hedna dhyso? | Mind your own business! |
| Pëth adhevî·s! | Just the thing! |
| Por dhâ, sos! | Cool! Good on you, mate! |
| Prat plos a wrusta! | That's a dirty trick [to play]! |
| Pywa! | Who?! What?! |
| Re'th fo crog! | Get knotted! |
| Re'm fay! | Gosh! Wow! |
| Re'm leowta! | Gracious [me]! Good grief! |
| Re'm pât! | I say! |
| Re'n ow thas! | Gosh! Wow! |
| Soweth! | Bad luck! More's the pity! |
| Spladn! | Brilliant! Splendid! |
| Te a ol hedna! | You'll be sorry! |
| Te a worr whans wheja ino'! | You make me sick! |
| Te javal! | You scoundrel! |
| Tety-valy! | Tut tut! |
| Tru! | Pity! |
| Tybyans dâ! | Good thinking! Good idea! |
| Wèl, goda-chauns re'th fo! | Well, good luck to you! |
| Yma· va owth hegasa ow dens! | He really gets my goat! |
| Yn tien! | Absolutely! |
| Yth esoma i'n nevow! | I'm over the moon! |

Here are some exclamations based specifically on religious ideas.

| | |
|---|---|
| A Dhuw! | Oh dear! |
| A Dhuw ker! | Dear God! |
| Aba·rth Duw! | For God's / Christ's / pity's sake! |
| Allelùya! | Halleluya! |
| Bednath Duw warnas! | Bless you! (to sneezer) |

| | |
|---|---|
| **Cres dh'y ena!** | God rest his / her soul! (when referring to deceased) |
| **Crows Crist[, painys trist]!** | Cross my heart [and hope to die]! |
| **Dh'y lawa!** | Praise be! |
| **Dùrsona dhis!** | God bless! |
| **Duw dyfen!** | God forbid! |
| **Grâss e dhe Dhuw!** | Thank God! |
| **In iffarnow heb gow!** | Bloody hell! |
| **Jesu a olas!** | Jesus wept! (John 11 35) |
| **Kê dhe'n jowl genes!** | Go to hell! |
| **Mollath Duw!** | Damn! Blast! |
| pronounced 'Mollatuw' | |
| **Re Varia!** | Gosh! Wow! |
| **Re Vyhal!** | Gosh! Wow! |
| **Re'n ebron dhâ!** | Good heavens! Heavens above! |
| **Wàr ow enef!** | Dear[y] me! |

## *And a few expressions not to use*

There are some 'outbursts' in current parlance that should really be avoided by speakers of more traditional Cornish. They are given here in Standard Cornish spelling for reference only.

| | |
|---|---|
| *dynargh!* | Prefer **wolcùm!** |
| *fatla genes?* | Prefer **fatl'yw genes?** |
| *meur ras brâs* | Prefer **gromercy milweyth** |
| *yn whir* | Prefer **in gwir** |

*Aria!*

This alternative to **Re Varia!** was noted by R. Morton Nance in his famous dictionary of 1938, on the basis of a dialect word in English. But there is no evidence for it in the surviving texts.

# APPENDIX

# PLACE NAMES

A dot has been inserted to show when the primary stress is not on the penultimate syllable, as elsewhere in the dictionary. Place names are usually written without diacritical marks, though u ù û are distinguished here as an aid to pronunciation.

Cornish place names have been taken from Craig Weatherhill, *A Concise Dictionary of Place-Names* (Evertype 2009), where you will find many more. I have occasionally adapted a vowel to Standard Cornish spelling.

## Cornwall

It is often difficult to identify the gender of a Cornish place name. Feminine gender is marked for a few names where it is well established (*e.g.* Kernow). Some may wish to treat names beginning with elements such as Lan- as feminine too, but this is left to personal preference. It is usual to refer to a city, town or village as hy in any event, because cyta, tre and treveglos are all feminine nouns.

**An E·denva** *f* The Eden Project
**An Lesard** Lizard Point
**An Tireth Uhel** North Cornwall
**Arwednek** (Falmoth) Falmouth
**Ash** Saltash
**Austol** St Austell
**Bosvena** Bodmin
**Bronel** Brannel
**Cambron** Camborne
**Carrek Loos i'n Coos** St Michael's Mount
**Din Kernowyon** Tintagel Castle
**Dowr Fala** The [River] Fal
**Dowr Tamer** The [River] Tamar
**Ewny Redru·dh** Redruth
**Fawy** The [River] Fowey; West Wivelshire
**Goon Bren** Bodmin Moor
**Helles** Helston
**Heyl** Hayle
**Kernow** *f* Cornwall
**Keryer** Kerrier

**Langordhow** Fowey (town)
**Lanstefan** Launceston
**Lanù·st** St Just (Penwith)
**Lanvausa** St Mawes
**Lanwedhenek** Padstow
**Lesnowyth** Lesnewth
**Logh** East Looe
**Lulyn** (Lùlyn) Newlyn
**Lys Kernow** New County Hall
**Lyskerwys** Liskeard
**Mahonyer** The Helford River
**Manahek** Meneage
**Pe·dera** Pydar
**Pedn an Wlas** Land's End
**Penwyth** Penwith
**Penza·ns** Penzance

**Porth Bian** West Looe
**Porth Ia** St Ives
**Porth Leven** Porthleven
**Pow E·reder** (Pow Erder) Powder
**Ros** Rame Peninsula; Roseland
**Ryslegh** East Wivelshire
**Stert** Torpoint
**Stradneth** Stratton
**Syllan** Scilly
**Tewyn Plustry** Newquay
**Trygor** Trigg
**Tryverow** (Trûrû) Truro
**Wade** Wadebridge

## *Rest of United Kingdom*

Caution should again be exercised about gender. Elements like Enys or Ker- may justify treatment of an entire name as feminine.

**An Orcados** The Orkneys
**An Vretan** *f* **Veur** Great Britain
**An Wlascor** *f* **Unyes** The United Kingdom
**Brystow** Bristol
**Dauns an Gewry** Stonehenge
**Dinedyn** Edinburgh
**Dowr Havren** The [River] Severn
**Dowr Tavos** (Tamys) The River Thames
**Enesow Heleth** (**Nessa** / **Pelha**) The [Inner / Outer] Hebrides

**Enesow Shetlond** The Shetland Isles
**Englond** (Inglond / Pow an Sowson) England
**Enys Gwyth** The Isle of Wight
**Enys Wedryn** Glastonbury
**Evrok** York
**Gwlas** *f* **an Hâv** Somerset
**Havren** *f* see **Dowr Havren**
**Kembra** *f* Wales
**Kere·sk** Exeter
**Kerge·nt** Canterbury
**Kergrau·nt** Cambridge
**Loundres** *f* London

**Mor Havren** The Bristol Channel
**Plymoth** Plymouth
**Pow Densher** Devon
**Resohen** Oxford
**Scotlond** (Alban) Scotland
**Wordhen North** Northern Ireland

## Rest of Europe

Cornish names derived from Latin names in *-a* may be treated as feminine.

**Albanya** Albania
**A·Idernes** Alderney
**An Alpow** The Alps
**An Chanel** The English Channel
**An Iseldiryow** The Netherlands
**An Mor Baltek** The Baltic [Sea]
**An Mor Cres** The Mediterranean [Sea]
**An Mor North** The North Sea
**An Repùblyk Check** The Czech Republic
**[An] Ûcra·yn** [The] Ukraine
An **Va·tycan** The Vatican
**An Vretan** *f* **Vian** Brittany
**Armenya** Armenia
**Austrya** Austria
**Belarù·s** Belarus
**Bosnya** Bosnia
**Bùlgarya** Bulgaria
**Co·rsyca** Corsica
**Co·sovo** Kosovo
**Creta** Crete
**Croacya** Croatia
**Cyprùs** Cyprus
**Denmark** (Pow an Danow) Denmark
**Dowr Donow** The [River] Danube
**Dowr Elb** The [River] Elbe
**Dowr Loyr** The [River] Loire
**Dowr Reyn** The [River] Rhine
**Dowr Ron** The [River] Rhone
**Dowr Seyn** The [River] Seine
**Enesow an Chanel** The Channel Islands
**Enesow Faro** (Enesow an Deves) The Faroe Islands
**[Enys] Manow** The Isle of Man
**Estonya** Estonia
**Ewrop** Europe
**Frynk** France
**Fynlond** Finland
**Garnsy** Guernsey
**Grenlond** Greenland
**Grûshya** Georgia
**Islond** Iceland
**I·taly** Italy
**Je·rmany** (Almayn) Germany
**Jersy** Jersey
**Jybraltar** Gibraltar

**Latvya** Lativia
**Lettow** Lithuania
**Lù·xemborg** Luxembourg
**Macedonya** Macedonia
**Majorca** Majorca
**Malta** Malta
**Menydhyow Pyre·n** The Pyrenees
**Moldova** Moldova
**Mo·naco** Monaco
**Montenegro** Montenegro
**Norwey** (Norgagh) Norway
**Polo·yn** Poland
**Portynga·l** Portugal
**Pow Beljyan** Belgium
**Pow Grek** Greece

**Pow Swyts** Switzerland
**Romanya** Romania
**Rùssya** Russia
**Sardi·n** Sardinia
**Sarkenys** Sark
**Serbya** Serbia
**Slovakya** Slovakia
**Slovenya** Slovenia
**Spayn** Spain
**Sweden** (Swe·dherwyk) Sweden
**Sy·cyly** Sicily
**Tùrky** Turkey
**Ù·ngary** Hungary
**Wordhen** Ireland

## *Rest of the World*

Cornish names derived from Latin names in *-a* may be treated as feminine.

**Afganista·n** Afghanistan
**A·fryca** Africa
**Ame·ryca Cres** Central America
**An Arctek / Antarctek** The Arctic / Antarctic
**An Bahamas** (Enesow Bahama) The Bahamas
**An Ca·wcasùs** The Caucasus
**An Gwastattiryow** The Steppes
**An Keheseth** The Equator
**An Kelgh Arctek / Antarctek** The Arctic / Antarctic Circle

**An Lohow Meur** The Great Lakes
**An Menydhyow Carnak** The Rocky Mountains
**An Meurbrasow** The Prairies
**An Mor Atlantek** The Atlantic [Ocean]
**An Mor Carrybean** The Caribbean [Sea]
**An Mor Caspyan** The Caspian [Sea]
**An Mor Cosel** The Pacific [Ocean]
**An Mor Du** The Black Sea

**An Mor Eyndek** The Indian Ocean
**An Mor Rudh** The Red Sea
**An Morblek Arabek** The Persian Gulf
**An Norvys** The World
**An Statys Unyes** (Statys Unyes Ame·ryca) The United States [of America]
**An Yst Cres** The Middle East
**An Yst Pell** The Far East
**A·raby Sawdek** Saudi Arabia
**Arhansin** *f* Argentina
**Asya** Asia
**Australya** Australia
**Banglade·sh** Bangladesh
**Bara·yn** Bahrain
**Bermûda** Bermuda
**Brasy·l** Brazil
**Ca·nada** Canada
**Cashmi·r** Kashmir
**Catar** (Qatar) Qatar
**China** (Catha·y) China
**Crymea** Crimea
**Cûba** Cuba
**Cùrdysta·n** Kurdistan
**Cùwa·yt** Kuwait
**Dowr A·mazon** The [River] Amazon
**Dowr Congo** The [River] Congo
**Dowr Ganjes** The [River] Ganges
**Dowr Jordan** The [River] Jordan

**Dowr Mysoury / Mysysypy** The [River] Missouri / Mississippi
**Dowr Nil** The [River] Nile
**Dowr Sen Lorens** The St Laurence [River]
**Dowrgleth Panama·** The Panama Canal
**Dowrgleth Sûez** The Suez Canal
**Dùba·y** Dubai
**Dyfeyth [an] Sahara** The Sahara [Desert]
**Ejyp** Egypt
**Enesow Falklond** (Enesow Malo) Falkland Islands (Malvinas)
**Enesow Felyp** The Philippines
**Ethiopya** Ethiopia
**Evrok Nowyth** New York
**Eynda** India
**Eynda-Catha·y** Indo-China
**Hayty** Haiti
**Hong-Cong** Hong Kong
**Indonesya** Indonesia
**Ira·k** (Ira·q) Iraq
**Ira·n** Iran
**I·srael** Israel
**Jamaica** Jamaica
**Japa·n** Japan
**Latyn-Ame·ryca** Latin America
**Loghlyn** Scandinavia
**Lybya** Libya
**Madagascar** Madagascar

**Malaysya** Malaysia
**Menydhyow Andes** The Andes
**Menydhyow Hyma·laya** The Himalayas
**Menydhyow Ùral** The Ural Mountains
**Me·xyco** Mexico
**Mongolya** Mongolia
**Myanmar** (Bùrma) Myanmar (Burma)
**Nepa·l** Nepal
**North-Ame·ryca** North America
**North-Corea** North Korea
**Pakysta·n** Pakistan
**Palesti·n** Palestine
**Pedn Ehel an North / Soth** The North / South Pole
**Penri·n an Corn** Cape Horn
**Penri·n an Govenek Da** The Cape of Good Hope
**Pow an Pùscas** Newfoundland
**Pow Tay** Thailand
**Selond Nowyth** New Zealand
**Soth-A·fryca** South Africa
**Soth-Ame·ryca** South America
**Soth-Corea** South Korea
**Sry-Lanca** Sri Lanka
**Sy·bery** Siberia
**Syngapo·r** Singapore
**Syrya** (Sùrry) Syria
**Taywa·n** Taiwan
**Trovan an Canker / Avar** The Tropic of Cancer / Capricorn
**Tùnisya** Tunisia
**Tybe·t** (Tubek) Tibet
**Vyetna·m** Vietnam
**Yemen** Yemen

## *Ethnicities, inhabitants, languages*

Standard Cornish has a system of nouns and adjectives for ethnicities, inhabitants, languages; but a full list of these words is outside the scope of a small dictionary. In conversation you can always use the name of the country to make a paraphrase. Thus, 'a Frynk' (from France) may be substituted for an adjective meaning 'French', and you can say 'den a Frynk' for 'Frenchman' and 'tavas Frynk' for 'French' (the language).

# KESCOWS NEBES MOY

If you find this dictionary useful you might also like to buy its companion volume *Kescows Nebes Moy*. Another 5000 words and phrases to enrich your Cornish. The material is presented in 50 classified sections, with many sub-divisions, to help you expand your vocabulary in particular areas of interest. The selection is especially suitable for those using traditional Cornish at home. The English-Cornish section is an index of this material, arranged alphabetically for easy access. An additional 300 idiomatic expressions are given in a separate section, and principles of Cornish word-building are described in an appendix.

Paperback, 350 pages.

Available from Agan Tavas. Price £9.95 + p&p.